D0504889

AUTHOR

HAYES, D.

CLASS

TITLE

The wars of the roses

The WARS of the ROSES

A History of Lancashire v. Yorkshire Cricket Matches

Written and compiled by Dean Hayes

The Parrs Wood Press
<u>MANCHESTER</u>

First Published 2000

THE PARRS WOOD PRESS
St Wilfrid's Enterprise Centre
Royce Road, Manchester, M15 5BJ
www.parrswoodpress.com

© Dean Hayes

U8478328

ISBN: 1 903158 11 7

This book was produced by Andrew Searle and Bob
Wells of The Parrs Wood Press and Printed in Great
Britain by:

Fretwell Print and Design
Healey Works
Goulbourne Street
Keighley
West Yorkshire BD21 1 PZ

CONTENTS

iv

v

ACKNOWLEDGEMENTS

The following organisations helped me considerably in the compilation of this book: Lancashire County Cricket Club, Yorkshire County Cricket Club, the British Newspaper Library, Manchester Central Reference Library, Bolton Central Library and the Harris Library. I would also like to thank Don Ambrose, Ben Hayes, Barry Rickman, Peter Stafford and Barry Watkins for their invaluable assistance. My gratitude also goes to Mick Pope, Tony Sheldon and the Lancashire Evening Post for providing the photographs and images.

FOREWORD

I HAVE HAPPY MEMORIES of the Roses fixtures from 1949 to 1968. There were some occasions when these matches proved to be harder than a Test match. Many was the time there would be seventeen or eighteen international cricketers within the two sides.

In 1952, when I played my first Test match for England at Headingley, it was straight after a Roses game. The atmosphere when I walked out in the Test match was nothing to compare with what I had experienced on the same ground a few days earlier.

To some players this was the biggest match of their career. I will never forget the 1949 match at Old Trafford. It was there that I shook hands for the first time with England's great opening batsman Len Hutton, later to become Sir Leonard, and his opening partner Cyril Washbrook. Brian Close, Frank Lowson and myself were making our Roses debut, and the gates were closed at 10.45 in the morning with thousands outside unable to get in. An agreement was reached between the two Captains and ropes were placed across all four corners of the ground and people were allowed to sit on the grass.

They were the days of the great Roses matches and I was fortunate to make dear friends both on and off the field. Yes, they are the matches I will never forget.

Fred Trueman

First Lancashire v. Yorkshire Match

Played at Whalley, June 20th, 21st, 22nd, 1867.

Lancashire, 1st Innings.	
A. N. Hornby c Stevenson b Freeman.	2
J. Ricketts b Greenwood	3
J. F. Leese c Freeman b Greenwood.	22
C. Coward b Greenwood	13
A. B. Rowley b Greenwood	0
G. Holgate c Anderson b Freeman.	8
Arthur Appleby b Freeman.	1
W. Hickton c Anderson b Freeman.	2
E. Leventon b Freeman	0
E. B. Rawlinson not out.	1
— Hibbert b Freeman	2
Extras	3
Total	**57**

Lancashire, 2nd Innings.	
A. N. Hornby b Freeman	3
J. Ricketts b Freeman	0
J. F. Leese b Freeman	4
C. Coward c Iddison b Greenwood	5
A. B. Rowley b Freeman	0
G. Holgate run out	21
Arthur Appleby b Greenwood	18
W. Hickton b Freeman	0
E. Leventon c Iddison b Greenwood	6
E. B. Rawlinson b Greenwood	14
— Hibbert not out	2
Extras	2
Total	**75**

Yorkshire, 1st Innings.	
J. Rowbotham c Hornby b Appleby	7
J. Thewlis b Appleby	1
E. Stevenson b Leventon	54
Roger Iddison b Appleby	14
J. E. Lee b Appleby	0
E. Dawson b Hickton	11
G. Anderson b Leventon	6
G. Freeman c Rawlinson b Hickton	28
J. Berry c Hibbert b Appleby	27
L Greenwood c and b Appleby	19
G. Atkinson not out	14
Extras	7
Total	**188**

Yorkshire won by an innings and 56 runs.   *Umpires: Wright and Rostron.*

LANCASHIRE v YORKSHIRE
at Whalley 20,21,22 June 1867

Yorkshire 188 (Stephenson 54, Appleby 6-62)
Lancashire 57 (Freeman 7-10) and 75 (Freeman 5-41, Greenwood 4-32)
Yorkshire won by an innings and 56 runs

The first-ever Roses match was played at the beautiful Whalley ground where Lancashire were greatly overmatched, especially in bowling power, and lost by an innings and 56 runs. The Manchester Courier newspaper went to great lengths to point out that the Lancashire team were not a fair representation of the county owing to the feeling of jealousy by some leading amateurs.

A number of the Yorkshire professionals, namely Anderson, Atkinson and Stephenson, were in dispute with the club but nevertheless they still played in the fixture, so it is highly unlikely that the Yorkshire committee had anything to do with the match.

Yorkshire won the toss and elected to bat, Ned Stephenson top scoring with 54 in his side's total of 188. Lancashire, who had Yorkshire's Gideon Holgate in their ranks, were dismissed for 57 and 75 with George Freeman taking seven for 10 and five for 41 and Greenwood three for 44 and four for 32 proving far too good for them.

LANCASHIRE v YORKSHIRE
at Old Trafford June 27,28,29 1867

Yorkshire 149 (Thewlis 44, Hickton 6-65) and 273 (Emmett 61, Smith 60,
A.Rowley 5-71)
Lancashire 159 (E.B.Rowley 55, Cuttell 4-38) and 98 (Emmett 5-46, Cuttell 5-46)
Yorkshire won by 165 runs

The second meeting between Lancashire and Yorkshire that year saw Yorkshire visit Old Trafford for the first time, yet the fixture was regarded as of little importance by the players or the public.

Yorkshire batted first and scored 149 with John Thewlis top scoring. He scored 44 as he and Gideon Holgate, now restored to Yorkshire's ranks, opened the innings with a good partnership, Holgate scoring 35. Towards the end of the Yorkshire innings, Roger Iddison knocked up a quick-fire 34.

Lancashire did well to score 159 with Edmund Rowley top-scoring with 55, while Willis Cuttell, later to play for Lancashire, taking four for 38 and Tom Emmett three for 57. In their second innings, Yorkshire scored

273, thanks mainly to Tom Emmett with 61 and William Smith with 60, and Iddison again got runs lower down the order with 38.

Needing 264 for victory, Lancashire were bowled out for 98 with both Cuttell and Emmett returning figures of five for 46.

YORKSHIRE v LANCASHIRE
at Middlesbrough September 2,3 1867

Lancashire 97 (Emmett 6-41, Freeman 4-48) and 68 (Freeman 5-25, Emmett 4-25)
Yorkshire 205 (Smith 90, Appleby 6-87, Ricketts 4-40)
Yorkshire won by an innings and 40 runs.

The third meeting between the two sides in the summer of 1867 took place at Middlesbrough where Yorkshire recorded their third win in as many games against their rivals.

Lancashire won the toss and decided to bat but were soon to regret their decision, being bowled out for 97 with Tom Emmett taking six for 61 and George Freeman four for 48. In reply, Yorkshire were given a good start when Darnton and Stephenson put on 55 for the first wicket, before local batsman William Smith scored a powerful 90 to give Yorkshire a first innings total of 205. Batting for a second time, Lancashire were dismissed for 68 with George Freeman taking five for 25 and Tom Emmett four for 25.

George Freeman had played in two of the three matches and had taken 21 wickets at a cost of 5.90 runs apiece.

YORKSHIRE v LANCASHIRE
at Holbeck July 9,10 1868

Lancashire 30 (Freeman 8-11) and 34 (Emmett 5-13, Freeman 4-12)
Yorkshire 250 (Savile 65, Iddison 57, Hickton 6-105)
Yorkshire won by an innings and 186 runs.

In the only Roses match to be played at Holbeck near Leeds, Lancashire won the toss and elected to bat. With only four regular players available, the Red Rose county knew that they were in for a difficult time and only Cornelius Coward reached double figures as they were shot out for just 30. George Freeman had figures of eight for 11, including a hat-trick, dismissing Burrows, Fred Coward and Storer.

By close of play on the first day, Yorkshire were 190 for seven with Savile and Iddison both having scored half-centuries. When play resumed

3

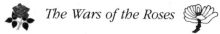

on the second day, the home side took their total to 250. Bill Hickton, who was the first Lancashire bowler to take all ten wickets, had figures of six for 105 from 57 overs.

In their second innings, Lancashire were again dismissed cheaply, being bowled out for 34 as Freeman (four for 12) and Emmett (six for 13) ripped through the side. Nine of the wickets to fall were clean bowled as Yorkshire won by an innings and 186 runs.

GEORGE FREEMAN (YORKSHIRE)

Regarded by W.G.Grace as the finest fast bowler he ever played against, George Freeman's youthful days were guided by the Revd Canon Owen, for over fifty years Vicar of Boroughbridge and a lifelong cricket enthusiast. As a 16-year-old, Freeman took six for 23 and nine for 15 for Boroughbridge against Knaresborough. Taking a clerical position with a Leeds solicitor, he quickly made a name for himself in local cricket and then, in 1863, moved to Edinburgh, combining work with pleasure as cricket tutor and Headmaster's secretary at the Grange House School.

Whilst on a visit home, he played in a match at York and his bowling was so impressive that a job was found for him with a Malton manure merchant. Thereafter, within the space of a season, Freeman's cricket career was transformed.

A fine bowling performance for a local 22 against the famous All England Eleven so impressed George Parr, the touring team's manager, that he engaged Freeman to play for the Eleven and got him a trial with Yorkshire. By 1867, Freeman had established himself as a regular member of the Yorkshire side and along with Tom Emmett startled the cricket world with a series of magnificent bowling feats. That year, Yorkshire won all its six matches, Freeman taking 51 wickets at a cost of 7.4 runs each. Against Lancashire at Whalley, Freeman took seven wickets for 10 runs and five for 41 in dismissing Lancashire for 57 and 75. The following year at Holbeck, bowling unchanged with Emmett, Freeman repeated the dose against the Red Rose county. Batting first, Lancashire were all out within an hour for 30, Freeman taking eight wickets for 11 runs, including the hat-trick. In the late autumn of 1868, Freeman was a member of the second team of English professionals to tour America, his tally of 107 wickets for 212 runs in six matches was phenomenal, even against such lowly opposition.

In 1869, George Freeman went into business as an auctioneer at Thirsk Stock Market but two years later, despite his continuing success on the cricket field and in the peak of health and form, he decided to retire from professional cricket and devote his full-time energies towards the development of his business career.

His last game for Yorkshire was in 1881, nearly ten years after his retirement from regular play; although nearing the age of 40, he showed he had lost little of his skill, taking nine wickets. Strange to relate, his valedictory innings of 60 was the highest of his entire first-class career.

In minor cricket, Freeman once hit 123 for Malton Twenty-Two against An All England XI attack that included Jemmy Shaw, George Tarrant and Dick Tinley. During his short full-time career, he took hundreds of wickets for the All England and United North Elevens and in 1866 for the United against Twenty-Two of Redcar, he took six wickets in eight balls including a wicket with each delivery of a four-ball over. Two weeks later he captured seven wickets with his first nine balls in a match at Tadcaster.

Freeman, who took 209 wickets at 9.47 runs each for Yorkshire, died from Bright's Disease on 18 November 1895 at the early age of 52.

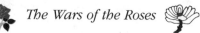

LANCASHIRE v YORKSHIRE
at Old Trafford June 29,30, July 1, 1871

Yorkshire 142 (Freeman 51, Reynolds 5-39) and 265 (Greenwood 50,
Emmett 48, Hickton 4-83)
Lancashire 90 (Emmett 5-34) and 95 (Emmett 6-51, Freeman 4-27)
Yorkshire won by 222 runs.

On the first day, Yorkshire were bowled out for 142 with George
Freeman's 51 the only innings of note. It was said that Fred Reynolds, the
Lancashire opening bowler, started the proceedings by bowling lobs. At
the close of play, Lancashire in reply were 53 for two but early the next
day were dismissed for 90 with Tom Emmett taking five for 34.

By the end of play, Yorkshire had put themselves into an unassail-
able position. Opening the innings was Andrew Greenwood, who had
scored 21 not out in the first innings. This time, he scored 50 and was well
supported by George Freeman with 37. Other Yorkshire players to score
runs lower down the order were Tom Emmett with 48 and George Pinder
with 35. These two batsmen added 48 for the eighth wicket as Yorkshire's
second innings totalled 265. Chasing 318 for victory, Lancashire were skittled out for 95 with Tom Emmett taking six for 51 to give match figures
of eleven for 85 and George Freeman four for 27. The two Yorkshire
bowlers bowled unchanged throughout the match and Emmett, in the
middle of some excellent bowling, sent down a formidable number of
wides, a favourite idiosyncrasy of his!

YORKSHIRE v LANCASHIRE
at Bramall Lane July 17,18,19, 1871

Lancashire 343 (Appleby 99, Hickton 55, Clayton 6-92) and 20-0
Yorkshire 191 (Iddison 54*, Appleby 5-87,Hickton 4-62) and 171
(Lockwood 48, Appleby 3-54)
Lancashire won by 10 wickets.

There were four changes in the Lancashire side for the return game
played at Sheffield, 18 days later. The visitors won the toss and elected to
bat, ending the first day on 253 for eight. Arthur Appleby and Bill Hickton
went on to add 111 for the ninth wicket. Appleby had the misfortune to
be out for 99, whilst Hickton scored 55. Lancashire reached 343 with

6

Clayton the pick of the Yorkshire bowlers taking six for 92. Joe Rowbotham, who had played for Yorkshire since 1861, twice refused to bowl after Lancashire had reached the 300 mark!

Richard Barlow, who was later to become one of Lancashire's finest professionals and whose opening partnerships with A.N.'Monkey' Hornby were to be a feature of county cricket, made his Lancashire debut in this match. In fact, when Yorkshire batted, Barlow bowled Johnnie West with his first delivery.

Yorkshire at one time were 96 for eight but thanks to Roger Iddison, with an unbeaten 54, they rallied to score 191. Forced to follow-on, the home side were in trouble again and with Appleby who had taken five for 87 in their first innings, taking three for 54 in the second, they were bowled out for 171, a lead of just 19 runs.

Lancashire had no problems in knocking off the required runs to register their first win in a Roses match.

LANCASHIRE v YORKSHIRE
at Old Trafford May 30,31, June 1, 1872

Lancashire 157 (Emmett 6-57) and 79 (Clayton 5-32, Emmett 5-42)
Yorkshire 93 (McIntyre 5-45, Appleby 4-42) and 100 (Appleby 4-44, McIntyre 3-50)
Lancashire won by 43 runs

Lancashire won the toss and opted to bat on a fairly flat Old Trafford wicket. Tom Emmett, Yorkshire's opening bowler, was in devastating form, taking six for 57 in Lancashire's total of 157. The home side would have been hoping for a much higher total but, as it transpired, they had scored the game's highest total! Lancashire's bowlers, Bill McIntyre and Arthur Appleby, bowled well in tandem to dismiss Yorkshire for 93. The home side had a first innings lead of 64 and it was just as well as Emmett and Clayton took five wickets apiece to help dismiss the home side for 79.

Yorkshire required 144 runs to win the opening Roses encounter of the summer. They made a steady start but Appleby and McIntyre picked up the wickets at regular intervals and Yorkshire were bowled out for 100 to leave Lancashire the winners by 43 runs.

YORKSHIRE v LANCASHIRE
at Bramall Lane July 15,16, 1872

Lancashire 89 (Emmett 5-32, Lockwood 4-40) and 76 (Lockwood 5-29, Emmett 4-32)
Yorkshire 55 (McIntyre 5-12, Watson 3-28) and 68 (McIntyre 6-19, Watson 3-32)
Lancashire won by 42 runs.

In a match when the bowlers were always on top, Lancashire were bowled out for 89 with Tom Emmett taking five for 32 and Ephraim Lockwood four for 40. Two of Lockwood's victims were stumped by wicket-keeper Pinder. Bill McIntyre, who headed this season's first-class averages with 41 wickets at 5.65 runs each, took five for 12 as the White Rose county were dismissed for 55. Lancashire had a first innings lead of just 34 but it proved priceless after Emmett and Lockwood again ran through the visitors batting with the latter bowler's deceptive slows accounting for five of the Lancashire batsmen including another two stumped by Pinder, who had eight victims in the match. Needing 111 for victory, Yorkshire fell 43 runs short as McIntyre finished with the remarkable match figures of eleven for 31.

LANCASHIRE v YORKSHIRE
at Old Trafford May 29,30, 1873

Lancashire 58 (Emmett 7-29, Hill 3-23) and 82 (Hill 5-24, Emmett 4-53)
Yorkshire 98 (Watson 4-27) and 43-1
Yorkshire won by 9 wickets.

In one of the shortest Roses matches on record, Yorkshire's opening bowlers, Tom Emmett and Allen Hill, bowled the home side out for 59. Emmett, who had figures of seven for 29, was almost unplayable, whilst Hill was so accurate that the batsmen had to play every delivery. In reply, Yorkshire fared only slightly better. Whilst their total of 98 gave them a valuable first innings lead of 40, it was the tight bowling of Arthur Appleby that caught the eye. The former Enfield professional sent down 50 overs of which 36 were maidens!

In their second innings, Lancashire were restricted to 82 as Tom Emmett produced match figures of eleven for 82 and Allen Hill eight for 47, with seven of his victims being clean bowled. Lancashire's Alec Watson couldn't reproduce his first innings performance and Yorkshire coasted to victory by nine wickets.

YORKSHIRE v LANCASHIRE
at Bramall Lane June 30, July 1, 1873

Yorkshire 63 (McIntyre 5-25, Watson 5-36) and 142 (McIntyre 5-48, Watson 4-62)
Lancashire 94 (Hillkirk 56, Emmett 6-45, Clayton 3-29) and 47 (Emmett 5-19,
Clayton 5-27)
Yorkshire won by 64 runs.

In yet another bowler's match, Yorkshire, who opted to bat first, were dismissed for 63 with Bill McIntyre and Alec Watson taking five wickets apiece. The visitors reached 94 thanks in the main to John Hillkirk, who scored over half their total.

Yorkshire's second innings started in much the same vein as their first before Joseph Rowbotham, who at 42, was the oldest member of the Yorkshire side, and last man Bob Clayton put on 52 valuable runs for the last wicket.

The Osset-born bowler then took five for 27 and with Tom Emmett, who was often the scourge of Lancashire, taking five wickets, the Red Rose county were bowled out for just 47.

LANCASHIRE v YORKSHIRE
at Old Trafford June 27,28,29, 1874

Yorkshire 96 (Watson 6-44, Appleby 3-46) and 96 (Appleby 4-26, Watson 4-35)
Lancashire 39 (Emmett 5-24, Hill 4-11) and 87 (Hill 6-27, Emmett 3-50)
Yorkshire won by 66 runs.

Lancashire won the toss and put Yorkshire in to bat. Thanks largely to a devastating display of bowling from Alec Watson, who took six for 44, the visitors were dismissed for 96. Only Joseph Rowbotham with an unbeaten 24 looked comfortable. This was followed by a very poor display of batting by Lancashire who collapsed to 39 all out, their lowest total of the Roses meetings with the exception of that strange match at Holbeck six years earlier. Tom Emmett took five for 24 and Allen Hill four for 11, whilst not one Lancashire batsman reached double figures!

Yorkshire then scored 96 again with Tom Emmett proving his all-round worth with a fighting innings of 29. Watson took another four wickets to have match figures of ten for 79. Set 154 to win, Lancashire were, in all honesty, never in with a chance. They were bowled out for 87 and all but Appleby, who was run out for a top score of 33, were clean bowled. Allen Hill took six for 27 in 28.3 overs to have match figures of ten for 38.

9

TOM EMMETT (YORKSHIRE)

As a boy, Tom Emmett bowled for the Illingworth club and, after learning how to break back the ball, was eventually invited to play for Halifax. He later spent three years playing as professional for Keighley, a post which included a winter job. For Keighley, in a match against Todmorden, he scored 199 not out and took six wickets, a performance that alerted Yorkshire to his talents.

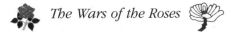

Emmett's first county match was against Nottinghamshire at Trent Bridge where he had innings figures of five for 33. Such was his immediate success that he headed the first-class averages in both 1866 and 1867. In the Roses match at Old Trafford in 1867, Emmett scored 61 and took five for 46. By now, he had establsihed himself as George Freeman's opening bowling partner, the pairing being one of the most formidable ever seen in county cricket.

In 1868, Emmett and Freeman ran through the might of Lancashire for 30 and 34 at Holbeck, Emmett's share being eight for 24. The following year came the most spectacular match analysis of Emmett's career when he took 16 wickets for 38 runs against Cambridgeshire, then a first-class county, as Yorkshire won by an innings and 266 runs.

Emmett was known as the 'Wicket and Wide Man' and was probably the first top-class bowler to make full use of the bowling crease in altering the angle of attack. He also altered his length by delivering the ball from behind the crease and was the first to bowl deliberatley wide of the off stump in the hope of inducing an edge. His best ball was his 'sostenutor' - a ball that would pitch on middle and leg and hit the off stump.

In 1871 at Old Trafford, Lancashire were bowled out for 90 and 95 with Emmett taking eleven for 85, bowling unchanged with Freeman in a 222 run win. At Sheffield he scored 64 not out and had match figures of thirteen for 90 as Yorkshire beat Nottinghamshire by 140 runs. He also took eleven wickets in each of the two matches against Lancashire in 1873. Also in the same season, Emmett made the only century of his career - 104 against Gloucestershire at Clifton.

In 1876-77, Emmett played in Australia, including a game which later became known as the first-ever Test Match. He was to play in seven of the first eight Tests and though he did not distinguish himself in the first two Tests, he later had figures of seven for 68 to become the first English player to take as many wickets in a Test.

In the close season of 1877-78, Emmett was appointed Yorkshire captain and though, according to his contemporaries, he was not an ideal leader, being over-modest with his bowling, he led the side for five seasons.

Emmett took 1,216 wickets for Yorkshire at an average of 12.71 and scored 6,315 runs at an average of 15.10, being the first bowler to take 1,000 wickets for the county.

On his retirement at the age of 47, Emmett became coach and groundsman at Rugby School, courtesy of Lord Harris's recommendation. He later became coach to Leicestershire but sadly the powers of alcohol overtook his enthusiasm for the game and he died in a fit of apoplexy in Leicester Asylum in June 1904.

YORKSHIRE v LANCASHIRE
at Bradford August 10,11,12, 1874

Lancashire 209 (Porter 61, Emmett 4-61)
Yorkshire 107 (McIntyre 5-31, Appleby 4-42) and 69 (McIntyre 8-35)
Lancashire won by an innings and 23 runs.

For the return meting, the first to be played at Park Avenue, Yorkshire were without the services of Hill and Rowbotham. Lancashire won the toss and thanks to a hard-hitting innings of 61 by Edward Porter, a Liverpool amateur, they scored 209. Tom Emmett was the pick of the Yorkshire bowlers, taking four for 61 in 61 overs!

George Ulyett, who had taken three for 35 in Lancashire's first innings, opened the batting for the home side. He was the only Yorkshire batsman to be at ease against the pace and swing of McIntyre and Appleby, who bowled out the White Rose county for 107. Following-on, Yorkshire again failed to come to terms with Lancashire's opening bowlers and in particular Bill McIntyre, who took eight for 35 to have match figures of thirteen for 66.

LANCASHIRE v YORKSHIRE
at Old Trafford June 24,25,26, 1875

Yorkshire 83 (Appleby 5-20) and 216 (Ulyett 50, McIntyre 5-96, Appleby 4-73)
Lancashire 154 (Hill 4-34) and 148-0 (Hornby 78*, Barlow 50*)
Lancashire won by 10 wickets.

Arthur Appleby and Bill McIntyre made early inroads into the Yorkshire top order and only a useful stand by George Ulyett and Tom Emmett helped the visitors to reach 83. Despite a devastating opening spell by Allen Hill, who clean bowled Barlow, Wright and Mills, Lancashire had moved into a strong position at 95 for five by the end of the first day. The Red Rose county were eventually dismissed for 154, a lead of 71 runs.

Yorkshire fought back well in their second innings with George Ulyett (50) and Tom Emmett (39) the chief run-getters. Some lusty blows by Clayton and Rowbotham lower down the order helped Yorkshire to total 216. Lancashire were left to score 146 for victory, a reasonably demanding total in those days.

Hornby and Barlow opened Lancashire's innings, walking to the wicket from separate pavilions situated on opposite ends of the ground, and by lunch on the final day had scored 30 runs without being parted. Yorkshire used five bowlers but nothing could disturb the opening pair, who knocked off the runs between them, Hornby scoring 78 not out and Barlow 50 not out.

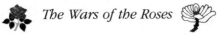

It was the first century opening partnership for Lancashire and was described at the time as an unparalleled feat. Hornby received a new cane-handled bat from Lancashire secretary Sam Swire and Barlow, who was hoisted shoulder high, was presented with the reward of six sovereigns.

YORKSHIRE v LANCASHIRE
at Bramall Lane July 12,13,14, 1875

Lancashire 112 (Hill 5-47) and 100 (Clayton 6-42, Hill 3-31)
Yorkshire 218 (McIntyre 5-92)
Yorkshire won by an innings and 6 runs.

Hornby and Barlow opened the batting for Lancashire and had taken the score to 34 when Barlow was brilliantly stumped by Yorkshire wicket-keeper Pinder. Wisden recounted the dismissal as follows: 'Barlow was superbly stumped by Pinder from the leg-side, a feat so cleanly and quickly done as to be unsurpassed in the annals of wicket-keeping.' In fact, Barlow was such a stone-walling batsman that it seemed something of a miracle for the cautious Lancashire opener to be stumped at all! Hill and Lockwood ran through the middle order and only some hefty blows by Coward, Appleby and Wright helped Lancashire to reach 112.

Despite losing Hicks, clean bowled by Appleby in the opening over of the Yorkshire innings, Clayton (44) and Lockwood (43) helped the home side to a lead of 106 runs.

Batting for a second time, Lancashire's hopes of saving the game depended heavily on Hornby and Barlow but both batsmen were clean bowled by Hill and Clayton respectively. Clayton went on to take six for 42, ably supported by Hill, whose second innings figures of three for 41 gave him a match return of eight for 88 in a match Yorkshire won by an innings and six runs.

LANCASHIRE v YORKSHIRE
at Old Trafford June 22,23,24, 1876

Lancashire 56 (Hornby 23* Hill 6-24, Armitage 4-30) and 98 (Hornby 43, Ulyett 4-14, Hill 3-28)
Yorkshire 138 (McIntyre 5-74) and 17-1
Yorkshire won by 9 wickets.

Yorkshire completely outplayed their rivals in this Old Trafford Roses match. The home side were bowled out for just 56 with opening batsman

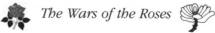

'Monkey' Hornby carrying his bat for 23 not out. Allen Hill bowled as destructively as ever to take six for 24 with five of his victims being clean bowled. He was well supported by Thomas Armitage, who took four for 30 with his lobs.

By the end of that first day, Yorkshire had been bowled out for 138 with Bill McIntyre the most successful Lancashire bowler, having figures of five for 74.

On the following day, Hornby again top-scored for Lancashire with 43 before he was caught by wicket-keeper Pinder off the bowling of George Ulyett. Destined to be one of the great figures in early Roses history, he made his mark with four for 14 off nine overs as Lancashire were dismissed for 98.

Requiring just 17 to win, Yorkshire lost Champion, bowled by McIntyre, and though no further wickets fell, McIntyre and Appleby bowled 23 overs before the target was reached.

YORKSHIRE v LANCASHIRE
at Bramall Lane July 10,11,12, 1876

Yorkshire 129 (McIntyre 5-47) and 86 (Appleby 6-33, McIntyre 4-51)
Lancashire 127 (Hill 3-22, Emmett 2-19) and 70 (Hill 6-28, Emmett 4-23)
Yorkshire won by 18 runs.

Yorkshire won both games this season, yet it didn't seem that would be the case at Bramall Lane when the home side were dismissed for 129. Bill McIntyre did the damage with five for 47, backed up by Alec Watson (three for 31) and Arthur Appleby (two for 40). Yet Yorkshire still managed to lead by two runs on the first innings. Hornby and Barlow were responsible for 74 of their side's total. Hornby hit 32 out of the first 35 runs whilst Barlow was the ninth batsman out for 42.

When Yorkshire batted again, Ulyett scored 20 but some fine fielding and bowling soon had the home side back in the pavilion for just 86 runs. Appleby (six for 33) and McIntyre (four for 51) bowled unchanged.

Lancashire's task of scoring 89 for victory seemed well within their capabilities, especially when they reached 62 for three. Then Allen Hill bowled Edmund Rowley and Vernon Royle without any addition to the score, Richard Howe at 64 and Arthur Appleby at 66. The last six wickets fell for eight runs, with Hill's last four overs being bowled for five wickets and one run!

Allen Hill finished with six for 28 and was well supported by Tom Emmett who took four for 23.

YORKSHIRE v LANCASHIRE
at Huddersfield July 12,13,14, 1877

Yorkshire 122 (Watson 4-55, Appleby 3-23) and 113 (Watson 5-45, Appleby 3-42)
Lancashire 207 (Appleby 69*, Ulyett 3-31, Emmett 3-53) and 29-1
Lancashire won by 9 wickets.

In this match at Fartown, Huddersfield, Yorkshire lost both openers, Greenwood and Bates, to Alec Watson with less than 10 runs on the board and never recovered. Only George Ulyett (39) and Ephraim Lockwood (28) played with any confidence as the home side were dismissed for 122. At the close of play on the first day, Lancashire were 78 for four with Richard Barlow unbeaten on 24. He added another 13 runs the following day before he was dismissed by Ulyett. Arthur Appleby, batting at number six, was Lancashire's top scorer with 69 not out in the visitor's total of 207 all out. In fact, so well did Appleby play that he was presented with a prize bat from the St John's club.

Having gained a first innings lead of 85, Lancashire went on the attack at the outset of the Yorkshire innings and, with the aid of some poor stroke play from the home side's top-order batsmen, grabbed some early wickets. At one stage, Yorkshire were 52 for five but a sixth wicket stand of 30 helped them to reach a total of 113. Top-scorer was Andrew Greenwood with 41, whilst for Lancashire, Alec Watson again impressed, taking five for 45.

Lancashire soon knocked off the 29 runs needed for victory, losing just one wicket in the process.

LANCASHIRE v YORKSHIRE
at Old Trafford August 9,10,11, 1877

Lancashire 215 (Hornby 88, Clayton 8-66) and 72 (Armitage 6-32, Clayton 4-38)
Yorkshire 144 (Patterson 5-99, Watson 4-46) and 108 (Patterson 5-40, McIntyre 3-35)
Lancashire won by 35 runs.

A.N. 'Monkey' Hornby with 88 and Richard Barlow with 24 began well for Lancashire by putting on 92 for the first wicket. Kershaw and Rowley also made useful contributions as the home side put 215 on the board. For Yorkshire, Clayton, aided by some terrific catches, took eight for 66 from 45.1 overs.

Lancashire's Cambridge Blue, Bill Patterson, bowled with great variation in flight to take five Yorkshire wickets and at 96 for eight it looked as though the visitors would struggle to avoid the follow-on. However,

15

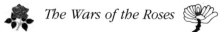

Armitage (30) and Clayton (18 not out) came together to save the follow-on and take Yorkshire to 144. By the close of play on the second day, Lancashire had been reduced to 38 for five in their second innings and the match now seemed to be swinging towards the White Rose county. Lancashire were all out for 72 just before lunch on the final day with Thomas Armitage taking six for 32. Clayton, who bowled unchanged with him, took four for 38 to finish with match figures of twelve for 104.

Needing 144 for victory, Yorkshire lost early wickets before Greenwood and Lockwood added 27 for the fourth wicket. There then came a collapse as Patterson and McIntyre took wickets with great rapidity, the former finishing with match figures of ten for 130 as the visitors were bowled out for 108 just before tea.

LANCASHIRE v YORKSHIRE
at Old Trafford July 11;12, 1878

Lancashire 267 (Hornby 78, Barlow 60, Ulyett 4-67)
Yorkshire 123 (A.G.Steel 5-49) and 118 (A.G.Steel 9-63)
Lancashire won by an innings and 26 runs.

After rain had delayed the start, Hornby and Barlow opened for Lancashire with a remarkable stand of 87 for the first wicket, during the course of which Hornby hit George Ulyett for four fours in one over. Hornby's was the first wicket to fall, caught by Armitage off the bowling of Lockwood for 78. At this time, Barlow was only nine but went on to score 60, adding 75 with Vernon Royle, who made 42 in Lancashire's total of 267.

When Yorkshire batted, only George Ulyett with 46 and Bates, with an unbeaten 21, played with any conviction and with Allan Steel taking five for 49, they were all out for 123.

When they followed-on, the visitors still found Steel to be in sparkling form. The all-rounder took nine for 63 with four of his victims being stumped by Dick Pilling - the 'Prince of wicket-keepers'. Yorkshire were all out for 118 just before seven o'clock on the second day, giving Lancashire victory by an innings and 26 runs. Steel, who bowled 89 overs in the match, had figures of fourteen for 112 - a truly remarkable performance.

ALLAN STEEL (LANCASHIRE)

Allan Gibson Steel was considered second only to W.G.Grace as the country's finest all-rounder in a career which ran through seventeen seasons from 1877 to 1893. He played in 162 first-class matches in that time but only 47 of them were for Lancashire!

He captained Lancashire only once, in 1886, and although he was never appointed county captain, he achieved a remarkable sequence as a winning captain - captaining Marlborough to victory over Rugby, Cambridge to victory over Oxford, the Gentlemen to victory over the Players, Lancashire to victory over Yorkshire and England to victory over Australia.

Steel scored a magnificent 87 against Sussex on his Lancashire debut in 1877 and a year later astonished the cricket world by taking 164 first-class wickets, 55 of them for Lancashire.

In 1878, Yorkshire were bowled out twice in a day with Steel taking fourteen for 112, including his best innings analysis of nine for 63. In 1881 Lancashire again romped home in the Roses match by eight wickets with a brilliant all-round display by Allan Steel. The Liverpool-born all-rounder scored 57 and 3 not out and took seven for 59 and six for 87. Yorkshire were again the opponents in 1886 when, after captaining England against Australia, Steel scored a magnificent 55 out of 112 and then, when Lancashire required 178 for victory, led the way with an unbeaten 80.

Playing for the MCC against Yorkshire at Scarborough in 1881, he made 106. It was one of eight first-class centuries, but his only hundred for Lancashire came in 1887 against Surrey at Old Trafford.

Allan Steel was a man for the big occasion and as a batsman was at his best for England against Australia. He toured Australia in 1882-83 and scored 135 not out in a Test match at Sydney. But probably his best innings for England was his 148 at Lord's in 1884. He came to the wicket with England 75 for three and scored his runs out of 238 made while he was in.

His career as a barrister developed quite quickly and after being called to the Bar at the Inner Temple when only 24, he became a QC when he was just 27. He had a large Admiralty practice and in 1904, when he was 46, he became Oldham Recorder.

When he died in 1921 at the age of 62, the County Club had been in existence fifty-seven years with such famous names as Hornby, MacLaren, Spooner, Briggs and Tyldesley, yet the 'Athletic News' was in no doubt that Steel was the best of them all - 'The greatest player Lancashire have ever produced.'

In his forty-seven matches for Lancashire, he scored 1,960 runs at an average of 29.25 and took 238 wickets at 13.16 runs each.

🌹 *The Wars of the Roses* 🌼

YORKSHIRE v LANCASHIRE
at Huddersfield August 8,9,10, 1878

Yorkshire 47 (Barlow 8-22) and 151-4 (Ulyett 91*)
Lancashire 123 (Bates 8-45)
Match Drawn

There was quite a turnabout in fortunes in the return game that summer despite Yorkshire being bowled out for 47 in their first innings. Richard Barlow took eight for 22 in 27.1 overs and the Lancashire opening batsman was still on the field at the close of play as the Red Rose county were 66 without loss in reply - 19 runs ahead of their rivals with all ten wickets still intact.

After Lancashire's first wicket had gone down at 74, they suffered a remarkable collapse. They were all out for 123 with Willie Bates emulating Barlow's feat by taking eight wickets for 45 runs. His figures would have been even better had he not been heavily punished early in the visitors' innings by Hornby, who top-scored with 43. At the close of play on the second day, Yorkshire were 151 for four with George Ulyett 91 not out after a magnificent display of attacking batsmanship.

With Yorkshire 75 runs ahead and six wickets in hand, the game was poised for an exciting final day, but, unfortunately, heavy rain prevented any further play.

RICHARD BARLOW (LANCASHIRE)

In his schooldays Richard Barlow used to practise with a crude bat, hewn from a rough piece of wood, and a ball pieced together with cloth and string. In his reminiscences he told how he would play truant from school and his methods of obtaining proficiency as a cricketer were thorough and workmanlike, two qualities he was to exhibit throughout his life.

The rough wickets of Barlow's day favoured the bowlers and it was often a considerable achievement for a batsman to keep his wicket at all. The long innings he played match after match, against some of the best bowling in England, were a measure of his technical ability and the efficacy of self-training. On numerous occasions, Barlow saved Lancashire from defeat by his resolute defence.

Twelve times he carried his bat through an innings and on many more occasions his was the last wicket to fall. Unfortunately, Old Trafford did not see what is generally reckoned to have been Barlow's finest innings. It was played at Trent Bridge for the North of England against the Australian touring team of 1884. The North scored 91 with Barlow making 10 not out and the Australians replied with 100. Spofforth, who had found the wicket in the first innings very much to his liking, prophesied that the Englishmen wouldn't make 60 in their second knock. After the first five wickets had fallen with 53 on the board it seemed that his prophecy wouldn't be far wrong. Then Nottinghamshire's Flowers joined Barlow and they added 158 for the sixth wicket. Barlow was last man out after scoring 101 without offering a chance in four-and-a-half hours. He completed a remarkable all-round performance by taking 10 wickets in the match for 45 runs!

Another noteworthy performance came at Trent Bridge in 1882 when he carried his bat through a Lancashire total of 69, of which Barlow in two-and-a-half hours, made only five! It was this innings which gave birth to the term 'stonewaller'.

Barlow's bowling was more than useful and he was one of the first cricketers to bat right-handed and bowl left. For Lancashire he took 736 wickets at 13.60 runs apiece. It was said that he had a special ball which he reserved exclusively for W.G.Grace whom hedismissed 31 times!

His all-round ability can be gauged from his record against Australia. He played in 17 Test matches, twelve of them in succession, scoring 591 runs and taking 35 wickets. To this day, Barlow is the only cricketer to be selected for England with the specific intention that he should open both the batting and the bowling.

Barlow was also a more than useful footballer and he achieved further distinction as a referee, taking charge of the famous FA Cup tie when Preston North End beat Hyde United 26-0.

Barlow's dedication to the game was shown in the house he built in Raikes Parade in Blackpool for 1,500 pounds. His initials were carved on stone over the door, his stained-glass window greeted the visitor at the vestibule and a gas lamp in the hall showed the names of famous Lancashire players, plus W.G.Grace. Richard Barlow even designed his own headstone for his grave in Layton Cemetery, Blackpool, close to the gates. It shows a set of stumps with the ball passing through middle and leg and at the bottom the words 'Bowled at Last!' He had also made sure that the stone would do him justice with the following inscription:

'Here lies the remains of Richard Gorton Barlow, died 31 July 1919, aged 68 years. For 21 seasons a playing member of the Lancashire County XI and for 21 seasons an umpire in county matches. He also made three journeys to Australia with English teams. This is a consecutive record in first-class cricket which no other cricketer has achieved.'

LANCASHIRE v YORKSHIRE
at Old Trafford July 10,11,12, 1879

Yorkshire 79 (A.G.Steel 7-34) and 69 (McIntyre 5-17, A.G.Steel 4-39)
Lancashire 180 (D.Q.Steel 52, Emmett 4-43, Bates 4-62)
Lancashire won by an innings and 32 runs.

After his fourteen for 112 at Old Trafford in 1878, Allan Steel was again the scourge of the Yorkshire batsmen. Only three of the visitors side managed double figures - Lockwood (28), Emmett (15) and Ulyett (10) as Steel finished with seven for 34. Wisden commented: 'It seems the best of England's batsmen find it difficult to master the ever-varying pace, pitch and curve bowling of Mr A.G.Steel, who makes his mark in match records against the cleverest of bats on all grounds.'

Despite losing Richard Barlow, clean bowled by Bates in the opening over of their innings, Lancashire replied with a total of 180. Top-scorer with the highest individual innings of the match was D.Q.Steel with 52. He was well supported by A.N.Hornby (36) and A.G.Steel (31). For Yorkshire, Bates and Emmett took four wickets apiece.

When Yorkshire batted a second time, only wicket-keeper George Pinder batting at number ten showed any resistance with an innings of 19 not out. Bill McIntyre took five for 17 off 23 overs whilst Allan Steel finished with match figures of eleven for 73 as Lancashire won by an innings and 32 runs.

YORKSHIRE v LANCASHIRE
at Bramall Lane August 11,12, 1879

Lancashire 87 (Ulyett 7-32) and 186 (Hornby 55, Royle 48, Emmett 5-38, Peate 4-54)
Yorkshire 353 (Bates 118, Ulyett 53)
Yorkshire won by an innings and 80 runs.

Yorkshire turned the tables at Bramall Lane, beating Lancashire by an innings and 80 runs in a one-side game. Lancashire won the toss and elected to bat but soon lost Barlow, run out after a mix-up with Hornby. Hornby (28) and Royle (21) batted with composure before George Ulyett bowled both batsmen within the space of three balls. Wickets then began to fall at an alarming rate with the last seven batsmen only mustering six runs as Lancashire were bowled out for 87. George Ulyett took seven for 32 with Ted Peate, playing in his first Roses game, taking two for 26 from 17 overs.

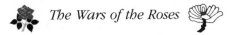

Ulyett then scored a quick-fire 53, adding 70 for the second wicket with Ephraim Lockwood, who scored 39. At the close of play on the first day, Yorkshire were 200 for six with Bates 53 not out. On the second day he progressed to 118 before being bowled by Barlow. It was a splendid innings and helped the home side to reach 353.

Needing 266 to prevent an innings defeat, Lancashire began well with Hornby and Barlow putting on 72 for the first wicket. Vernon Royle backed up Hornby's fighting half-century with an innings of 48 before losing his off stump to Emmett. The Yorkshire bowler went on to take five for 38 as the lower order batsmen failed to sustain the improvement and were bowled out for 186. Peate again showed immense promise with four for 54.

LANCASHIRE v YORKSHIRE
at Old Trafford August 5,6,7, 1880

Lancashire 132 (Peate 6-56) and 47 (Peate 8-24)
Yorkshire 125 (Nash 6-32) and 4-0
Match Drawn

In a game that was continually interrupted by rain, it has to be said that certain victory was snatched from Yorkshire who, when the wet weather finally closed in, needed 51 to win with all ten wickets intact.

After a delayed start, Hornby and Barlow put on 45 for the first wicket, with Hornby the first out for 42. The Lancashire captain had been judged lbw to the bowling of Bill Bosomworth, who was playing in his first game for Yorkshire for five years. Lancashire were all out for 132 with Ted Peate taking six for 56.

After losing the early wicket of Ulyett, Tom Emmett (44) and Ephraim Lockwood (41) began to take the Lancashire attack apart, but when both fell to George Nash in the space of a few balls, wickets began to fall with amazing rapidity. Nash ended with figures of six for 32 from 42.3 overs!

This feat was completely eclipsed by Yorkshire's Ted Peate, who took eight for 24 off 38 overs as Lancashire collapsed to 47 all out. Richard Barlow carried his bat through this catastrophic innings for 10 not out!

Needing just 55 for victory, Yortkshire were four without loss when further rain fell, washing out most of the last day's play.

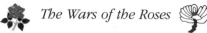

TED PEATE (YORKSHIRE)

Ted Peate began his career as a fast bowler in Yeadon in 1875, joining a troupe called Treloar's Cricket Clowns which included acrobats. He later spent the winter practising in the Yeadon shed where he worked as a warp-twister. Peate was spotted at Scarboroiugh by the Revd. E.S.Carter, who recommended him to Yorkshire. Eventually he was given a trial with the Colts in 1879 and, much to everyone's amazement, he took seventeen wickets for 33 runs in the match! Immediately promoted to the first team, Peate's first two games for the county were all but washed out, but on his third appearance against Kent at Bramall Lane, he had match figures of twelve for 77.

Though Peate was not a great spinner of the ball, tending to rely on flight, length and variations of pace, there was no doubt that he could be deadly if there was any help in the wicket. However, he was not just a 'bad-wicket' bowler and when he toured Australia in 1881-82, he demonstrated that to great effect. On virtually perfect batting strips, he had returns of eight for 57 against Murdoch's XI, six for 100 against New South Wales and six for 30 against Victoria. During the following summer, when the Australians visited England, Peate took 63 Australian wickets at 12.90, twice as many as any other English bowler.

In 1883, whilst playing on his home-town ground of Holbeck, Peate took eight wickets for five runs as Surrey were bowled out for just 31. Peate's best figures for Yorkshire came three years later when he took nine for 21 against Sussex. In eight seasons of first-class cricket, Ted Peate took 1,033 wickets at 13 runs apiece. A year after his most successful return, his county career was ended by Lord Hawke. One of the reasons given for his dismissal was his failing eyesight but he may well have fallen foul of his Lordship.

When Ted Peate died at the age of 45, having played league cricket for several years, Wisden spoke in its obituary of 'his death ostensibly through pneumonia but for some time as a result of his way of life, he had been in a poor condition'.

Yorkshire wicket-keeper David Hunter remembered Ted Peate as 'the finest left-arm slow bowler I ever saw. He had a beautiful action and was extraordinarily accurate, seldom, if ever, losing his length.'

YORKSHIRE v LANCASHIRE
at Bramall Lane July 12,13,14, 1880

Lancashire 125 (Bates 4-50, Peate 3-34) and 17-0
Yorkshire 154 (Emmett 51, A.G.Steel 7-63)
Match Drawn.

After an absorbing first day's cricket, no play was possible after lunch on the second day and the game fizzled out into a tame draw.

Lancashire won the toss and elected to bat but fine bowling by Bates and Peate reduced the Red Rose county to 37 for seven. When wicket-keeper Dick Pilling joined Johnny Briggs, a stubborn resistance was offered. It was due to their batting that a total of 125 was reached, Pilling ending unbeaten on 44.

Though Allan Steel took some early wickets in Yorkshire's first innings, the home side had reached 126 for six by the time stumps were drawn at the end of the first day. Tom Emmett, who was 48 not out, added three runs to his overnight score before becoming another of Steel's victims. The Lancashire all-rounder finished with seven for 63 as Yorkshire were bowled out for 154.

In the minutes that remained up to lunch, Hornby and Barlow took Lancashire to 17 without loss. Just before the restart, a thunderstorm accompanied by torrential rain washed out play for the rest of the day. After more rain the following day, the ground was unfit for play and the match abandoned.

YORKSHIRE v LANCASHIRE
at Bramall Lane July 4,5,6, 1881

Lancashire 162 (Hill 3-36) and 196 (Barlow 69, Ulyett 3-33, Bates 3-51, Peate 3-54)
Yorkshire 163 (Lockwood 73, Miller 5-46) and 145 (Nash 4-26)
Lancashire won by 50 runs.

A crowd of 14,000 filled Bramall Lane to watch a Roses match between two sides that had each won their last five county games. With the exception of Lancashire all-rounder Allan Steel, both sides were at full strength.

Lancashire made a very solid start with Hornby and D.Q.Steel adding 51 for the second wicket after Barlow had been run out with 31 on the board. Hornby was Lancashire's second wicket to fall, being stumped by Hunter off the bowling of Peate for 46. Robinson and Briggs also got amongst the runs but from 152 for four, Lancashire collapsed to 162 all out with the last four batsmen all failing to score! All the Yorkshire bowlers took wickets with Hill the most successful with three for 36.

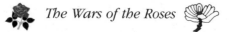

By the end of the first day, Yorkshire were 155 for seven with Ephraim Lockwood batting brilliantly for his innings of 73. Lancashire's top scorer Hornby even took a wicket with his lobs when Tom Emmett was stumped by Pilling off his second delivery. The three remaining wickets fell early the next day to leave Yorkshire with a lead of just one run.

Lancashire's second innings began badly when Hornby was bowled by Bates for four, but with Richard Barlow scoring 69, helped by some useful contributions from D.Q.Steel, Briggs and Miller, the visitors finally reached 196.

Needing the same score for victory, Yorkshire soon lost Ulyett to a splendid catch in the covers by Hornby and Bates, who slipped when going for a quick single and was run out. However, Lockwood and Emmett stood firm and took the score at the end of the second day to 76 for two. But then a heavy overnight thunderstorm put a completely different complexion on the game. George Nash bowled well to take four for 26 and as wickets continued to tumble, Yorkshire were all out for 145, leaving Lancashire the winners by 50 runs.

LANCASHIRE v YORKSHIRE
at Old Trafford July 28,29,30, 1881

Yorkshire 96 (A.G.Steel 7-59) and 185 (Emmett 75, A.G.Steel 6-87)
Lancashire 212 (Hornby 69, A.G.Steel 57, Emmett 5-42) and 70-2 (Hornby 50)
Lancashire won by 8 wickets.

It had been arranged to play this Roses match on the new ground at Liverpool but, owing to the unsatisfactory state of the wicket, the match was switched to Old Trafford.

Despite a number of early morning showers, Yorkshire on winning the toss, elected to bat. Their innings started disastrously when Allan Steel, back in the Lancashire side following injury, removed both openers, Hall and Bates. Only the Lockwoods, Henry with 32 and Ephraim with 15, along with Tom Emmett (20), succeeded in reaching double figures, whilst Steel, aided by some magnificent fielding, finished with figures of seven for 59.

Hornby and Barlow were still there for Lancashire at the close of play but the latter was run out for 26 early the following day. Hornby went on to top score with 69 whilst Allan Steel followed up his outstanding display of bowling with a hard-hit 57. Vernon Royle, who had run out Ephraim Lockwood in spectacular style in what was his first appearance of the season, scored an unbeaten 19 as Lancashire's innings closed on 212.

By the end of the second day, Yorkshire were in real trouble at 96 for seven with Steel again the major wicket-taker. A surprise was in store

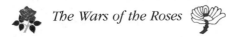

for the few spectators who decided to turn up for the final day's play. The last three wickets put on no less than 91 runs with the best stand being one of 70 between Peate and Emmett. Lancashire tried several bowling changes before Barlow clean bowled Emmett for 75. The pick of the Lancashire bowlers was again Allan Steel, who finished with match figures of thirteen for 146.

Needing 70 to win, Lancashire lost two wickets in reaching their goal. 'Monkey' Hornby followed up his first innings score with a quick-fire 50.

YORKSHIRE v LANCASHIRE
at Bramall Lane July 24,25,26, 1882

Lancashire 152 (Peate 4-63, Emmett 2-0) and 75 (Emmett 6-34, Peate 4-29)
Yorkshire 98 (Ulyett 53, Watson 6-32) and 67-4
Match Drawn.

This Roses match was played for the benefit of Yorkshire's Ephraim Lockwood, who for the last 16 years had been a much respected professional for the White Rose county. Sadly, the weather was wet and the game ended in a draw, albeit very much in Lancashire's favour.

The visitors won the toss and elected to bat, but play didn't get underway until 2.15 pm and shortly after 5.00 pm, the rain came down again. Stumps were drawn, Lancashire having lost three wickets in scoring 61 runs. Rain again delayed the start of the game on the second day until after lunch. Lancashire were all out for 152 with Richard Barlow top-scoring with 32. Ted Peate took four for 32 whilst Tom Emmett took two wickets without conceding a run.

Yorkshire, it seemed, had found a strong opening partnership in Ulyett and Hall. Ulyett, known as 'Happy Jack', was a big, cheerful extrovert, keen on his glass of ale, while Hall was slightly built, a Methodist preacher and a teetotaller. They made quite a remarkable reply, posting 60 for the first wicket in a little over three-quarters of an hour. Hall was the first to fall for six with Ulyett being dismissed shortly afterwards for a well-hit 53. With Alec Watson taking six for 32, Yorkshire were bowled out for 98, the two opening batsmen being responsible for more than half the total.

In Lancashire's second innings, only former Yorkshire batsman Edward Roper (27) and 'Monkey' Hornby (19) reached double figures as the Red Rose county were dismissed for 75. Emmett took six for 34 off 20 overs and he was well supported by Peate, who repeated his achievement of the first innings in taking four wickets.

Needing 130 for victory, Yorkshire had scored 67 for four when stumps were drawn.

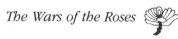

LANCASHIRE v YORKSHIRE
at Old Trafford August 3,4,5, 1882

Lancashire 218 (Barlow 68, Peel 5-41) and 97 (Peate 5-25)
Yorkshire 158 (A.G.Steel 5-81) and 141 (Crossland 3-37, Barlow 3-41)
Lancashire won by 16 runs.

In one of the most exciting Roses matches of recent years, Lancashire won the toss and elected to bat. They were indebted to Richard Barlow, who, after helping Hornby put on 65 for the first wicket, held the innings together, scoring 68. There were useful contributions from Pilling (30) and Yates (24) before the last wicket pairing of Watson and Crossland did some hard hitting to bring the total up to 218. Yorkshire's most successful bowler was Bobby Peel, playing in his first season of county cricket. He took five for 41 off 30 overs.

Yorkshire lost two early wickets when both Lord Hawke and George Ulyett were stumped by Pilling off the bowling of John Crossland. The visitors batted quite steadily on the second day but only Ted Peate with 38 stayed at the wicket for any length of time. When the last wicket fell, Yorkshire were 60 runs adrift of their rivals.

It was Peate again, this time with the ball, who came to Yorkshire's rescue, taking five for 25 in Lancashire's second innings total of 97. In fact, if Barlow (28) and Royle (19) hadn't held up Yorkshire's attack, Lancashire's total would have been much lower.

Yorkshire required 158 to win and Peate and Emmett put on 35 for the first wicket before Peate, who had a fine match, was out for 21. Emmett went for 38 and by lunch on the final day, Yorkshire were 86 for six. Stell Haggas (16) and Irwin Grimshaw (15) took the score to 124 before the eighth wicket fell. The last wicket went down with Lancashire the winners by 16 runs in a pulsating finish.

Unfortunately, the match was tainted by both sides claiming that its opponents' umpire favoured his own side!

LANCASHIRE v YORKSHIRE
at Old Trafford July 5,6, 1883

Lancashire 79 (Harrison 7-43) and 120 (Ulyett 4-25)
Yorkshire 143 (Watson 6-46) and 58-2
Yorkshire won by 8 wickets.

Lord Hawke, who had made his Yorkshire debut some two years earlier, was missing from the side when they visited Old Trafford at the beginning of July. Lancashire too were under strength with both Steel and Royle missing through injury.

Lancashire won the toss but failed to make good use of what seemed a good batting wicket. They were all out for 79 with the last seven wickets going down for just 24 runs. Yorkshire's opening bowler George Harrison, known as 'Shoey' because of his cobbling trade, took seven for 43, clean bowling five of the Lancashire batsmen.

Yorkshire's innings began in much the same way as the home side's before Louis Hall (43) and Ephraim Lockwood (31) put on 40 for the third wicket. The White Rose county were all out for 143 early the second day with Alec Watson having taken six for 46. Needing 64 runs to make the visitors bat again, Lancashire made a spirited reply but on reaching 94 for three, four wickets fell without a run being added! George Ulyett took four for 25 and Tom Emmett three for 13 as Lancashire were bowled out for 120.

Needing only 57 for victory, Yorkshire lost two wickets with only 20 on the board but then an unbroken third wicket stand of 38 between the first innings heroes, Hall and Lockwood, took the visitors to an eight-wicket win.

YORKSHIRE v LANCASHIRE
at Bramall Lane July 16,17, 1883

Lancashire 83 (Ulyett 5-16, Harrison 5-22) and 127 (Harrison 3-37)
Yorkshire 93 (Crossland 4-10) and 119-2 (Ulyett 61)
Yorkshire won by 8 wickets.

Yorkshire completed the double over Lancashire this year, their margin of victory at Bramall Lane being the same as at Old Trafford.

The game itself lasted for two days but such was the interest that over 19,000 spectators were attracted to the Sheffield ground.

Lancashire made a dreadful start, losing their first three wickets to the bowling of Harrison for just seven runs, but then a stand of 47 between Frank Taylor (30) and Richard Barlow (28) gave them some hope. It wasn't to be and the visitors were all out for 83. George Ulyett took five for 16 including the hat-trick - his victims, Hornby, Briggs and Watson all being clean bowled. George Harrison's sheer speed saw him take five for 22, again all clean bowled. When Yorkshire went in, wickets fell so fast that it didn't seem that they would even reach the total of their visitors. However, thanks to some brave hitting by Emmett and Hunter, they amassed 93, a lead of ten runs.

27

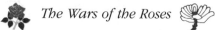

Lancashire collapsed to 68 for seven in their second innings before an eighth wicket stand of 31 between Richard Barlow (33) and Vernon Royle (38) allowed them to reach 127.

Yorkshire soon set about their task of making 118 for victory with the sustained hitting of George Ulyett bringing him 61 runs out of 94 for the first wicket in what was a brilliant innings. Louis Hall scored 30 and Yorkshire reached their target for the loss of only two wickets.

LANCASHIRE v YORKSHIRE
at Old Trafford June 26,27, 1884

Lancashire 123 (E.E.Steel 51, Ulyett 5-38) and 154 (H.B.Steel 48, Peate 4-43)
Yorkshire 181 (Crossland 4-45) and 97-7
Yorkshire won by 3 wickets.

This was another exciting Roses match, the result of which was in doubt until the last over.

Lancashire won the toss but then proceeded to give one of the worst batting displays of the season, losing their first five wickets for 34 runs, all to the bowling of George Ulyett. E.E.Steel, the youngest of the four brothers to appear for Lancashire this season, came to the wicket and scored 51 out of 73 runs added whilst he was at the crease. Pilling and Crossland added 16 for the last wicket to take Lancashire to a first innings total of 123. Ulyett, who broke the back of the Red Rose county's first innings, finished with five for 38.

Though Yorkshire made a much better start with their first four batsmen reaching double figures - Ulyett (20) Hall (21) Bates (16) and Lee (23) - six wickets were down when the score reached 90. Peel then batted well for 37 before Hunter and Harrison made useful lower order contributions.

Batting for a second time, Lancashire found themselves 58 runs in arrears and after losing their first four wickets for 26 were still 32 runs short of making Yorkshire bat again when the Steel brothers, H.B. (48) and E.E. (30 not out), helped the home side to a total of 154. Ted Peate was the pick of the Yorkshire bowlers, his four for 43 including the wickets of Lancashire's opening batsmen, Hornby and Barlow.

Yorkshire were set 97 to win but lost two wickets with just seven runs on the board. Lee (19) helped the visitors to 41 before the third wicket went down. Barlow and Watson grabbed a wicket apiece to leave Yorkshire 44 for five before Ulyett and Lord Hawke took the score to 69 for six when the latter batsman was dismissed for 22. Ulyett then began

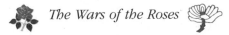

Yorkshire 1884

Back row: Peate, Emmett, H.Turner (scorer), Harris, Hunter
Middle row: Rawlin, Lee, Hall, Peel, Ulyett
Front row: Bates, Grimshaw

to hit out and made 32 in taking Yorkshire to 92 for seven before he was out. Despite some near misses, there were no further dismissals and so Yorkshire won by three wickets.

YORKSHIRE v LANCASHIRE
at Bramall Lane July 14,15, 1884

Yorkshire 128 (Bates 66, Barlow 7-38) and 72 (Barlow 6-28)
Lancashire 170 (Briggs 75*, Peate 7-46) and 31-4
Lancashire won by 6 wickets.

In what was Allen Hill's benefit match, Yorkshire batted first, but the only noteworthy features of their innings were the patient defensive cricket of Louis Hall and the adventurous stroke-play of Willie Bates. Hall spent two-and-a-quarter hours at the wicket in compiling his 28 whilst Bates' innings of 66 contained seven fours. After Bates had been dismissed, the last seven Yorkshire wickets fell for 19 runs. Richard Barlow had figures of seven for 38 from 39.2 overs.

29

At the close of play on the first day, Lancashire were only 23 runs behind Yorkshire's total of 128 with six wickets in hand. When play resumed on the second day, Briggs, who had been 34 not out, carried his bat for a really admirable 75. Peate that morning took four more wickets for only 15 runs to finish with seven for 46 from 45.3 overs.

Yorkshire went in to bat for a second time needing 42 runs to make the visitors bat again. Barlow again took early wickets and half the White Rose side were out at lunch with just 15 runs on the board. Afterwards, and despite four of Yorkshire's remaining batsman achieving double figures, Lancashire were left with the task of making 31 runs to win. Richard Barlow took six for 28 to finish with match figures of thirteen for 66. His bowling performance must have gone to his head, for he was stumped by Hunter off the bowling of Peate without a run on the board. In fact, Lancashire lost four wickets, the other three to Bates, before reaching their target. Sadly for Allen Hill the match did not extend into the third day.

LANCASHIRE v YORKSHIRE
at Old Trafford June 18,19,20, 1885

Lancashire 168 (Hornby 61, Peel 4-22, Harrison 4-64) and 138 (Emmett 7-50)
Yorkshire 158 (Grimshaw 74, Watson 4-34, Barlow 4-54) and 75-6
Match Drawn.

Ted Peate and George Harrison took two early wickets apiece as Lancashire slumped to 47 for four. Frank Taylor and 'Monkey' Hornby added 90 for the fifth wicket before the former was adjudged lbw to Peel. The Yorkshire bowler later bowled Hornby for 61 and finished with four for 22 as the home side were bowled out for 168.

After Bates had been run out for four, Hall and Grimshaw took the score to 117 before the latter batsman was bowled by Barlow for a faultless 74. On the second day, Watson and Barlow bowled well and Yorkshire's last eight wickets added just 41 runs to give Lancashire a ten run lead on first innings.

Lancashire again lost early wickets and were indebted to Leach (39) and captain Hornby (34), who added 42 for the fifth wicket. Tom Emmett bowled extremely well, taking seven for 50 from 34 overs as Lancashire were dismissed for 138.

Yorkshire's openers had just come down the pavilion steps when heavy rain ended play for the day before they could begin their task of getting 149 runs for victory. A close finish was expected on the final day

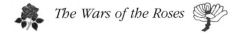

but a series of heavy showers meant that when stumps were drawn, Yorkshire were 75 for six.

YORKSHIRE v LANCASHIRE
at Huddersfield July 23,24,25, 1885

Lancashire 232 (Robinson 80, Bates 6-85) and 214 (Kemp 109, Peate 6-44)
Yorkshire 301 (Bates 98, Preston 59, Briggs 4-96) and 148-2 (Bates 82*)
Yorkshire won by 8 wickets.

Willie Bates destroyed Lancashire's top-order with a fine display of bowling, removing Hornby, Lancashire and Briggs in his opening spell and finishing with six for 85. Cambridge University student George Kemp made a useful 37 before Walter Robinson, who had played seven first-class matches for Yorkshire, scored 80, receiving good support from the last few batsmen. In fact, the last four wickets put on 153 of Lancashire's first innings total of 232.

Ulyett and Hall made a good start for Yorkshire, putting on 56 at a run a minute before the former was stumped for 40. The major feature of the second day's play was the batting of Willie Bates. He was 19 not out at the close of the first day's play and went on to make 98 out of 141 before being bowled by Alec Watson. The home crowd were very impressed by his performance and made a collection which totalled some £14. Yorkshire, with Preston (59) and Emmett (45 not out) making useful contributions, were bowled out for 301, a lead of 69 runs.

At the close of play, Lancashire, who had lost both openers, Hornby and Barlow, were 81 for two with Kemp 38 not out. On the final day, Kemp went from strength to strength and in an innings of 109, scored 17 fours. Unfortunately for the visitors, no-one else could play the Yorkshire attack with such confidence and with Ted Peate taking six for 44 from 41 overs, the home side were left to make 148 for victory in just under three hours.

The game looked to be heading for a draw after Watson had removed Ulyett and Grimshaw but Bates (82 not out) and Preston (39 not out) played magnificently and Yorkshire won by eight wickets with just under an hour still to play.

Willie Bates had an outstanding match, scoring 180 runs and capturing seven wickets.

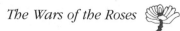 *The Wars of the Roses*

LANCASHIRE v YORKSHIRE
at Old Trafford July 8,9,10, 1886

Yorkshire 133 (Ulyett 64, Barlow 6-58) and 156 (Barlow 6-53)
Lancashire 112 (A.G.Steel 55, Emmett 7-33) and 178-6 (A.G.Steel 80*)
Lancashire won by 4 wickets.

Yorkshire made a good start to the Roses match and at lunch were 89 for two. However, the afternoon session saw Lancashire take the remaining eight wickets for just 44 runs with Richard Barlow finishing with six for 58 off 43 overs. For Yorkshire, George Ulyett scored 64, almost half his side's total. Lancashire were then bowled out for 112 with Allan Steel, who was captaining the side in the absence of 'Monkey' Hornby, scoring 55. The only other Lancashire player to reach double figures was Johnny Briggs with 23. Tom Emmett took seven for 33 off 32 overs - a magnificent piece of bowling.

Yorkshire began their second innings in bad light and after Barlow had bowled Ulyett without a run on the board, Watson took three more quick wickets to leave the visitors on 37 for four. Lord Hawke (33) and Bobby Peel (32) both played well to take the Yorkshire total to 156.

Set 178 to win, Lancashire lost four early wickets as Emmett and Peel tore through the home side's top order. Allan Steel then proceeded to dominate the Yorkshire attack to score a glorious unbeaten 80 as Lancashire reached the required total with four wickets to spare.

YORKSHIRE v LANCASHIRE
at Dewsbury July 29,30,31, 1886

Yorkshire 112 (Briggs 5-57, Watson 4-52) and 107-7 (Watson 5-25)
Lancashire 53 (Bates 6-19, Emmett 4-10)
Match Drawn.

The only-ever Roses match to be played at Dewsbury produced a rain-spattered draw.

It was not until 4.15 pm on the first day that a start could be made and then, on a wicket completely saturated, Yorkshire scored 97 for seven. A complete collapse was avoided by the stubborn batting of Ulyett (31) and Preston (30) who helped the home side to reach a total of 112 after the entire second day had been lost to rain.

The wicket on the final day was extremely treacherous with 20 wickets falling for 175 runs. Lancashire were bowled out for just 53 with Willie Bates taking six for 19. The only Red Rose county batsman to reach

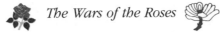

double figures was Johnny Briggs with 20. The visitors last eight wickets fell for just 13 runs!

In their second innings, Yorkshire lost early wickets to Alec Watson but Willie Bates (30) and George Ulyett (32) made sure the White Rose county didn't collapse and when stumps were drawn, the home side were 107 for seven.

YORKSHIRE v LANCASHIRE
at Bradford August 8,9,10, 1887

Yorkshire 590 (Lee 165, Hall 160, Ulyett 67, Lord Hawke 58)
Lancashire 303 (Robinson 111*, Hornby 69) and 317-8 (Hornby 92, Eccles 57, Hall 4-122)
Match Drawn.

In the year of Queen Victoria's Jubilee, Yorkshire's first innings total of 590 was the highest of all Roses' totals and contained half-centuries by George Ulyett and Lord Hawke and hundreds from Louis Hall and Fred Lee. Lee was one of Yorkshire's many young cricketers from the Huddersfield district. He had a meteoric but sadly short cricketing career in the 1880s before dying at the age of 39.

Ulyett began well, making 67 out of 89 in just 56 minutes before Lee joined Hall to add 280 for the second wicket in just under three-and-a-half hours. Fred Lee was dismissed for 165, the highest score of his career, though he had been dropped in the deep when he had scored 19. Hall and Lord Hawke were at the wicket when stumps were drawn with Yorkshire's total standing at 434 for two. Hawke went early the following day for 58 out of a partnership of 74. Bates then hit a quick-fire 38 before Louis Hall was fifth out at 529. His innings of 160 took six hours 40 minutes and during that time he didn't offer one single chance. The home side were eventually all out just after lunch with Lancashire's Alec Watson having taken four for 118 from 113.2 overs!

'Monkey' Hornby and Barlow put on 84 for Lancashire's first wicket with the former batsman making 69, but by mid-afternoon the visitors were 99 for six. Robinson joined Barlow and the two batsmen took the score to 167 before the Lancashire opener fell victim to Emmett. Robinson batted well into the third day, scoring an unbeaten 111 out of Lancashire's first innings total of 303.

Following on 287 behind, Lancashire faced a difficult task in batting all day to save the match. However, the wicket played as well as on the first day and with Hornby (92) and Joe Eccles (57) in splendid form, the Red Rose county ended the final day on 317 for eight, just 30 runs ahead with two wickets left.

LORD HAWKE (YORKSHIRE)

It was at his Slough prep school that Martin Hawke's love of cricket began. After Slough came Eton where Hawke was given his colours for the 1878 Harrow match. While he was there his family moved to Wighill Park, Tadcaster, a step that was to qualify him to play for Yorkshire. During the summer holidays he was honoured by an invitation to play for the Yorkshire Gentlemen and in this way his first contact with the county was established.

When Martin Hawke was twenty-one, he went up to Cambridge where he gained his Blue the following year by knocking up 58 out of 89 in a match at the Oval. That event prefaced three happy years in the University eleven culminating in his captaincy in 1885.

In his last year at Cambridge he scored 73 in the MCC match at Lord's against the bowling of the redoubtable A.G.Steel and Barnes.

Lord Hawke always maintained that he owed his introduction to Yorkshire cricket to a certain Canon Carter, a keen amateur. So keen indeed, that on one occasion while conducting a church service, he was heard to exclaim 'Here endeth the first innings!'

When Tom Emmett resigned the Yorkshire captaincy in 1883, it was offered to Martin Hawke, two years before he was due to come down from Cambridge. He accepted the honour with gratitude and thus found himself in the remarkable situation of skippering his county a couple of years before he was invited to do the same thing for his university.

Hawke's first century for Yorkshire was scored in 1886 when he made a chanceless 144 against Sussex at Hove and that same year, he hit up a fiery 63 against Middlesex at Lord's. The following season he again scored a century and the next milestone in his career came in 1887-88 when he captained his first unofficial team to Australia.

The team suffered only one defeat but for Martin Hawke the tour proved a tragedy when news of his father's death sent him hurrying homewards before the tour could be concluded.

For several years under Hawke's leadership, Yorkshire was in the doldrums but they began to pull out in 1890 when he headed the batting averages. But it took three more years of gruelling work, particularly in fielding, in which Yorkshire were specially weak, before they finally carried off the County Championship; after which they repeated the achievement eight times during Hawke's twenty-seven years of captaincy.

An outstanding match was the one played in the 1896 championship year against Warwickshire when Yorkshire compiled the record score of 887. Four separate centuries went towards this total, Hawke himself making 166 and Bobby Peel 210 not out in a record eighth wicket partnership of 292.

The year of 1900 was one of Lord Hawke's proudest, for Yorkshire not only won the championship again but he had the exhilarating experience of leading an unbeaten side. Hawke notched a couple of London centuries that year,

one at the Oval where he made 126 against Surrey and another at Lord's where he was 107 not out for the MCC against Oxford University.

Perhaps the most important reform introduced by Lord Hawke into Yorkshire cricket was the payment of winter salaries, a measure that was greatly appreciated by his men.

It must not be forgotten that it was Lord Hawke who planted the white rose on the Yorkshire caps and blazers, an idea which came to him after seeing the red rose of Lancashire. After his retirement from the captaincy in 1910 he became president of the county, a position he held until his death.

However, it is as a power at Lord's as President of MCC 1914-1919, Treasurer of MCC 1932-1938 and England selector 1899-1909 and after 1933 that Lord Hawke is chiefly remembered today.

35

LANCASHIRE v YORKSHIRE
at Old Trafford August 25,26,27, 1887

Lancashire 129 (Emmett 3-38) and 246 (Robinson 92)
Yorkshire 414 (Lord Hawke 125, Peel 66, Hall 62, Briggs 4-119)
Yorkshire won by an innings and 39 runs.

Since the first meeting of these two sides earlier this summer, Lancashire had won four matches in succession and were favourites to win this match, the last first-class fixture of the season.

Lancashire won the toss and elected to bat on what seemed a good wicket. However, the Red Rose county batsmen failed to make full use of their opportunities and with Emmett, Preston and Peel all bowling well, were all out for 129.

Bates and Hall opened the batting for Yorkshire, the former having scored 33 when he was the first wicket to fall at 37. Hall was joined by Fred Lee, who had made 57 when he was brilliantly caught by Hornby on the square-leg boundary. At the close of play, the visitors were 162 for two. Hall failed to add to his overnight score of 62, whilst both Ulyett and Lord Hawke were dropped before they had reached double figures. They proceeded to take the score up to 240 before Ulyett was caught and bowled by Barlow for 44. Lord Hawke was joined by Bobby Peel and they added 107 for the fifth wicket before Peel was dismissed for 66. Lord Hawke went on to score 125, his only century for the county that summer as Yorkshire totalled 414.

Needing 285 to avoid an innings defeat, Lancashire made a disappointing start, losing their first five wickets with less than 30 on the board. Frank Sugg then hit 34 before Walter Robinson set his stall out to save the game. Encouraged by the stubborn resistance of Baker (16) Yates (23) Watson (35) and Pilling (17 not out), Robinson went on to score 92 before being adjudged lbw to Wade, the pick of the Yorkshire bowlers.

YORKSHIRE v LANCASHIRE
at Bramall Lane July 2,3,4, 1888

Lancashire 54 (Wade 6-29, Peel 4-23) and 35-0
Yorkshire 80 (Napier 4-0, Briggs 4-37)
Match Drawn.

The first two days of this Roses clash were completely washed out by the incessant rain which fell at Bramall Lane.

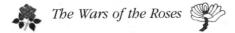

When play finally got underway at the start of the third day, Lancashire were skittled out for 54 in an hour and a three-quarters. Saul Wade and Bobby Peel bowled unchanged for Yorkshire to record figures of six for 29 and four for 23 respectively.

Lancashire's Johnny Briggs, who along with Yorkshire's Bobby Peel had been selected in Wisden's 'Six Great Bowlers' that season, bowled well and had figures of four for 37 as the home side reached 80 for five, seemingly heading for a good lead on the first innings. It was then that the Reverend John Napier was put on to bowl. The clergyman, in what was his one and only Roses match, proceeded to finish off Yorkshire's first innings with a spell of four wickets in 14 balls without conceding a run. He took the last two wickets in two balls, yet never bowled for Lancashire again!

There was no chance of a result to the game but Hornby and Barlow rattled up 35 runs without loss before the rain came.

LANCASHIRE v YORKSHIRE
at Old Trafford July 19, 20, 1888

Lancashire 79 (Peel 5-32, Wainwright 3-9) and 82 (Peel 7-30)
Yorkshire 51 (Briggs 6-24, Watson 3-9) and 111-8 (Barlow 3-14, Watson 3-21)
Yorkshire won by 2 wickets.

On a wicket that suited the bowlers, Lancashire batting first were skittled out for 79 with only Frank Sugg (27) batting with any conviction. Bobby Peel took five for 32 and Ted Wainwright three for nine from 10 overs.

For Yorkshire, opening batsman Louis Hall batted 45 minutes without scoring a run, whilst only George Ulyett (18) and Henry Hill (11) managed double figures. With Johnny Briggs taking six for 24 and Alec Watson three for nine from 11 overs, Yorkshire stumbled to a deficit of 28 runs.

A devastating spell of bowling by Bobby Peel in the last session of the first day reduced Lancashire to 13 for five and the only thing that was certain was that play would not go into a third day! On the following morning, Peel continued to take wickets and finished with seven for 30 as Lancashire, for whom George Baker made 36 runs, were bowled out for 82.

Yorkshire were set 111 to win but after losing early wickets to Briggs and Watson, were indebted to Ulyett (30) and Peel (20) who helped take the score to 90 for five. But then Lancashire's Richard Barlow took three quick wickets and the result was in doubt right up to the finish - Yorkshire reaching their target with two wickets to spare.

BOBBY PEEL (YORKSHIRE)

The second in the remarkable succession of slow left-arm bowlers - Ted Peate, Peel, Wilfred Rhodes and Hedley Verity - who rendered such brilliant service to Yorkshire over a period of sixty years, he first played for the White Rose county in 1882, taking nine for 29 in the match against Surrey at Sheffield.

Peel's career overlapped that of Ted Peate by five years and though the latter was the senior bowler, Peel seemed quite content to play the lesser role. His career didn't really blossom until Peate's departure in 1887, although in those five seasons they were together Peel took 163 wickets. From 1888 to his own departure in 1897, Bobby Peel took a further 1,273 wickets. In 1887, when he completed the 'double', he took five Kent wickets for 14 runs in an innings and with 43 runs in a low-scoring match, helped largely in a victory by four wickets. In the same season 11 Leicestershire wickets fell to him for 51 runs at Dewsbury, five in the first innings for four runs! A year later he took eight Nottinghamshire wickets in an innings for 12 runs, while in 1892 five wickets for seven runs and eight for 33 in the match against Derbyshire at Headingley was an outstanding performance. He did even better in 1895 against Somerset, 15 wickets falling to him in 36 overs for 50 runs, nine for 22 in one innings. At Halifax in 1897, a month before his county career ended, Peel dismissed eight Kent batsmen in an innings for 53 runs to help give Yorkshire an innings victory with 103 runs to spare in two days.

Peel toured Australia no less than four times, an extraordinary accomplishment at that time. At Sydney in 1894, Australia, set 177 to win, were 113 for two at the close of the penultimate day's play. The result seemed a foregone conclusion but strong sunshine followed heavy rain during the night and with Peel and Briggs at their best, the remaining eight wickets fell for 53 runs to give England victory by 10 runs.

Peel also enjoyed a large share in winning the deciding match of that tour. He took seven wickets and scored 73 in a stand of 152 with Lancashire's Archie MacLaren to help England win by six wickets. At the Oval in 1896, Peel, who played in 20 Tests for England, helped dismiss Australia for 44. Peel's share in the victory by 66 runs was eight wickets for 53 runs thus recording his one hundredth Test wicket against them, the first Englishman to reach that landmark.

Besides his great achievements as a bowler, Peel hit 10 centuries for Yorkshire. His highest innings was 226 not out against Leicestershire in 1892 and four years later he scored 210 not out in a Yorkshire total of 887 agsinst Warwickshire at Edgbaston, a Yorkshire and County Championship record.

Bobby Peel's departure from cricket is one of the saddest of stories. He turned up drunk for a game at Bramall Lane - too drunk even to stand - but insisted on presenting himself to Yorkshire captain Lord Hawke on the field at the start of play - before, so legend has it, relieving himself against the sightscreen - Peel was of course sacked.

Afterwards he played league cricket for a good number of years, notably for Lancashire League club Accrington. Thankfully, he and Lord Hawke later made up and Peel returned to his beloved county to help with scouting and coaching.

YORKSHIRE v LANCASHIRE
at Huddersfield July 18,19, 1889

Lancashire 81 (Ulyett 7-50) and 153 (Ulyett 5-52)
Yorkshire 160 (Lord Hawke 50*, Mold 6-76) and 71 (Mold 7-35)
Lancashire won by 3 runs.

In one of the most remarkable Roses matches ever played, Yorkshire, who had yet to win a first-class game that season, lost by three runs after dominating the early stages of the game.

Lancashire won the toss and elected to bat but their batsmen had no answer to the bowling of Peel and Ulyett and half the side were out with the score on 21. Johnny Briggs (25) and Alec Watson (16 not out) were the only batsmen to reach double figures, whilst George Ulyett, who bowled with great pace, took seven for 50. Lancashire's last wicket fell just on the stroke of the lunch interval and so when play began in the afternoon, the home side began their first innings.

Arthur Mold bowled from the same end as Ulyett had done and was equally successful, removing both openers, Hall and Wade. However, Frank Lee came to the rescue of the White Rose county, hitting 42, mainly in boundaries, before he fell to a good catch by Baker off the bowling of Mold. Lord Hawke, who was dropped when he had scored five, went on to record the highest score of the match - 52 not out - as Yorkshire reached 160, a lead of 79. For Lancashire, Arthur Mold took six for 76 and Johnny Briggs three for 58.

By the close of play, George Ulyett had removed the first four Lancashire batsmen with only 22 runs on the board. Everything pointed to an easy win for the home side when play got underway on the second day as Lancashire, with six wickets to fall, still wanted 57 runs to avoid an innings defeat.

Only five runs had been added to their overnight score when Lancashire lost their fifth wicket, that of Mold, also to the bowling of Ulyett. Frank Ward was then joined by Johnny Briggs and the two of them took the visitors to within one run of making Yorkshire bat again. The stand of 51 runs seemed to put heart into Lancashire's lower order and after useful contributions from Baker, Peel and Watson, the Red Rose county were eventually all out for 153.

Yorkshire needed 75 to win but in the space of eight overs, Mold had dismissed Wade, Lee, Hall and Ulyett whilst only nine runs had been scored. Peel and Wainwright added useful runs before the former was brilliantly run out by a direct throw. Wainwright continued to hit out but

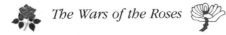

Frank Ward took a simple catch after the Yorkshire batsman had mis-hit a Mold delivery. That eighth wicket fell at 63 after which Whitehead and Hunter took Yorkshire to within four runs of victory before Mold uprooted Whitehead's middle stump. There was no addition to the scoring when, with all the fielders surrounding the last man, Lancashire's captain 'Monkey' Hornby caught Middlebrook off Mold's bowling to give the visitors victory by three runs. There is little doubt that Lancashire's victory owed much to the batting of Briggs, who top-scored in each innings, and the bowling of Mold, who had match figures of thirteen for 111.

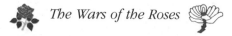

GEORGE ULYETT (YORKSHIRE)

George Ulyett was born in Pitsmoor, Sheffield and learned to play cricket with a team of boys in Crabtree Vilage, who challenged local teams to play for money! In time, he worked his way up to become a professional at Bradford and it was there on the old Horton Road ground that he first came to the attention of Yorkshire after he had dismissed W.G.Grace.

Ulyett went on to become one of the finest cricketers the county has ever produced. Though he opened the innings, Ulyett was renowned as a hitter and was once credited with clearing the players' seats at Lord's in 1878, dropping the ball into the gravel behind the pavilion - a hit of 109 yards! As a bowler, Ulyett bowled fast-medium with a break-back and had the ability to make the ball lift off a length.

He was the first Englishman to score two fifties in a Test match and also produced some fine bowling performances against Australia, including seven for 36 at Lord's in 1884. That match also saw Ulyett take what is still regarded as the most remarkable catch ever seen to help dismiss George Bonnor.

Nicknamed 'Happy Jack' his career for the county extended over twenty years. The greatest professional batsman of his time, he scored 14,264 runs at 24.25 with a highest of 199 not out against Derbyshire in 1887. His benefit match that year lasted only two days but a subscription list was opened and in the end the fund topped £1,000, a handsome sum for those days. He played his last match for the White Rose county in 1893 before leaving to become landlord of the Vine Hotel in Sheffield.

Sadly, Ulyett was only in his forty-seventh year when his life was cut short. Despite carrying a heavy cold he insisted on attending the Yorkshire v Kent match at Bramall Lane on a damp day in June 1898. According to A.A.Thomson, Ulyett met George Hirst on the pavilion steps and said 'I'm finished, young 'un'. Hirst, who was taken aback, replied, 'Nay, never in this world.' But, sadly, Ulyett's premonition was correct for within the space of a few days he had died from an acute attack of pneumonia.

Wisden said of George Ulyett's death - 'A finer cricketer the county has never produced. He was for years the best bat in the team and if he had not been able to get a run, he would have been worth his place for his bowling and his fielding.'

LANCASHIRE v YORKSHIRE
at Old Trafford August 1,2, 1889

Yorkshire 117 (Briggs 5-47, Mold 4-55) and 139 (Briggs 5-52)
Lancashire 215 (Hornby 78, Ulyett 4-77) and 43-0
Lancashire won by 10 wickets.

There was a lot of interest in this return meeting, not only because of the close fight between the counties at Huddersfield, but because since then Yorkshire had beaten Gloucestershire, who had defeated Lancashire.

Accurate bowling by Briggs and Mold accounted for most of Yorkshire's top order batsmen, with the exception of Louis Hall, who top-scored with 38. Briggs went on to take five for 47 and Mold four for 55 in the visitors total of 117 all out.

By the close of play on the first day, Lancashire had reached 151 for two. 'Monkey' Hornby went on to score 78, the Lancashire captain being well supported by Frank Sugg (32) and Albert Ward (27). On the second day, Lancashire were dismissed for 215 with Yorkshire's George Ulyett finishing with four for 77.

When Yorkshire batted for a second time, it was again only Louis Hall who was able to play the bowling of Briggs and Mold with any confidence. The Yorkshire opener scored 48 out of the White Rose county's second innings total of 139. Briggs again captured five wickets to finish with match figures of ten for 99.

Barlow and Eccles knocked off the 43 runs needed, giving Lancashire victory by 10 wickets.

LANCASHIRE v YORKSHIRE
at Old Trafford July 10,11,12, 1890

Lancashire 161 (Briggs 52, Whitwell 4-24, Peel 4-69) and 187 (Paul 65, Briggs 54, Whitwell 4-59)
Yorkshire 88 (Mold 8-38) and 2-2
Match Drawn.

Rain caused several interruptions on the second day of this Roses clash and prevented any cricket at all on the third day.

After Bobby Peel had removed both Lancashire openers, Albert Ward and George Baker, very cheaply, Johnny Briggs proceeded to play a splendid innings for his side, scoring 52 out of the home side's total of

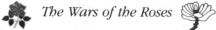

161. By the end of play on the first day, Yorkshire had been reduced to 60 for seven with Arthur Mold, Lancashire's Northamptonshire-born pace-man, claiming all seven victims. Bowling unchanged with Alec Watson, Mold finished with eight for 38 off 25.4 overs as the visitors were bowled out for 88.

Again Lancashire lost early wickets before Briggs and Paul began to hit out. Briggs scored 54, his second half-century of the match before he was bowled by Whitwell, the Yorkshire bowler going on to take four for 50. Arthur Paul was the game's top scorer, being run out for 65 as Lancashire made 187.

Needing 259 runs to win the match, Yorkshire made a dreadful start with both Louis Hall and Jack Brown bowled without troubling the scorers. At the close of play, Yorkshire were 2 for two, torrential rain on the Saturday preventing Lancashire from a most likely victory.

YORKSHIRE v LANCASHIRE
at Huddersfield July 17,18,19, 1890

Yorkshire 90 (Mold 9-41) and 57 (Watson 5-19, Mold 4-35)
Lancashire 175 (Baker 51, Peel 6-43)
Lancashire won by an innings and 28 runs.

Arthur Mold's outstanding form this season continued into the return Roses clash at Huddersfield.

Despite no play being possible on the first day due to heavy rain, Lancashire dismissed the home side for 90 in a little over two hours. Opening batsman George Ulyett scored exactly half his side's total and was the one noteworthy feature of Yorkshire's batting display. For Lancashire, Arthur Mold was virtually unplayable, taking nine for 41 off 31.1 overs, including eight for 13 off his last 8.1 overs.

Though the Lancashire innings lasted no longer than Yorkshire's, the stroke play was so effective that the visitors obtained a lead of 85 runs. Top scorer was George Baker with 51, whilst Kemble (35) and Sugg (30) offered valuable support.

Despite rain preventing any more play that day, Yorkshire's second innings proved even more disastrous than their first. Though Hall and Ulyett got Yorkshire off to a good start, the bowling of Mold and Watson, who again bowled unchanged throughout the innings, helped to dismiss the White Rose county for 57.

Lancashire's victory by an innings and 28 runs was thanks mainly to the efforts of Arthur Mold, who ended with match figures of thirteen for 76.

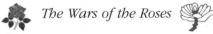

ARTHUR MOLD (LANCASHIRE)

Never having been taught a trade, Mold pursued cricket from boy-hood, advancing from Middleton Cheney in Northamptonshire to Banbury, where he played as professional in 1885 and 1886. One of Banbury's matches was against the Free Foresters, for whom Lancashire's Arthur Appleby was playing. He was very impressed by Mold's bowling and in 1887 he was taken on to the Old Trafford staff.

After two years qualification period he made his mark as one of the fastest bowlers in the country. He took thirteen Yorkshire wickets for 111 runs at Huddersfield and finished third in the national bowling averages with 102 wickets at 11.83 runs each.

In 1890 Mold again took over a hundred wickets and endeared himself further to Lancastrian hearts with two outstanding performances against Yorkshire, taking nine for 40 at Old Trafford and thirteen for 76 in a big Lancashire victory at Huddersfield.

Though there were doubts about his action, W.G.Grace had no doubts and pronounced him 'the fairest of fast bowlers'. Mold celebrated the good doctor's support of his action by taking 129 wickets in the following season at 12.62 runs apiece. In two games against Somerset, Mold took 26 wickets at a total cost of 240 runs.

In 1892 Mold was chosen as one of Wisden's Five Cricketers of the Year. Again he took over a hundred wickets, thirteen of them against Middlesex when he hit the stumps ten times. When Somerset were beaten inside a day, Mold took eight for 40 and against Kent at Tonbridge he had career best figures of nine for 29. In the summer of 1893 Mold took 142 wickets at slightly over 15 runs apiece and was chosen to play for England in three Tests against Australia - sadly he didn't do himself justice.

The seasons of 1894 and 1895 were Mold's most successful campaigns in first-class cricket. In each season he amassed over 200 wickets in all matches. Against Somerset he took seven for 10 in their first innings, including a hat-trick, and then, ten balls later, three wickets in four balls. In the magnificent summer of 1895, when W.G.Grace scored his thousand runs in May, Mold helped to restore the balance by taking 182 Championship wickets at 13 runs each. He had sixteen for 111 against Kent at Old Trafford and fif-teen for 85 against Nottinghamshire at Trent Bridge (including a spell of four wickets in four balls).

Injuries began to plague the fast bowler but he continued to take over a hundred wickets a season with the exception of 1900, when he took 97 to finish second to Wilfred Rhodes in the national averages! It was that season that Mold encountered the first signs of trouble that was to later end his career when he was no-balled by Australian umpire Jim Phillips. Mold bore himself with considerable dignity throughout the unfortunate controversy. There was a great deal of sympathy for Mold's view that if there was any doubt to the legality of his action, he should have been stopped at the beginning of his career since to label him a 'thrower' at the end of it detracted somewhat from the merit of his performances.

But these performances were great. For Lancashire alone in his twelve seasons, he took 1,541 wickets at 15.15 runs each in 259 matches. His average of nearly six wickets a match has not been bettered by any of the great Lancashire bowlers.

YORKSHIRE v LANCASHIRE
at Bradford June 15,16,17, 1891

Lancashire 278 (Crosfield 82*, Peel 7-90) and 72-2
Yorkshire 181 (Ulyett 55, Briggs 6-80) and 168 (Wardall 51, Briggs 5-41, Mold 5-89)
Lancashire won by 8 wickets.

A.N. 'Monkey' Hornby the Lancashire captain was run out before a run had been scored but the visitors recovered to score 278. Top-scorer was

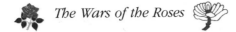

Sydney Crosfield with a hard-hitting unbeaten 82 and he was well supported by Yates (49) and Mold (40).

Yorkshire began well and by the close of play were 51 without loss with George Ulyett doing the bulk of the scoring. On the second day, Johnny Briggs began to weave his magic and after dismissing Ulyett for 55, proceeded to take six for 80 from 51 overs as Yorkshire were bowled out for 181. Following-on, Wardall and Hall reduced the deficit by 86 runs but after both batsmen had been clean bowled by Mold, Hall for 48 and Wardall for 51, the remaining Yorkshire batsman succumbed. Mold finished with five for 89, whilst Briggs took five for 41 to have match figures of eleven for 121.

Needing 72 for victory, Lancashire lost two wickets, both to Peel, but an unbeaten 32 from Richard Barlow helped them to an eight wicket win.

LANCASHIRE v YORKSHIRE
at Old Trafford July 30,31 August 1, 1891

Lancashire 288 (Sugg 75, A.Ward 70, Peel 3-80)
Yorkshire 150 (Peel 69*, Briggs 6-76) and 89 (Briggs 8-46)
Lancashire won by an innings and 49 runs.

Sadly, only three-quarters of an hours play was possible on the first day, during which time Lancashire scored 32 for the loss of Richard Barlow's wicket. Despite heavy overnight rain, play on the second day started on time. Surprisingly, Sugg and Ward had few problems and added 118 for the second wicket before the former batsman was dismissed for 75. Ward went for 70 before useful contributions from Yates and Crosfield helped the home side to a total of 288.

Yorkshire lost their first three wickets for four runs as Johnny Briggs and Alec Watson began to make full use of a rapidly deteriorating Old Trafford wicket. However, Yorkshire's Bobby Peel played with great determination, scoring an unbeaten 69, but the White Rose county failed to save the follow-on, being 138 runs adrift of Lancashire's first innings total.

Following a solid opening partnership by Hall and Ulyett, Yorkshire collapsed to the fine bowling of Johnny Briggs who took eight for 46. The only other Yorkshire player to put up a fight was Ted Wainwright, who top-scored with 29 following his first innings score of 26. Briggs finished with match figures of fourteen for 122 as Lancashire won by an innings and 49 runs in a game in which Arthur Mold played but was unable to bowl!

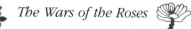

YORKSHIRE v LANCASHIRE
at Bramall Lane June 6,7, 1892

Lancashire 118 (Peel 6-43) and 101 (Hirst 4-32, Peel 3-27)
Yorkshire 159 (Briggs 5-43) and 63-6 (Watson 4-36)
Yorkshire won by 4 wickets.

After A.N. 'Monkey' Hornby had been stumped by Hunter off the bowling of George Hirst before a run had been scored, Lancashire's next three batsmen played with great concentration. Frank Sugg was the Red Rose county's top-scorer with 39, whilst Ward and MacLaren gave useful support. Lancashire were all out for 118 with Bobby Peel taking six for 43 off 30 overs.

By the close of play, the home side had scored 100 for three with Bobby Peel the county's top-scorer with 33. However, they lost another four wickets in passing Lancashire's total before eventually being all out for 159. Johnny Briggs was the pick of the Lancashire bowlers, taking five for 43 off 39 overs.

Finding themselves 41 behind, Lancashire cleared off the arrears for two wickets but later on, they were only nine runs ahead with five men out. In the end they were only able to set Yorkshire a victory target of 61, as tight bowling by Hirst (four for 32) and Peel (three for 27) restricted the visitors to a total of 101.

However, Lancashire didn't give up the ghost and with Watson and Briggs bowling well, reduced Yorkshire to 33 for six. It was only some brave hitting by Wainwright and Tunnicliffe that saw the White Rose county home.

LANCASHIRE v YORKSHIRE
at Old Trafford August 1,2,3, 1892

Lancashire 471 (A.Ward 180, Briggs 115, Smith 80, Peel 4-79)
Yorkshire 209 (E.Smith 57, Briggs 8-113) and 179 (Tunnicliffe 50, Watson 5-55, Briggs 5-96)
Lancashire won by an innings and 83 runs.

The Roses match at Old Trafford proved to be the biggest defeat yet suffered by Yorkshire, who lost by an innings and 83 runs.

Lancashire lost Frank Sugg with 24 on the board before Albert Ward and Arthur Smith put on 189 for the second wicket. When Smith left for 80, Briggs joined Ward in a stand of 113 for the fourth wicket before Ward's epic innings of 180, which included 28 fours in a stay of over four hours at the crease, came to an end. Johnny Briggs scored 115 in two-

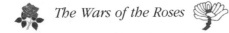
JOHNNY BRIGGS (LANCASHIRE)

One of cricket's most gifted all-rounders of the last twenty years of the nineteenth century, Johnny Briggs was a Nottinghamshire man by birth. When he was 14, the year after his father had become the first professional at Widnes Cricket Club, Johnny along with the rest of his family moved from Sutton to make their home there.

Briggs played in the Lancashire Colts XI in May 1879 and made his first-class debut against his native county Nottinghamshire while still only 16. He made 36, the highest score in the Lancashire innings, before being run out. His bowling improved when he reduced his pace to slow-medium but probably the main reason for Johnny Briggs' development as a left-arm spinner was the increased share of the attack he was required to take when Crossland was disqualified from playing for Lancashire.

Briggs played 33 times for England - thirty-one times against Australia and twice against South Africa. He toured Down Under with a team captained by Arthur Shrewsbury in 1884-85 as a batsman and scored 121 in the second Test at Melbourne. In 1885, the year of Crossland's disqualification, he topped the Lancashire bowling averages with 79 wickets at 10.50 runs apiece, but his real emergence as a left-arm spinner of Test calibre dated from 1886 when he was picked for all three matches against Australia. At Lord's he was the most successful bowler with match figures of eleven for 74 as England won by an innings. At the Oval he took six for 58 and scored 53 as England had another innings win. Briggs toured Australia with the Shaw and Shrewsbury teams of 1886-87, 1887-88 and 1888-89. In the first Test of 1886-87, England won by 13 runs after being dismissed for 45 in their first innings. Briggs top-scored with 33 in England's second innings and in recognition of his part in the recovery, the Prince of Wales (later to become King Edward VII) presented him with a gold medal bearing his initials set in a pattern of seven diamonds.

In 1888 he topped the bowling averages with 160 wickets and scored 800 runs. Wisden introduced its gallery of Six Great Bowlers for the first time and Johnny Briggs was one of the chosen six. Two days after marrying Alice Burgess at Widnes, he was playing for Lancashire against Surrey at Aigburth where he scored 186, the highest score of his career, and shared in a stand of 173 for the last wicket (still a Lancashire record) with Dick Pilling.

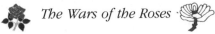
Playing for England against South Africa at Cape Town, he took seven for 17 and eight for 11 as the tourists won by an innings and 292 runs. He created new Test records by his analysis of eight for 11 (all bowled) and fifteen for 28 all in the same day's play. The fifteen wicket record still stands as the most taken by one bowler in a day in Test cricket.

In 1891-92 he toured Australia again with Stoddart's team and in the second Test at Sydney ended Australia's innings with a hat-trick. Briggs is still the only cricketer to have scored a hundred and performed the hat-trick in Tests.

For Lancashire, Johnny Briggs took 1,696 wickets at 15.60 runs apiece and scored over 10,000 runs in his twenty seasons of first-class cricket. He is the only player to have scored 10,000 runs and taken over 1,000 wickets for the county and his tally of wickets has only been bettered by Brian Statham.

In 1899 he was brought back for the Headingley Test against Australia and after taking three for 53 in 30 overs he suffered an epileptic seizure and was admitted to Cheadle Royal Mental Hospital. After an improvement in his condition he was discharged and he played one more season for Lancashire. It was a glorious finale for the little man as he took 120 wickets at 17.40 runs apiece, including all ten wickets for 55 runs in Worcestershire's first innings at Old Trafford.

Before the 1901 season began he was readmitted to Cheadle Royal and though his condition seemed to improve he had a relapse and on 11 January 1902 one of the greatest cricketers and characters of the game breathed his last.

and-a-half hours and George Baker hit a quick-fire 49 as Lancashire reached 471 at almost 70 runs per hour. Peel and Wainwright took Lancashire's last six wickets for 37 runs.

There was early rainfall on the second day which affected the wicket and Yorkshire's batsmen were soon in trouble except for schoolmaster Ernest Smith who made a fighting 57 in an hour and a half, with John Tunnicliffe also showing his fighting qualities with an unbeaten 31. Briggs took eight for 113 as Yorkshire were all out for 209.

When Yorkshire followed-on 262 runs behind, Tunnicliffe, who had batted at number eight in the first innings, opened with Lord Hawke. At the end of play on the second day, Yorkshire were 74 for one with Tunnicliffe undefeated. After he had completed a fighting half-century early on the last day, the rest of the Yorkshire side fell to the bowling of Briggs and Watson, who took five wickets apiece as the White Rose county were dismissed for 179, leaving Lancashire the victors by an innings and 83 runs.

YORKSHIRE v LANCASHIRE
at Headingley June 19, 20, 1893

Yorkshire 107 (Mold 6-40, Briggs 4-56) and 53 (Briggs 8-19)
Lancashire 169 (MacLaren 54, Peel 5-28)
Lancashire won by an innings and 9 runs.

After making a good start to the season, Yorkshire gave one of their worst displays for a good number of years in the first Roses' meeting of the summer.

Winning the toss, Yorkshire made a solid start on a wicket that favoured the bowlers. Sellers, Wardall and Tunnicliffe all batted well and at 80 for two, the home side looked well set. However, following Tunnicliffe's dismissal, the remaining Yorkshire batsmen were quite helpless against the bowling of Briggs and Mold, the last eight wickets falling for just 27 runs!

Archie MacLaren was in splendid form, his innings of 54 helping Lancashire to a close of play total of 128 for six. Bobby Peel bowled well, taking five for 28 off 23 overs as Lancashire added a further 41 runs to their overnight score.

Though few in the ground expected Yorkshire to win the match, no-one expected the game to end as quickly as it did. Needing 62 to make Lancashire bat again, the Yorkshire batsmen, with the exception of Wardall (25), had no answer to Johnny Briggs' bowling. He took eight for 19 off 15 overs to finish with match figures of twelve for 75 and was instrumental in the visitors winning the match by an innings and nine runs.

LANCASHIRE v YORKSHIRE
at Old Trafford August 7, 8, 1893

Lancashire 64 (Peel 4-15) and 50 (Peel 6-24, Wainwright 4-8)
Yorkshire 58 (Briggs 6-35, Mold 4-20) and 51 (Briggs 5-25, Mold 2-13)
Lancashire won by 5 runs.

Prior to one of the most sensational games of cricket in the history of the Roses history, Yorkshire and Lancashire occupied the two leading positions in the County Championship.

Despite threatening rain, a Bank Holiday crowd of over 10,000 were present at midday and though a heavy storm delayed the start of play until after lunch, this number increased to 22,554 - the highest attendance for a match at Old Trafford at that time.

The wicket looked slow and difficult and wasn't likely to improve over the next few days, so on winning the toss Lancashire captain Sydney

Crosfield elected to bat. The home side made a disastrous start and were 22 for four when the players had to leave the field following a heavy shower. Tinsley was dismissed directly after the resumption without any addition to the score. Ward, who batted two hours for his 19, and Baker (21) took the score to 56 but the tail collapsed and Lancashire were all out for 64.

When Yorkshire went in to bat, Brown, Tunnicliffe and Peel reached double figures as Briggs and Mold, bowling unchanged, dismissed the visitors for 58. Briggs took six for 35 and Mold four for 20 in an innings that lasted just one hour and 50 minutes!

By the close of play on the first day, Lancashire had scored seven without loss. However, just before play started on the second day, rain followed by strong sunshine made the wicket even more difficult. Peel and Wainwright in particular were virtually unplayable and Lancashire were dismissed for 50.

Needing 57 for victory, Yorkshire's opening pair of Sellers and Jackson took the score to 24 before Bill Oakley, who had replaced Mold, appealed for leg before against Jackson. The Yorkshire batsman ran halfway down the wicket as the ball he thought he had hit ballooned down the leg-side but Sellers, thinking he had been given out, did not move and Jackson was run out! The incident obviously upset Sellers and he was bowled by Oakley soon afterwards. Ernest Smith hit three successive boundaries but just before lunch he was given out caught by Crosfield at cover point, though the Yorkshire supporters in the crowd didn't feel the ball carried. At lunch, Yorkshire were 42 for six, needing another 15 runs for victory. The Lancashire bowlers, and Briggs in particular, stuck to their task and with just six runs needed for victory, Briggs pitched a ball up for Ulyett to hit. His audacity was rewarded when Albert Ward took a magnificent catch on the boundary to give Lancashire victory by five runs and Briggs match figures of eleven for 60.

LANCASHIRE v YORKSHIRE
at Old Trafford May 14,15, 1894

Lancashire 50 (Hirst 7-25, Peel 2-24) and 98 (Peel 4-56, Hirst 3-31)
Yorkshire 152 (Briggs 5-62, Mold 4-74)
Yorkshire won by an innings and 4 runs.

The bad weather, which had threatened to delay the start of what was Johnny Briggs' benefit match, cleared up, but the wicket that had been prepared had been covered up and Lord Hawke, not wanting to risk playing on it, demanded that a new one be marked out.

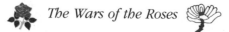

There was an extraordinary start to the game as Lancashire's first four batsmen - Hornby, Ward, MacLaren and Sugg - were all dismissed without a run on the board! The home side struggled to 17 for seven, of which 14 runs had been scored by the beneficiary. The only other Lancashire players to reach double figures were Kemble (18) and Baker (17 not out) as the Red Rose side were dismissed for 50. Yorkshire's George Hirst was in devastating form with the ball taking seven for 25.

Though Yorkshire only lost two wickets in passing Lancashire's total, Briggs then produced a spell of bowling that reduced the visitors to 76 for seven. The total was then doubled as Jack Mounsey, who was only playing due to an injury that forced Sellers to miss the game, scored 36 and wicket-keeper David Hunter an unbeaten 21.

Lancashire began their second innings at the start of play on the second day but were all out for 98 before lunch. Baker, who was unbeaten in the first innings, was again not out, top-scoring with 20. Peel took four for 56 whilst Hirst's figures gave him a match analysis of ten for 56.

YORKSHIRE v LANCASHIRE
at Bradford August 6,7,8, 1894

Yorkshire 183 (Tunnicliffe 56, E.Smith 52, Mold 6-63, Briggs 4-69) and 217
(E.Smith 58, Briggs 7-91)
Lancashire 181 (A.Ward 50, Peel 3-35) and 102 (Jackson 4-14)
Yorkshire won by 117 runs.

In a match played for Bobby Peel's benefit, Yorkshire, who won the toss and elected to bat, lost three wickets with just 14 runs on the board. But then Ernest Smith and John Tunnicliffe added 99 for the fourth wicket in just three-quarters of an hour before the former was caught by Briggs off the bowling of Mold for 52. Tunnicliffe went on to score 56 before Briggs uprooted his off stump. The only other Yorkshire player to master the Lancashire bowlers was Ted Wainwright who made 36. Arthur Mold took six for 63 and Johnny Briggs four for 69.

Archie MacLaren and Albert Ward put on 91 for Lancashire's first wicket before the former batsman was bowled by Jackson for 43. Ward went on to score 50 but the rest of the Lancashire side, with the exception of Tindall (25), failed to do themselves justice and they were all out for 191, two runs behind the Yorkshire total.

Ernest Smith was again Yorkshire's hero when the home side batted for a second time, scoring 58 before being caught and bowled by Arthur Mold. Briggs finished with figures of seven for 91 as Yorkshire scored 217. Following the fall of Yorkshire's last wicket there was no time left for

Lancashire to start their innings in search of the 220 runs needed for victory.

Heavy rain fell during the night, so when Lancashire began their second innings they found Yorkshire's bowlers, and in particular Stanley Jackson, almost unplayable. Jackson took four for 14 as the Red Rose county were skittled out for 102, leaving Yorkshire the victors by 117 runs.

YORKSHIRE v LANCASHIRE
at Bramall Lane June 3,4,5, 1895

Lancashire 166 (Peel 4-41, Hirst 4-87) and 304 (Paul 87, A.Ward 68, Sugg 58, Hirst 5-63)
Yorkshire 161 (Briggs 5-62, Mold 4-60) and 164 (Mold 7-68)
Lancashire won by 145 runs.

Lancashire won the toss and elected to bat but on a fairly soft wicket lost wickets at regular intervals to the fine bowling of Peel (four for 41) and Hirst (four for 87) and were all out for 166.

Yorkshire in reply struggled to 43 for six, but with Denton (44 not out) Wainwright (35) and Lord Hawke (34) batting well lower down the order, the home side were five runs short of Lancashire's total when the last wicket fell. Johnny Briggs took five for 62 and Arthur Mold four for 60.

After Archie MacLaren had been run out for three, Albert Ward and Arthur Paul added 144 runs for the second wicket. Though they both played and missed on a number of occasions, Ward (68) and Paul (87) stuck to their task well in difficult conditions. Frank Sugg also batted well, scoring 58 as the visitors went on to score 304.

Needing 310 to win, Yorkshire's first four batsmen were all clean bowled by Arthur Mold with only 33 runs on the board. Peel hit a quick-fire 40 and Lord Hawke was still there on 45 not out when Mold grabbed Yorkshire's tenth and his seventh wicket. Mold finished with seven for 68 from 40.2 overs as Lancashire won by 145 runs.

LANCASHIRE v YORKSHIRE
at Old Trafford August 5,6,7, 1895

Lancashire 103 (Peel 5-47) and 227-8 (Jackson 4-44)
Yorkshire 270-7dec (Jackson 76, Lord Hawke 61*, Moorhouse 50)
Match Drawn.

The return game that summer at Old Trafford had lost nothing of its interest, a fact borne out by 25,331 spectators passing through the turnstiles on the first day.

55

Lancashire batted first on a slow wicket, taking over three hours to make 103. The Yorkshire fielding was faultless and Bobby Peel bowled well to take five for 47 from 35.3 overs.

Yorkshire's opening batsmen presented a strong contrast as Jackson and Mitchell put on 96 in eighty minutes before they were separated. Jackson was in outstanding form but when he was brilliantly run out for 76, it signaled the start of a mini-collapse and Yorkshire ended the day on 146 for five.

Unfortunately, rain prevented any play on the second day, but on the final day Moorhouse and Lord Hawke put on 120 runs in an hour and a half, enabling the visitors to declare at 270 for seven. Moorhouse made 50 whilst Lord Hawke was undefeated on 61.

Lancashire were 167 behind and in danger of suffering an innings defeat but all the top order batsmen contributed to their total of 227 for eight when stumps were drawn. Jackson had bowled beautifully to take four for 44 from 32 overs, whilst for Lancashire, Archie MacLaren led the way with a fighting 46 before he was bowled by the game's Man-of-the-match, Stanley Jackson.

LANCASHIRE v YORKSHIRE
at Old Trafford May 4,5,6, 1896

Lancashire 150 (Sugg 74, Peel 4-54) and 139 (Paul 52, Milligan 4-28, Jackson 4-30)
Yorkshire 123 (Briggs 5-44) and 168-8 (Mold 4-49)
Yorkshire won by 2 wickets.

It was following the dispute between Lancashire and Yorkshire, who couldn't agree to the date the contest should be played, that this important fixture had to be decided in the first week of the season. Despite the early date, the match produced one of the most exciting struggles of the whole summer.

After Peel had made early inroads into the Lancashire top order, Frank Sugg made 74 out of 87 in just 75 minutes as the home side were bowled out for 150. Peel was Yorkshire's most successful bowler with four for 54. When Yorkshire batted only Bobby Moorhouse with an innings of 43 could cope with the masterly bowling of Johnny Briggs, who dismissed the visitors first five batsmen for 44 runs. Yorkshire too were bowled out on the first day, 27 runs adrift of Lancashire's total.

Next day, Jackson and Milligan took four wickets apiece for Yorkshire but Arthur Paul, batting with extreme care, scored 52 in a little over three hours.

Yorkshire were left with 167 runs to win. Fortunes fluctuated throughout the day as Ted Wainwright (47) and Stanley Jackson (41) first gave Yorkshire the edge before Arthur Mold (four for 49) and Johnny

Briggs (three for 55) brought Lancashire back into the game. At the close of play on the second day, Yorkshire were left with 18 to get with two wickets in hand. These runs were easily obtained the next morning without the fall of another wicket.

YORKSHIRE v LANCASHIRE
at Headingley July 20,21,22, 1896

Yorkshire 190 (Tunnicliffe 62, Mold 5-94, Briggs 4-52) and 209 (Mold 6-67)
Lancashire 169 (Haigh 5-55) and 107 (Peel 5-29)
Yorkshire won by 123 runs.

Yorkshire made a good start in the return match with Jackson, Tunnicliffe and Brown helping the home side to 124 for two. Tunnicliffe went on to score 62 before he became one of Mold's five victims in a Yorkshire total of 190.

Despite Archie MacLaren making his first appearance for Lancashire since the previous summer, the Red Rose county lost their first six wickets for 94 runs - MacLaren's share being 32. John Tyldesley and George Baker batted well, but with Schofield Haigh taking five for 55 Lancashire were all out for 169.

In Yorkshire's second innings, nine members of the side reached double figures although George Hirst was top-scorer with 38. Lancashire's Arthur Mold took six for 67 in the home side's total of 209 to finish with match figures of eleven for 161.

Lancashire had to get 231 to win and although Rowley and MacLaren took the score to 74 after the early dismissal of Albert Ward, Bobby Peel took five for 29 as the visitors ten men (Hallam was ill and couldn't bat) were bowled out 124 runs short of their target.

YORKSHIRE v LANCASHIRE
at Bradford July 19,20,21, 1897

Yorkshire 345 (Moorhouse 61, Denton 59, Mold 4-98) and 66 (Hallam 4-17, Cuttell 4-43)
Lancashire 354 (MacLaren 152, A.Ward 55, Jackson 4-100)
Match Drawn.

With both Yorkshire and Lancashire occupying high positions in the County Championship, there was great interest in the game, a fixture set aside for the benefit of the Yorkshire wicket-keeper David Hunter.

57

Yorkshire batted for the whole of the first day, making 323 for nine with Bobby Moorhouse top-scoring with 61 and David Denton making a quick-fire 59. The home side were eventually all out for 345, a total which owed much to the poor fielding of Lancashire.

The visitors' opening pair, Archie MacLaren and Albert Ward, then proceeded to put on 167 for the first wicket in less than two hours before Ward was dismissed for 55. Sadly, heavy rain then fell and play was abandoned for the day. MacLaren, who was playing in his first match of the season, went on to score 152 before he was brilliantly caught by Moorhouse off the bowling of Hirst. Lancashire were bowled out for 354, a lead of nine runs, and though the game seemed to be heading for a draw, there was some sensational cricket before this outcome was reached.

Cuttell and Hallam reduced Yorkshire to 38 for eight and at half-past five, the home side found themselves only 29 runs on with the last two batsmen together. Fortunately for the White Rose county, Haigh (15 not out) and the beneficiary Hunter (12) saved their side.

LANCASHIRE v YORKSHIRE
at Old Trafford August 12,13,14, 1897

Yorkshire 160 (Jackson 59, Hallam 6-61) and 100 (Cuttell 5-31, Briggs 4-46)
Lancashire 286 (Sugg 122)
Lancashire won by an innings and 26 runs.

Despite losing John Tunnicliffe without a run on the board, Yorkshire recovered to score 160. Top-scorer was Stanley Jackson with a fine innings of 59 before, like Tunnicliffe, he fell to the bowling of Willis Cuttell. However, it was Albert Hallam who did most of the damage with six for 61.

MacLaren and Ward gave Lancashire a solid start before Frank Sugg went to the wicket. Though he played some risky shots and twice might have been run out, he scored 122 in his three-and-a-half hours at the wicket, adding 73 for the ninth wicket with Willis Cuttell.

When Yorkshire batted for a second time, 126 in arrears, it was Sheffield-born Cuttell that did the damage, as the visitors lost half thee side for just 19 runs following heavy overnight rain. Though Milligan (24) and Lord Hawke (35 not out) played some plucky cricket, the result was inevitable and with Willis Cuttell taking five for 31 from 25 overs, Lancashire won by an innings and 26 runs.

58

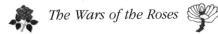

YORKSHIRE v LANCASHIRE
at Bramall Lane June 11,12,13, 1898

Yorkshire 316 (Brown 144, Milligan 62, Mold 4-81) and 253-2 dec (Jackson 134*,
Tunnicliffe 102)
Lancashire 288 (Cuttell 85*, Sugg 70) and 140-5
Match Drawn.

When the two sides met at Bramall Lane in a match set aside for Ted
Wainwright's benefit, Yorkshire were undefeated and Lancashire had the
next best record in the County Championship.

Yorkshire kept their opponents in the field for the whole of the first
day, the great feature of their batting being a fine innings of 144 by Jack
Brown. Despite the opener's attacking play, Yorkshire were 134 for six
before Brown and Milligan (62) added 115 for the seventh wicket. With
Wilfred Rhodes later hitting a quick-fire 33, Yorkshire reached 316.

Though Frank Sugg hit freely for Lancashire, scoring 70, the visitors
had slumped to 183 for seven when Johnny Briggs joined Willis Cuttell.
Thanks to their brilliant hitting - Briggs scoring 47 and Cuttell an unbeat-
en 85 - Lancashire finished just 28 runs behind Yorkshire's total.

After Yorkshire's first innings centurion Jack Brown had trod on his
own wicket to give Briggs an early success, Tunnicliffe (102) and Jackson
(134 not out) put on 206 for the second wicket - a truly remarkable batting performance.

Lancashire were set 282 to win in three hours and, with Stanley
Jackson taking three early wickets, seemed to be heading for defeat. With
one and a half hours left to play, Lancashire were 84 for five but first
innings hero Willis Cuttell was joined by Stoddart and these two saved the
game for the Red Rose county.

LANCASHIRE v YORKSHIRE
at Old Trafford August 12,13,14, 1898

Lancashire 112 (Smith 3-12, Jackson 3-25) and 64 (Smith 3-8, Jackson 3-27)
Yorkshire 114 (Cuttell 4-47) and 63-0
Yorkshire won by 10 wickets.

On a wicket which favoured the bowlers, Lancashire seemed to have
gained a big advantage in winning the toss. In a game played for the benefit of George Baker, Archie MacLaren and Albert Ward made a splendid
start for the home side, the former scoring 47 out of 56 runs for the first

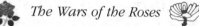

Yorkshire 1898

wicket in less than an hour. Lancashire's score stood at 96 for four when Ernie Smith was introduced into the visitor's attack. He took three for 12 from nine overs, including the wicket of Ward for 30, as the innings came to a startling conclusion for the addition of just 16 runs.

Brown and Tunnicliffe put on 48 in half-an-hour for Yorkshire's first wicket but then came another collapse as the White Rose county ended the first day on 98 for nine. Yorkshire's last wicket pairing of Haigh and Hunter took the score to 114, whilst Cuttell produced Lancashire's best figures with four for 47.

In the home side's second innings, Albert Ward batted for an hour-and-a-half for his 19 but otherwise the Yorkshire bowlers were completely on top, dismissing Lancashire for 64 runs.

Yorkshire were expected to make the 63 runs needed for victory but no-one was prepared for such an emphatic win as Brown and Tunnicliffe, in less than an hour, hit off the runs without being separated.

YORKSHIRE v LANCASHIRE
at Bramall Lane June 26,27,28, 1899

Lancashire 203 (MacLaren 126, Rhodes 4-91) and 157 (Rhodes 4-50)
Yorkshire 115 (Mold 4-44, Briggs 3-48) and 186 (Hirst 63*, Briggs 7-76)
Lancashire won by 59 runs.

Despite some rain on the evening prior to the start of the game, the wicket in this match at Bramall Lane didn't give the bowlers too much assistance. However, in Lancashire's first innings only Archie MacLaren made more than twenty. The old Harrovian, who opened the batting with Ward, scored 126 in an exhibition of strong defence and well-timed hitting. For Yorkshire, Rhodes took four for 91 and he was well supported by Haigh and Hirst who captured three wickets apiece. By the close of play, the home side had scored 63 for two.

On the second day, Mold and Ainsworth bowled well, Yorkshire's remaining eight wickets adding just 52 runs to the overnight total. Mold finished with four for 44, whilst Ainsworth took three for 11.

Wilfred Rhodes was again Yorkshire's most successful bowler in Lancashire's second innings, taking four for 50 as the Red Rose county were dismissed for 157. Jack Brown took three for 3, including the wicket of Johnny Briggs, whose quick-fire innings of 40 allowed Lancashire to set Yorkshire 246 to win.

Brown, who had already hit four boundaries, was bowled by Briggs in the last over of the day whilst attempting a huge leg-side hit. Rain Delayed the start of play on the final day and it was almost three o'clock when the game resumed. The home side had little option but to try and bat out for a draw but fine innings from Tunnicliffe (41) and Hirst (53 not out) meant that at 150 for five, with an hour-and-a-half to play, Yorkshire were still in with a chance. Briggs then weaved his magic, bowling the home side out for 186 and finishing with seven for 76.

LANCASHIRE v YORKSHIRE
at Old Trafford August 3,4,5, 1899

Yorkshire 344 (Mitchell 84, Jackson 68, Denton 64) and 222-5 (Denton 101*)
Lancashire 450 (MacLaren 116, Ward 78, JT Tyldesley 65, Sharp 50, Cuttell 50,
Smith 5-90)
Match Drawn.

After John Tunnicliffe had been bowled by Webb without a run on the board, Jackson (68) and Denton (64) put on 126 for the second wicket. Frank Mitchell later hit 84 before being bowled by Lancaster. George Hirst and Ernie Smith both hit 48 enabling Yorkshire to reach a first innings total of 344.

Lancashire lost two early wickets to the bowling of Wilfred Rhodes before Johnny Tyldesley and Archie MacLaren added 81 for the third wicket. After Tyldesley had become Rhodes' third victim, clean bowled for 65, MacLaren and Ward put on 125 for the fourth wicket, though both batsmen were often in difficulties. Ward went for 78 whilst MacLaren went

61

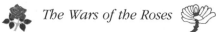

on to score 116. Both Cuttell and Sharp later hit half-centuries in a Lancashire innings of 450.

There were four hours play left when Yorkshire began their second innings facing the possibility of defeat. However, these fears were dispelled by a fine opening partnership between Jackson (43) and Tunnicliffe (36) followed by a magnificent unbeaten century by David Denton, an innings which helped save the game for Yorkshire.

ARCHIE MACLAREN (LANCASHIRE)

Archie MacLaren was a Manchester man by birth though his family came originally from Scotland. His father, James MacLaren, was for many years Treasurer and later President of the County Club. Young Archie spent much of his time at Old Trafford in his formative years and had the benefit of some careful coaching.

Attending Elstree School in London, he was coached by Vernon Royle, one of Lancashire's greatest ever cover points, so that when he arrived at Harrow there was already considerable natural; talent as well as much acquired wisdom. In his first match at Lord's at the age of 15 he distinguished himself by scoring 55 and 67 against Eton. In 1890, in his fourth year, he hit 76 in a total of 133 when only one other boy attained double figures.

Only a month later he made his first-class debut for Lancashire and scored 108 in just over two hours in the win over Sussex at Hove. In 1894, when Sydney Crosfield, who had been appointed captain, was unable to undertake the duties, MacLaren was appointed to take over. He was then only 22 and though his first season in charge didn't set Old Trafford ablaze with excitement, there was a great improvement in 1895 when Lancashire finished runners-up in the Championship and MacLaren achieved a personal distinction in the Somerset match at Taunton.

Despite not having played first-class cricket for five weeks, he went in first and hit the somerset bowling for 424 runs in ten minutes under eight hours. MacLaren's innings was composed of one six, 62 fours, 11 threes, 37 twos and 63 singles. He hit three more centuries that summer and they were made successively in eight days. MacLaren, who had taken up the offer of being a Prep Schoolmaster at Harrow, didn't join Lancashire until midway through the 1896 season but quickly hit form with a double century against Kent and averaged around the fifty mark as he led Lancashire to runners-up spot for the second year running.

MacLaren led the Lancashire side through the successful seasons of 1900 to 1907 and in 1904 they were unbeaten champions. His first-class career spanned the years between 1890 and 1914 and in that period he scored 15,735 runs in 307 matches for Lancashire at an average of 33.34. These figures seem modest in comparison with the records of modern batsmen until it is remembered that MacLaren played his cricket on pitches of variable quality and frequently they were quite unplayable.

MacLaren played 35 times for England between 1894 and 1909, scoring 1,931 runs at an average of 33.87. He was a member of Stoddart's side which toured Australia during the winter of 1894-95, scoring 120 in the Melbourne Test. Three years later MacLaren hit hundreds at Sydney and Adelaide. In 1901-02 MacLaren accepted an invitation which the MCC had earlier declined and took a team out to Australia. He scored a century in the Sydney Test, two hundreds against New South Wales at Sydney and another against Victoria at Melbourne. His last century innings against Australia was at Trent Bridge in 1905 when MacLaren, who captained England in 22 Tests, made a masterly 140.

In 1921, it seemed certain that the all-conquering Australians, who had won the Test series against England with ease, would end their tour without being beaten. MacLaren, who had retired from active cricket, declared that he could pick a team to beat the triumphant Australians. Calling his team 'An England XI' they won the game by 28 runs after being bowled out for 43 in the first innings!

Even at the age of fifty-one, MacLaren played for MCC against New Zealand in Wellington in 1923 and scored 200 not out!

He became county coach in the 1920s but, towards the end of his spell, had a dispute with the Lancashire committee and ended his long association with the county club.

YORKSHIRE v LANCASHIRE
at Bradford June 11,12,13, 1900

Yorkshire 230 (E.Smith 56, Hirst 50, Cuttell 5-115) and 64-6 dec
Lancashire 96 (Rhodes 8-43)
Match Drawn.

With both counties unbeaten in the Championship, a large crowd was present as Yorkshire recovered from a bad start to make 230 in their first innings. George Hirst (50) and Ernie Smith (56) added 64 in half-an-hour, Cuttell bowling unchanged took five for 115 from 52.2 overs.

Wilfred Rhodes dismissed both MacLaren and Ward without a run on the board, but then bad light followed by a violent thunderstorm ended play two hours early. On the second day, Rhodes bowled magnificently and a Lancashire follow-on seemed inevitable. But then Jack Sharp, the Everton and England footballer, hit out with great confidence to score 32 not out as the visitors were bowled out for 96. Wilfred Rhodes finished with eight for 43.

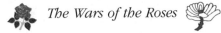

This meant that Yorkshire had to bat again and, though Lancashire were without Briggs and Mold, some excellent bowling by Sharp and Hallam reduced Yorkshire to 64 for six. Lord Hawke then declared the Yorkshire innings closed but, as he did so, the heavens opened and Lancashire, who had two-and-a-half hours left to make 199 for victory, were prevented from taking up the challenge.

Stumps were finally pulled up just after four o'clock, it having been agreed to stop play at half-past five in order that the Yorkshire side might get away for their match against Essex at Leyton early the following morning.

The Yorkshire players were convinced that if they had been able to force the follow-on, they would have won the game before the weather broke up.

LANCASHIRE v YORKSHIRE
at Old Trafford July 19,20,21, 1900

Yorkshire 235 (Hirst 59, Tunnicliffe 51) and 146 (Wainwright 50, Cuttell 5-51,
Sharp 4-51)
Lancashire 228 (Cuttell 63, MacLaren 52, Haigh 5-59) and 20-2
Match Drawn.

When the two counties met in the return match at Old Trafford, both had identical playing records, having won eleven and drawn four matches. The game, which both sets of players and supporters were looking forward to, saw Yorkshire lose Jack Brown without a run on the board. Tunnicliffe (51) and Denton (38) redressed the situation before George Hirst, with a hard-hit 59, became one of Jack Sharp's three victims. Yorkshire who were all out for 235, reduced the home side to 63 for four by the close of play.

Early the next day, Lancashire lost two further wickets with just 98 on the board, but then Cuttell joined captain Archie MacLaren and the two of them added 87 before MacLaren was out for 52. Cuttell went on to top-score with 63 before he was bowled by Hirst. The two of them took Lancashire to within seven runs of the Yorkshire total. Schofield Haigh was the best of the White Rose county's attack, taking five for 59.

On the last day, Yorkshire had only scored 84 for eight against some fine bowling by Sharp and Cuttell when Ted Wainwright, with 50, played one of his best innings of the season. Haigh stayed with him for an hour-and-a-quarter and scored 19 as Yorkshire's second innings ended on 146.

Needing 154 to win, Lancashire were 20 for two when stumps were drawn - the result meaning that both teams maintained their unbeaten record.

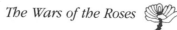

LANCASHIRE v YORKSHIRE
at Old Trafford May 27,28, 1901

Lancashire 133 (Hirst 5-54, Rhodes 5-67) and 44 (Hirst 7-28)
Yorkshire 134 (Sharp 5-89) and 44-1
Yorkshire won by 9 wickets.

The Old Trafford wicket had been fairly fiery all season and when Lancashire had first use, they found it no different against the bowling of Rhodes (five for 67) and Hirst (five for 54). Dismissed for 133, the only Lancashire batsman for which the wicket posed few problems was Jack Sharp, who made 30 not out.

Sharp was also the home side's best bowler as Yorkshire too found the wicket difficult. The White Rose county had lost five wickets for 44 runs when Hirst (40) and Wainwright (35) came to their rescue and gain a one run lead on first innings. Jack Sharp finished with five for 89.

In Lancashire's second innings, the Yorkshire fielding was outstanding and some good catches, notably by Tunnicliffe and Wainwright, were taken. George Hirst bowled magnificently to take seven for 28 as Lancashire were bowled out for just 44 and finish with match figures of twelve for 77. Hirst was also the game's top-scorer and one of only three players to hit more than 20 in either innings.

Chasing 44 to win, Yorkshire lost just one wicket in reaching their target.

YORKSHIRE v LANCASHIRE
at Headingley August 5,6,7, 1901

Yorkshire 319 (Mitchell 106, Hirst 58, Sharp 5-109) and 175-5 (Denton 62, Mitchell 54)
Lancashire 413 (MacLaren 117, Ward 100, A.Eccles 59)
Match Drawn.

The Bank Holiday match, which had been set aside for Jack Brown's benefit, was, in financial terms, the best that any professional cricketer up to that time had enjoyed. However, on the opening day, a crowd of 30,891 passed through the turnstiles and, as no adequate provision had been made for dealing with such a number, there was a good deal of delay with play after lunch not resuming until almost 3.30 pm.

With such a large crowd encroaching onto the playing area, the boundaries were decidedly short but Yorkshire at first failed to make good

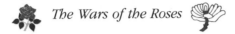

use as Sharp took three early wickets. Brown (37) and Mitchell took the score to 70 before the latter batsman was joined by Hirst. They added 122 for the fifth wicket in a little over an hour. Mitchell scored 106 in his stay at the wicket, scoring 19 fours. Hirst, who made 58, and Lord Hawke, with 55, helped the home side to a total of 319.

For Lancashire, MacLaren (117) and Ward (100) both batted well, adding 154 for the third wicket. Ward went on to add a further 107 runs with Alec Eccles, who made 59. Passing Yorkshire's total for the loss of four wickets, the visitors had a lead of 94 runs when their last man was dismissed. However, Ward had batted too slowly and there was little time left for the Red Rose county to try and force a victory.

In their second innings, Yorkshire scored 175 for five after being 31 for three, with both Denton and that man Mitchell both scoring half-centuries.

YORKSHIRE v LANCASHIRE
at Bramall Lane May 19, 20, 1902

Lancashire 72 (Jackson 3-5, Haigh 3-20, Rhodes 3-29) and 54 (Jackson 5-8, Rhodes 4-25)
Yorkshire 148 (Barnes 6-39)
Yorkshire won by an innings and 22 runs.

A shower just before midday delayed the start of this Roses clash by half-an-hour, but when play did get underway MacLaren and Ward, Lancashire's opening batsmen found Rhodes and Hirst difficult to get away. MacLaren was adjudged lbw to Rhodes and Johnny Tyldesley was bowled by Hirst as Lancashire struggled to 34 for two. That was the score at the close of play as a series of heavy showers limited play to just a few more over from which there was no addition to the score.

Next day, though Ward and Hallows took the score to 52 before the third wicket fell, the last seven wickets went down for the addition of only 20 runs with Stanley Jackson taking three for 5.

The wicket was still very difficult when Yorkshire went in to bat but Jackson, Brown and Taylor played each ball on merit and by the time Lancashire's total had been passed, the home side had lost only two wickets. Brought back for a second spell, Sydney Barnes took five wickets for 23 runs to finish with six for 39 as Yorkshire were bowled out for 148.

No batsman reached double figures in Lancashire's second innings as they were shot out for 54. Wilfred Rhodes bowled unchanged to take four for 25, whilst Stanley Jackson took five for 8 off seven overs to finish with match figures of eight for 13 as well as scoring 33, the game's highest score.

LANCASHIRE v YORKSHIRE
at Old Trafford August 4,5,6, 1902

Lancashire 243 (MacLaren 53, EE Steel 53, Haigh 5-62)
Yorkshire 499-5 (Hirst 112*, Denton 108*, Jackson 82, Tunnicliffe 59, Taylor 55, Washington 55)
Match Drawn.

Despite heavy rain preventing any play on the final day, the match set aside for Albert Ward's benefit was a financial success, the Lancashire batsman receiving over £1,700.

The wicket was slow and Lancashire, having won the toss, elected to bat. Archie MacLaren had scored 53 when he was stumped by Hunter off the bowling of Rhodes whilst attempting to force the pace. E.E.Steel also scored 53 whilst Jack Sharp made 48, and though a number of the other batsmen made useful contributions, the Red Rose county were all out for 243. Schofield Haigh finished with five for 62, all of his victims being clean bowled.

On the second day, Yorkshire, resuming on their overnight score of 31 for 0, soon lost Brown but then Tunnicliffe (59) and Washington (55) added 100 runs in an hour-and-a-half for the second wicket. Taylor (55) and Jackson (82) then put on 105 for the fourth wicket and Jackson and Denton 81 for the fifth. With Denton and Hirst at the wicket, the Lancashire bowlers, with the exception of Sydney Barnes, lost their length and the Yorkshire batsmen added 178 in an hour-and-three-quarters. By the close of play, Yorkshire were 256 runs ahead with five wickets in hand, Denton being 108 not out and Hirst 112 not out. Sydney Barnes took one for 24 in 46 overs!

LANCASHIRE v YORKSHIRE
at Old Trafford June 1,2,3, 1903

Yorkshire 360 (Denton 98, Lord Hawke 79, E.E.Steel 5-88) and 215 (Denton 84, Brearley 6-81)
Lancashire 230 (J.T.Tyldesley 73, MacLaren 53, Jackson 7-61) and 254-3 (Garnett 122, J.T.Tyldesley 52)
Match Drawn.

After Brown and Tunnicliffe had given Yorkshire a good start, David Denton played some splendid cricket in scoring 98. There followed a middle order collapse against some fine bowling by E.E.Steel, who finished with five for 88 including the wicket of Lord Hawke for 79 after he

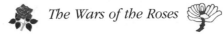

and Whitehead had put on a record 108 for the last wicket.

With Hirst injured and Rhodes and Haigh out of form, Johnny Tyldesley and Archie MacLaren both scored half-centuries as the home side threatened to overhaul Yorkshire's total of 360 with ease. However, after lunch on the second day, Jackson was reintroduced into the attack and he proceeded to take six wickets for 20 runs as Lancashire were dismissed for 230.

When Yorkshire batted a second time, Denton was again the county's top-scorer with 84. He was well supported by Jackson (48) and Schofield Haigh (28 not out) but the remaining Yorkshire batsmen had no answer to the pace of Walter Brearley, who took six for 81.

Lancashire needed 346 for victory and though throughout the game Yorkshire had held the upper hand, the home side, thanks to a fighting innings of 122 by Harold Garnett, ended the game just 92 runs short with seven wickets still in hand.

YORKSHIRE v LANCASHIRE
at Bradford August 3,4,5, 1903

Lancashire 233 (A.Eccles 61, Cuttell 51, Haigh 5-56, Rhodes 5-91) 168 (Sharp 56, Rhodes 8-61)
Yorkshire 238 (Hirst 58, Barnes 4-94) and 164-5 (Hirst 69*, Barnes 4-60)
Yorkshire won by 5 wickets.

Aided by a number of dropped catches, MacLaren (39) and Spooner (33) put on 58 for the first wicket. The Lancashire innings then collapsed against the bowling of Rhodes and Haigh in that seven wickets went down for the addition of 39 runs. Alex Eccles, with 61, and Willis Cuttell, with 51, added 85 for the ninth wicket as the visitors' innings ended on 233.

By the close of play, Brown and Tunnicliffe, the Yorkshire openers, were still there with 46 runs on the board. Overnight rain helped the bowlers on the second day but not before Hirst had scored a hard-hit 58. Sydney Barnes took four for 94 as Yorkshire were bowled out for 238, a lead of just five runs.

With Wilfred Rhodes bowling at his best, Lancashire were in trouble from the outset of their second innings. Only Jack Sharp with 56 seemed to have any answer to the Kirkheaton-born bowler who took eight for 61.

Yorkshire set 164 to win, lost Tunnicliffe, Denton and Jackson with 48 on the board and though Hirst again batted well, half the side were out with 53 runs still needed. With Barnes bowling well, it seemed that the match could go either way, but Rhodes joined Hirst (69 not out) and the two batsmen hit off the remaining runs in an hour to give the home side a five wicket victory.

69

WILFRED RHODES (YORKSHIRE)

Wilfred Rhodes was a unique cricketer. For Yorkshire, he scored 31,098 runs at 30.04 and took 3,597 wickets at 16.02 runs apiece. He played in 58 Tests for England, scoring 2,325 runs at 30.19 and captured 127 wickets at 26.96 runs each.

He learned to bowl on a patch of grass cut by his father near their home in Kirkheaton. Practice went on throughout the summer and winter in a woodshed and to measure his power of spin, he would coat one side of the ball with chalk. On the highly prepared uncovered pitches of his youth, Rhodes could turn the ball wickedly but as pitches improved and covering began, he turned to flight and length.

For a short spell he worked in the engine sheds at nearby Mirfield, virtually having to run the three miles to Kirkheaton to begin play at 2.30 pm on a Saturday afternoon. A spell of labouring ended when Galashiels made him an offer to become a professional. It was while he was waiting to be called up for a trial with Warwickshire that Bobby Peel was sacked and Rhodes called up for an end-of-season trial against the Colts. In April 1898 he played in the opening match against MCC at Lord's and after match figures of six for 33 was retained for the next game against Somerset. Rhodes took thirteen for 45 and finished the season with 154 wickets at 14.60 runs each. In his second season of first-class cricket, Rhodes ousted Lancashire's Johnny Briggs from the Test team, making his debut at Trent Bridge in W.G.Grace's final Test.

In 1902 he and George Hirst made history at the Oval in the fifth Test against Australia. Needing 263 to win, England were reduced to 48 for five on a turning pitch, but Gilbert Jessop hit 104 out of 139 in 75 minutes and when last man Rhodes joined Hirst, 15 runs were still needed.. Hirst is supposed to have said 'We'll get 'em in singles', which they did but both denied that any words were spoken! Rhodes toured Australia in 1903-04 as a bowler and improving batsman and returned in 1911-12 as Jack Hobbs' opening partner! After exactly half of his 58 Tests, Rhodes had batted in all eleven positions for England. He was the most durable of Test cricketers, enjoying the longest international career of all time and being the oldest to appear at that level.

He played his final match in 1930 at the end of the first Test rubber in the Caribbean. Four years earlier he had been recalled at the age of 48 to play a vital role in that historic win at the Oval which regained the Ashes. Rhodes was the first England cricketer to complete the Test 'double' and the first from any country to extend it to 2000 runs and 100 wickets.

70

Wilfred Rhodes played in more first-class, county and Championship matches than any other cricketer. His bowling was relentlessly accurate and with subtle variations of flight, angle, pace and spin, and coupled with a brief approach to the wicket, meant that he could bowl for hours without tiring.

His best performances with the ball for Yorkshire came against Essex at Leyton when he took nine for 28 in 1899 and nine for 39 in 1929. Rhodes also performed the hat-trick twice, against Kent at Canterbury in 1901 and against Derbyshire at Derby in 1920. His batting was based on a tenacious defence and careful placements. His was the tough, dour, pragmatic approach that typifies the Yorkshire spirit. He scored three double-centuries for the White Rose county, notably 267 not out against Leicestershire at Headingley in 1921. During his twenty-nine seasons in the Yorkshire side, he helped the county to a remarkable twelve Championships.

He later coached at Harrow School until his sight began to fade. Even after it deserted him completely in 1952, he remained a frequent visitor to matches and became an uncannily accurate judge of a batsman's timing from the sound of the ball being hit.

LANCASHIRE v YORKSHIRE
at Old Trafford May 23,24,25, 1904

Yorkshire 293 (Rhodes 94*, Haigh 84, Brearley 6-110) and 34-3
Lancashire 273 (Spooner 126, Sharp 52, Jackson 6-91, Myers 3-9)
Match Drawn.

This Whit-Monday match would normally have been played at Headingley but in order to ensure that George Hirst's benefit was a huge success, the Lancashire committee agreed to the fixtures being switched.

Yorkshire won the toss and elected to bat but with Walter Brearley bowling at his most fierce, they struggled to 126 for eight with six of the wickets falling to Brearley. However, Rhodes and Haigh saved them by putting on 162 for the ninth wicket. Haigh was bowled by Sharp for 84 whilst Rhodes was left undefeated on 94 when the last wicket went down.

At the end of the first day, Lancashire were 45 for one with Hirst having picked up the wicket of Garnett. On the second day Lancashire, in the face of some good bowling by Jackson who took six for 91, got within twenty of their opponents' total. They were indebted to Spooner,

Lancashire - County Champions 1904
Back row: Sharp, Cuttell, W.Findlay, Kermode, L.O.S.Poidevin, Hallows, Heap
Front row: Tyldesley, A.H.Hornby, A.C.Maclaren, R.H.Spooner, H.G.Garnett

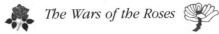

who on a rain-affected wicket scored a masterly 126, and Sharp, who hit 52 lower down the order.

By the close of play, Cuttell had removed both Yorkshire openers and Hallows had accounted for Denton to leave the visitors on 34 for three.

Sadly, heavy rain prevented any play on the third day when had it been possible to get a full day in, a close finish was likely.

YORKSHIRE v LANCASHIRE
at Headingley August 1,2,3, 1904

Yorkshire 403 (Smith 98, Hirst 65, Tunnicliffe 55, Hawke 54)
Lancashire 173 (A.H.Hornby 59, Hirst 6-42) and 163-3 (J.T.Tyldesley 108*)
Match Drawn.

During the three days of this Roses match set aside for the benefit of George Hirst, who had given Yorkshire twelve years splendid service, 78,661 came through the Headingley turnstiles, giving the all-rounder record proceeds.

Sent in to bat by Lancashire captain Archie MacLaren, the home side kept the Red Rose county in the field for seven hours whilst scoring 403 runs. That total seemed a long way off when Yorkshire were 146 for five. Ernie Smith was dropped before he had scored and he made the visitors pay by scoring 98 before being bowled by Hallows. He was well supported by Hirst (65), Tunnicliffe (55) and Lord Hawke (54) as Lancashire's bowlers had a very disappointing day.

When Lancashire went in to bat, Hirst removed Spooner, MacLaren and J.T.Tyldesley in his first three overs. Five wickets were down for 43 before Poidevin (40) and Hornby (59) took the visitors to 173. Following-on 230 behind, Lancashire lost a couple of early wickets, but with J.T.Tyldesley in fine form and Hallows and Poidevin offering stubborn resistance, Lancashire were 163 for three when stumps were drawn. Tyldesley was 108 not out, one of his finest innings in a Roses game.

LANCASHIRE v YORKSHIRE
at Old Trafford June 12,13,14, 1905

Lancashire 399 (J.T.Tyldesley 134, Spooner 109, Haigh 6-74)
Yorkshire 133 (Brearley 5-31) and 214 (Rhodes 65, Kermode 6-70)
Lancashire won by an innings and 52 runs.

A huge Bank Holiday crowd of 24,461 saw Spooner and Tyldesley put on 253 for the second wicket in 160 minutes after MacLaren had been dismissed for four. Both batsmen rode their luck, Tyldesley having made just

14 when he was badly missed by Tunnicliffe at slip off the bowling of Hirst and Spooner had scored 37 when a ball hit his off stump without dislodging the bails! Spooner was eventually bowled by Haigh for 109 whilst Tyldesley was fifth out at 297 for a well-hit 134. Cutting was the feature of his innings, but it also brought his downfall as he played on to a ball from Haigh, who finished with six for 74 as Lancashire were bowled out for 399 just before the close of play.

Rain on the second day gave much more help to the bowlers and Brearley (five for 31) and Kermode (three for 51) got the ball to lift dangerously. Denton with 41 and Jackson with 34 were the only Yorkshire batsmen to last any length of time.

Following-on 266 behind, Yorkshire again found the Australian-born Kermode a handful, the seamer taking six for 70 as Lancashire won with ease by an innings and 52 runs. Only Wilfred Rhodes with 65 seemed capable of averting the inevitable but he paid the price with some painful blows to the body.

JOHNNY TYLDESLEY (LANCASHIRE)

'John Thomas' or JT as he became known was regarded as the greatest professional batsman Lancashire had ever had until his brother Ernest finished up with more runs. JT was generally regarded by people who had the good firtune to see them both play as the superior player.

Born at Roe Green near Worlsey, Johnny Tyldesley played his early cricket with those two villages before going to play with Little Lever in the Bolton League and from there to Old Trafford on trial.

After several noteworthy performances for the 2nd XI he was given his first-class debut against Gloucestershire and scored 33 not out in Lancashire's second innings. In the following game against Warwickshire at Edgbaston, Tyldesley made 152 not out. Though he was unable to maintain this form he showed his liking for the Edgbaston wicket again in 1897 with a century in each innings of Lancashire's game with Warwickshire, followed by 174 against Sussex at Old Trafford. In 1898, JT scored almost 2,000 runs in all first-class matches including his first double century for the county in the match against Derbyshire. Test recognition followed in 1899 when Tyldesley played the first of 31 matches for his country. From then until 1909 he was an automatic choice for Test sides and in 1902 he was the onlyprofessional to be picked for his batting alone in a year when the England team included some of the finest amateur talent ever to grace it.

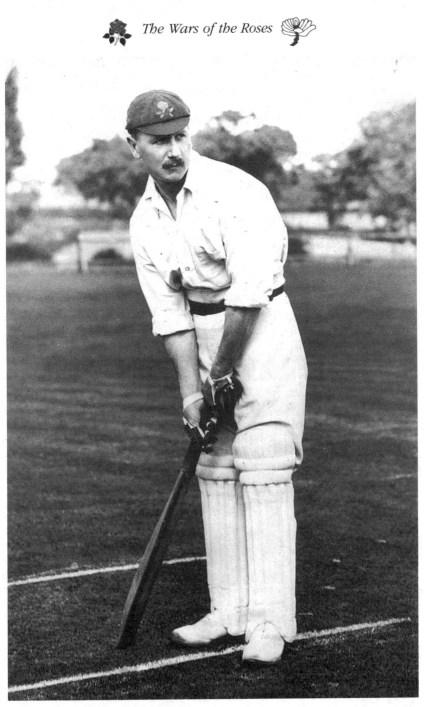

In Lancashire's match against Essex that season he had just reached his century, but the Red Rose county still needed 15 to win with three wickets in hand. A storm was on the way and as Claude Buckenham, Essex's opening fast bowler, tore in, Tyldesley made 16 runs in an over accompanied by thunder and lightning and two minutes later the Old Trafford ground was under water!

Between 1899 and 1909, Tyldesley scored 1,661 runs in Test matches at an average of 30.75. There are England batsmen who have made more runs at a better average but it should be remembered that Tyldesley's runs were made against top-class bowling on indifferent wickets. He hit three centuries against Australia - at Edgbaston in 1902 and two in 1905 at Headingley and the Oval. His fourth Test hundred, the first in sequence, was made at Cape Town in Lord Hawke's South African tour of 1898-99.

But it is as a Lancashire cricketer that Johnny Tyldesley is best remembered. His record for the county is astonishing. He scored 31,949 runs at an average of 41.38. His younger brother Ernest scored 2,000 more runs but he played 66 more innings than Johnny. His list of centuries includes hyndreds against every county playing in the Championship. At Edgbaston, always a happy hunting ground, his performances were legendary. There he scored no less than eleven centuries in county and representative games.

Tyldesley's highest innings of 295 was played at Old Trafford in 1906 against that season's county champions, Kent. Twice he hit two centuries in a match - against Warwickshire at Edgbaston in 1897 and against Hampshire at Old Trafford in 1910. In 1897 and again in 1904 he hit three hundreds in successive innings and still shares with Archie MacLaren the record Lancashire fourth wicket partnership of 324 against Nottinghamshire at Trent Bridge in 1904.

When cricket resumed in 1919 he was persuaded to play although at almost 41, he would have preferred to have retired. He scored three more centuries, one of them a massive 272 against Derbyshire at Chesterfield. His 1,000 runs that season were his nineteenth in succession. His last appearance came four years later when as county coach he was asked to captain the side in place of the injured Jack Sharp.

YORKSHIRE v LANCASHIRE
at Bramall Lane August 7,8,9, 1905

Yorkshire 76 (Brearley 7-35) and 285 (Denton 96, Rhodes 74, Brearley 6-122)
Lancashire 177 (MacLaren 51, Rhodes 5-66) and 140 (Rhodes 4-49)
Yorkshire won by 44 runs.

In a game which swung one way and then the other, Yorkshire emerged as winners by 44 runs.

It didn't seem as if that would be the case in the opening session as the home side were dismissed for 76 in a little over an hour-and-a-half. Walter Brearley took seven for 35 and Billy Cook three for 35, whilst only Stanley Jackson with 30 looked comfortable.

Lancashire's first three batsmen, MacLaren (51) Spooner (42) and J.T.Tyldesley (33) got them off to a good start and by the close of play on the first day, the Red Rose county were 87 runs ahead with two wickets in hand. Jackson polished off the tail early the following morning to finish with four for 15, whilst Wilfred Rhodes took five for 66.

In Yorkshire's second innings, Brearley clean bowled bothTunnicliffe and Rothery but then came a great partnership between Jackson and Denton, the pair adding 143 for the third wicket. Jackson (45) also fell to Brearley as did Rhodes, whose innings of 74 brought rapturous applause from the home crowd. Denton's innings was a brilliant one but he fell four runs short of what would have been a magnificent hundred.

Needing 185 for victory, Lancashire lost both MacLaren and Spooner towards the end of the second day and finished on 50 for two. On the final morning, the Lancashire batsmen struggled against the bowling of Rhodes (five for 49) and Haigh (three for 22) as Yorkshire won this most exciting of struggles.

YORKSHIRE v LANCASHIRE
at Bradford June 4,5,6, 1906

Lancashire 67 (Hirst 6-20, Haigh 4-30) and 151 (Haigh 5-35)
Yorkshire 177 (Hirst 58, Brearley 6-66) and 42-4
Yorkshire won by 6 wickets.

On a wicket that seemed to pose very few problems, only Spooner (18) and Tyldesley (16) reached double figures as Lancashire reached 56 for five at lunch. The last five wickets fell for 11 runs as Hirst (six for 20) and Haigh (four for 30) dismissed the visitors for just 67.

Yorkshire passed this total for the loss of four wickets, one of which was that of David Denton, given out in unusual circumstances. Brearley, taking a return from the Yorkshire batsman very low down near his ankles, threw the ball up, but was then preparing to bowl again when MacLaren appealed. The umpire at the bowler's end was unsighted but gave Denton out after consulting with the square-leg umpire! With Hirst batting very sensibly for 58, the home side secured a lead of 110 runs on the first innings.

After Lancashire had lost MacLaren bowled by Hirst without a run on the board, Spooner (42) and Tyldesley (37) almost pulled the game round, taking the visitors to within 26 runs of the deficit before another wicket went down. However, only Sharp with 31 provided any resistance as Schofield Haigh ran through the lower order to finish with five for 35.

Yorkshire lost four wickets in scoring the 42 runs for victory with Walter Brearley, who also had two simple chances off his bowling dropped, taking three for 17.

LANCASHIRE v YORKSHIRE
at Old Trafford August 6,7,8, 1906

Yorkshire 291 (Tunnicliffe 82, Kermode 4-54) and 193 (Hirst 85, Harry 4-53)
Lancashire 280 (Sharp 84, J.T.Tyldesley 65, Hirst 5-67) and 97 (Rhodes 5-49)
Yorkshire won by 107 runs.

The Old Trafford match, which was set aside for John Tyldesley's benefit, ended in a win for Yorkshire by 107 runs, but such a result looked unlikely until the third morning.

After Harry Dean had clean bowled Wilfred Rhodes, Tunnicliffe (82) and Denton (44) repaired the damage with a century partnership. Apart from Rhodes, the only other Yorkshire batsman to fail to get into double figures was George Hirst as the visitors totalled 291. Lancashire missed the pace of Walter Brearley, who failed to win selection following a disagreement with the county's committee. Alex Kermode bowled almost as fast, taking four for 54.

For Lancashire, Tyldesley (65) and Sharp (84) helped the Red Rose county come within 11 runs of Yorkshire's total but at one stage it looked as if they would have little trouble in passing their score. That they didn't was down to George Hirst who took five for 67.

By close of play on the second day, Yorkshire were 77 for five with Kermode removing Tunnicliffe, Rhodes and Denton.

Following overnight rain, Rhodes and Ernie Smith realised that the

78

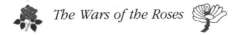

wicket was only going to remain docile for a short time and they had to make runs while the going was good. Hirst scored a superb 85, whilst Smith fell to a marvellous catch by Tyldesley off the bowling of Harry for 46.

Needing 205 for victory, Lancashire soon lost MacLaren, who in sheer exasperation hit his own wicket as he attempted an audacious stroke. Rhodes was the chief tormentor, taking five for 49, supported by Haigh with three for 8, as Yorkshire ran out easy winners.

LANCASHIRE v YORKSHIRE
at Old Trafford May 20,21,22, 1907

Lancashire 275 (Tyldesley 98, Sharp 85, Hirst 4-90) and 109 (Rhodes 6-46)
Yorkshire 248 (Rhodes 68, Cook 5-46)
Match Drawn.

After winning the toss, Lancashire batted first under a grey Old Trafford sky. Though they were without MacLaren and Hornby, there were good performances from Tyldesley, Poidevin and Sharp. Tyldesley, whom Poidevin helped put on 106 for the third wicket, hit brilliantly after the latter batsman had been dismissed for 43. After giving a faultless display of batting in his three hours at the crease, Tyldesley threw his wicket away, being stumped by Hunter off the bowling of Rhodes for 98. Jack Sharp, the England international footballer, also played well after a slow start, making 85 out of Lancashire's total of 275.

Unfortunately, not a ball could be bowled on the second day, but with Tunnicliffe (48) batting for over two hours and Rhodes (68) batting adventurously with Haigh (40), once the follow-on had been avoided Yorkshire ended their innings just 27 runs behind the home side.

When Lancashire batted a second time, Tyldesley showed himself to be England's best bad-wicket batsman with a fine innings of 42. Rhodes took six for 46 and Deyes three for 19, but despite Lancashire being bowled out for 109 on a fast-deteriorating wicket, there was no real hope of a finish.

YORKSHIRE v LANCASHIRE
at Headingley August 5,6,7, 1907

Lancashire 136 (Hornby 55, Rhodes 6-71) and 179 (Rhodes 5-67)
Yorkshire 183 (Rhodes 69, Dean 4-49) and 133-1 (Tunnicliffe 63*)
Yorkshire won by 9 wickets.

Following an attractive opening partnership between Spooner and

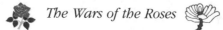

MacLaren, and a spell of hard-hitting from A.H.Hornby, Lancashire were 92 for three at lunch. But in less than hour after play had resumed, Rhodes (six for 71) and Hirst (four for 50) had bowled the visitors out for 136.

Yorkshire started badly and half their side were out with just 40 runs on the board as Dean and Harry clean bowled each of their victims. Then Rhodes and Wilkinson, the Sheffield left-hander, pulled the game round, adding 95 for the sixth wicket. Myers also gave Rhodes more valuable assistance and Yorkshire finished 47 runs in front.

In Lancashire's second innings, Hornby was again in fine form, being run out for 46, whilst amateur Harry Stanning gave him useful support with an innings of 42. By lunch on the final day, Lancashire were 112 runs ahead with five wickets in hand, but then Rhodes dismissed the last four batsmen for the addition of just 20 runs, leaving Yorkshire to make 133 for victory.

Tunnicliffe and Jackson, in his only game of the season, put on 58 for the first wicket before the latter batsman was dismissed by Dean for 35. Tunnicliffe was then joined by Denton, for whose benefit this game was played, and they took Yorkshire to the required total without any further loss.

YORKSHIRE v LANCASHIRE
at Bramall Lane June 8,9,10, 1908

Yorkshire 209 (Denton 71, Brearley 7-116) and 210 (Newstead 61*, Brearley 5-89)
Lancashire 129 (Tyldesley 63, Hirst 6-41) and 97 (Hirst 5-47, Rhodes 4-30)
Yorkshire won by 193 runs.

Thanks largely to some cavalier batting by David Denton, Yorkshire were 127 for three at lunch but a devastating spell of bowling from Walter Brearley saw him take five wickets in quick succession to leave the home side on 155 for eight. Some hard hitting by Newstead (35), with Hunter holding up his end, helped Yorkshire to reach 209 before the last wicket was taken. Brearley finished with seven for 116 from 33 overs.

After losing three early wickets, Lancashire were indebted to Tyldesley and Spooner, who took the score to 102 for three. The following day, Hirst (six for 41) and Newstead (four for 49) disposed of Lancashire's last seven wickets for 27 runs, leaving Yorkshire with a first innings lead of 80. For Lancashire, John Tyldesley scored almost half his side's total with a fighting innings of 63.

After nine wickets had fallen for 116 runs in Yorkshire's second innings, Newstead (61 not out) and Hunter (38) put on 94 for the last wicket, leaving the visitors needing 291 for victory.

With Schofield Haigh having broken a finger and thus unable to bowl, Yorkshire relied heavily on Hirst and Rhodes and the two great cricketers didn't let them down. Tyldesley again top-scored with 35 but the Red Rose county never came in sight of the runs required and were bowled out for 97 with Hirst taking five for 47 and Rhodes four for 30.

LANCASHIRE v YORKSHIRE
at Old Trafford August 1,3,4, 1908

Yorkshire 206 (Denton 63, Brearley 7-81) and 243 (Denton 51, Brearley 6-115)
Lancashire 144 (Newstead 4-45) and 115 (Newstead 5-44, Hirst 4-60)
Yorkshire won by 190 runs.

On a wicket which gave the bowlers some assistance, Yorkshire started badly, losing both openers, Rhodes and Hardisty, to the bowling of Brearley. Denton and Wilkinson put on 87 for the third wicket but both fell in quick succession to MacLeod. George Hirst batted in determined fashion, scoring 46 not out, but the remaining Yorkshire batsmen were destroyed by the pace of Brearley who took seven for 81.

Jack Newstead was Yorkshire's best bowler and he had captured three of the wickets to fall when play ended with Lancashire on 120 for seven. He added to his tally early the following morning to finish with four for 45 as the home side were bowled out 62 runs short of the Yorkshire total.

In Yorkshire's second innings, Rhodes and Hardisty made amends for their first innings failures with an opening partnership of 75. Denton followed up his good form in the first innings by hitting another half-century, although he was dropped after he had scored just two. Rothery and Bates added useful runs towards the end of the innings as Yorkshire were dismissed for 243. Walter Brearley was again Lancashire's best bowler, finishing with match figures of thirteen for 196 from 58.1 overs.

Needing 306 to win, Lancashire's batsmen were up against it, as a cross-wind helped Yorkshire's opening bowlers, Rhodes and Newstead. Only Spooner, with a fighting knock of 33, put up any resistance as Rhodes (four for 60) and Newstead (five for 44) bowled the White Rose county to victory by 190 runs.

WALTER BREARLEY (LANCASHIRE)

Walter Brearley played no first-class cricket until he was 26 years of age, though he had played a fair amount of club cricket, gaining a reputation as a fast bowler, first with Bolton and then with Manchester.

He made his debut for Lancashire at Hove in 1902 but his start was modest and it wasn't until the following season, when he took 69 wickets in his fifteen games, that he created any impression. In 1904, Brearley came into his own as Lancashire ran away with the Championship. Considered the best amateur fast bowler in the country, he would have taken more than the 95 wickets he did take if he had not missed several of Lancashire's August matches through injury. In what was a comparitively short career, Brearley had his first brush with authority at the end of that 1904 season. He was left out of the Lancashire side for the Champion County v Rest of England game and immediately announced his retirement from county cricket! Happily for all concerned the matter was settled amicably before the start of the 1905 season.

The 1905 season was Brearley's finest as he took 133 wickets at 19 runs apiece for Lancashire and 181 in all matches. His best performance came in the match against Somerset at Old Trafford. He took nine for 47 before lunch on the first day and when the visitors batted again accomplished the remarkable performance of taking four wickets in four balls. He went on to take eight for 90 in the innings and ended with a formidable match analysis of seventeen for 137.

His form that season led to him gaining recognition at Test level, playing in the last two Tests against Australia at Old Trafford and the Oval. On his home ground he had match figures of eight for 126, helping England to an innings victory. In that season of 1905, playing for Lancashire, the Gentlemen and England, Brearley took the wicket of Victor Trumper six times in nine innings spread over five matches. As at the end of the previous season there was a further difference of opinion or a sense of grievance and once again he submitted his resignation. Though he played in a few games, Brearley didn't return to the Lancashire side until 1908 and celebrated his return with 148 wickets in Championship matches and selection as one of Wisden's 'Five Cricketers of the Year'.

In the summer of 1909, Brearley took nine for 80 against Yorkshire at Old Trafford but still couldn't prevent a Lancashire defeat. That season, the volatile Brearley had yet another brush with authority when on the first morning of the second Test at Lord's, he was approached by Archie MacLaren to play for England. Brearley, however, was of the opinion that he should have been picked for the original side selected and refused the invitation.

A great believer in keeping fit, he never smoked until cricket was over for the day, though Gilbert Jessop said that when Walter went out to bat, he would light a cigarette, leave it burning in an ashtray and have a more than even chance of being back in time to finish smoking it before the tobacco had burned through! It was also said that the eccentric Brearley could vault a full-sized Billiard table!

For the county in his all-too-brief career, he took 690 wickets at 18.70 runs each. He brought a fresh breeze to Lancashire's matches in Edwardian days and Old Trafford was always a livelier place for his presence and for the cricket he played there.

LANCASHIRE v YORKSHIRE
at Old Trafford May 31, June 1,2 1909

Yorkshire 133 (Brearley 9-80) and 78 (Huddleston 8-24)
Lancashire 89 (Haigh 7-25, Hirst 3-34) and 57 (Hirst 6-23, Haigh 2-11)
Yorkshire won by 65 runs.

In spite of a series of heavy rain showers restricting play on the opening day, and bad light forcing the umpires to end play an hour-and-a-half early on the second day, this match produced some wonderfully exciting cricket.

On a wicket not particularly suited to him, Walter Brearley bowled magnificently to take nine for 80 as Yorkshire were bowled out for 133. David Denton, who was dropped when he was 16, was his side's top-scorer with 48. On the second day, the wicket had not only cut up but was made even more difficult by strong sunshine. Lancashire began reasonably well enough and were 54 for three at lunch. In the afternoon session, Haigh was virtually unplayable and finished with seven for 25, including a hat-trick in which each of his victims were clean bowled.

With a lead of 44 runs on the first innings, Yorkshire's second innings started in semi-darkness and when bad light eventually stopped

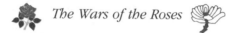

play, were 44 for four. Huddleston in the evening twilight had taken three for 15 but the following morning his off-breaks, bowled slightly quicker than normal, saw him take five for nine to finish with eight for 24 as Yorkshire were bowled out for 78.

Set 123 to win, Lancashire made a disastrous start and lost their first five wickets for six runs as George Hirst ran through the top-order. There was a spirited sixth wicket stand by Heap and Hornby but three brilliant catches after lunch gave Yorkshire victory by 65 runs. Though Hirst had taken six for 23, he was the least successful of the game's four successful bowlers!

SCHOFIELD HAIGH (YORKSHIRE)

Schofield Haigh began his career with Armitage Bridge and before long was noticed by Yorkshire's opening batsman Louis Hall, who at that time was in the habit at the end of each season of taking a team up to Scotland. On Hall's recommendation, Haigh was engaged by Aberdeen, but after three summers playing for them he joined Perth. It was here that he first began experimenting in shortening his run, slowing his pace and developing spin. The turning point of his career came when he met with great success for a Scottish side against Lancashire, prompting the Yorkshire authorities to realsise that he might make a first-rate county bowler..

After a brilliant trial against Durham at Barnsley in 1896, Haigh was given an opportunity to play first-class cricket when chosen to play against Australia at Bradford. Yorkshire lost the match by 140 runs but in the Australian's second innings, Haigh took eight for 78.

In his early days, Haigh took a great deal out of himself, finishing his delivery with a tremendous plunge, but as time went on, he modified his style and economised his strength. When the conditions were helpful, he was without doubt one of the most difficult bowlers of his generation.

He was not an opening bowler, although England once believed him to be. He played four times for England against Australia - at Lord's and Headingley in 1905, at Lord's in 1909 and at Old Trafford in 1912 - but against top-class batsmen on flat surfaces, he was far less successful. However, in 1898-99 he helped Trott dismiss the South Africans for 35 when he produced his best Test figures of six for 11. When he toured South Africa again in 1905-06, Haigh took 162 wickets at an average of 10.83 including four wickets in four balls against the Army at Pretoria.

His partnership with Hirst and Rhodes produced the formidable attack which brought Lord Hawke's famous side four Championships in five seasons (1898-1902) and eight titles during Haigh's career. Haigh took 100 wickets in a season 11 times and headed the national bowling averages on five occasions. His best figures were nine for 25 against Gloucestershire at Headingley in 1912, whilst he performed the hat-trick for Yorkshire against Derbyshire at Bradford in 1897, against Somerset at Sheffield in 1902, against Kent at Headingley in 1904 and against Lancashire at Old Trafford in 1909.

Haigh was also a keen fielder and a determined and often underrated lower-or-middle-order batsman who once rattled up a hundred before lunch against Nottinghamshire in 1901.

Haigh, who took 1,876 wickets for Yorkshire at a cost of 15.61 runs each, was a humorous, friendly man whose premature death after seven popular years as coach at Winchester College was much mourned.

YORKSHIRE v LANCASHIRE
at Bradford August 2,3,4, 1909

Yorkshire 159 (Heap 4-46, Brearley 4-65) and 146 (Heap 7-49)
Lancashire 120 (Hornby 51, Rhodes 7-68) and 85 (Rhodes 6-40)
Yorkshire won by 100 runs.

The return match played for Schofield Haigh's benefit, on a bowler's wicket at Park Avenue, produced more runs than the first game but still bore a considerable resemblance to that struggle.

A series of heavy showers meant that play on the first day didn't get underway until almost five o'clock. Benny Wilson's watchful defence brought him the reputation of being a dull batsman but in just over the hour's play that was possible, he scored 47, helping Yorkshire to finish on 111 for four. The next morning, Heap dismissed four batsmen in fourteen balls for five runs as Yorkshire were bowled out for 159.

For Lancashire, Spooner made 47 out of 63 in brilliant style and, with Hornby hitting 51, it seemed as though the Red Rose county would have little trouble in overtaking the Yorkshire total. However, the remaining Lancashire batsman fared badly against Rhodes, whose figures of seven for 68 restricted the visitors to 120.

With the exception of Denton, who hit powerfully for his 37 runs, the Yorkshire batsmen had no answer to Heap, the slow left-hander taking seven for 49 off 25.3 overs as Yorkshire were dismissed for 146.

Lancashire never looked like getting the 186 runs demanded of them and were all out in an hour-and-three-quarters. Rhodes, as in the first innings, had bowled marvellously, finishing with match figures of thirteen for 108, leaving Yorkshire the winners by exactly 100 runs.

YORKSHIRE v LANCASHIRE
at Headingley May 16,17,18, 1910

Lancashire 229 (John Tyldesley 51, Hirst 4-55) and 61 (Hirst 9-23)
Yorkshire 152 (Brearley 5-86, Dean 4-42) and 40-2
Match Drawn.

Unfortunately rain prevented any cricket from being played on the third day when Yorkshire with eight wickets to fall wanted 99 runs to win.

Hornby, Hartley and in particular Tyldesley gave Lancashire a good start but after lunch wickets began to tumble until Huddleston and Dean,

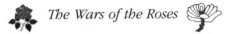

both noted for their bowling, put bat to ball to take the visitors to 229.

When Yorkshire went in to bat, they found Brearley in fine form, the Bolton-born bowler taking four of the first five wickets to fall for very few runs. The tail-enders staged a slight recovery, aided by a series of mistakes in the field, but when last man and top-scorer Schofield Haigh was dismissed for 27, Yorkshire were 77 runs behind Lancashire's total.

George Hirst then proceeded to produce one of the greatest bowling feats of his career. Almost unplayable, Hirst twice took two wickets with successive balls, hit the stumps eight times and finished with nine for 23 after his first four wickets had cost just five runs. Having dismissed Lancashire for 61, Yorkshire began the task of scoring 139 for victory but amid the encircling gloom ended the day on 40 for two.

Supporters of both sides felt that if play had been possible on the third day,that their side would have won!

GEORGE HIRST (YORKSHIRE)

A blunt, loyal, tenacious Yorkshireman, George Hirst was one of the most illustrious cricketers to grace the Golden Age. Figures alone tell only part of the story of Hirst, but they show unmistakably his supreme prowess as an all-round cricketer. Between his first county game for Yorkshire in 1889 and his last in 1929, Hirst scored 32,024 runs at 34.73 and took 2,481 wickets at a cost of 18.02 runs each.

The measure of Hirst's ability is best reflected in that he accomplished the double 14 times, a number only surpassed by his friend from Kirkheaton Wilfred Rhodes. His incredible output of 2,385 runs and 208 wickets in 1906, and even his record Yorkshire score of 341 made against Leicestershire in 1905, are achievements that are unlikely ever to be equalled.

Success in county cricket came slowly to him but after some seasons of quiet progress, he established himself in 1896 by scoring 1,122 runs and taking 104 wickets. Leicestershire, who were Yorkshire's opponents when Hirst made his 341 also suffered from his bowling as well as his batting. Twice he did the hat-trick against them, once in a match in 1907 when he had figures of fifteen for 63.

On the 24 occasions that Hirst played for England, he achieved only a few noteworthy performances. In 1902 at Edgbaston, Hirst and Rhodes bowled out Australia for 36, their lowest total in any Test. In the next match, the Australians met Yorkshire, who bowled them out for 23 with Hirst taking five for nine.

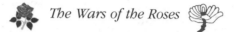

In the final Test of that summer, Hirst and Rhodes helped England to a one wicket victory with a last-ditch stand of 15 prefaced by Hirst's alleged (but disclaimed) command 'We'll get 'em in singles'.

In 1907, Hirst had innings figures of nine for 45 against Middlesex, whilst the following summer he played a notable part in the dismissal of Northamptonshire for 27 and 15 by taking twelve wickets for 19 runs! His best bowling figures for Yorkshire are nine for 23 against Lancashire at Headingley in 1901, eight of them being clean bowled. When he asked for the ball as a memento, Schofield Haigh, who had taken the other wicket, said, 'Nay we mun cut t'ball in half. We took 'em between us, George.'

In addition to his ability with bat and ball, Hirst was also a remarkable fielder, usually at mid-off where many of his 602 catches came from thundering drives.

When war broke out in 1914, Hirst, who was almost forty-four, continued playing league cricket, only claiming expenses when the club that had engaged him wasn't short of funds. He returned to play for Yorkshire in 1919 and hit 180 not out against MCC in the first match. Although he continued to play for Yorkshire until 1929,

he made few appearances after starting his 18-year engagement with Eton College where his kindliness, patience and deep knowledge of the game made him a great natural coach.

Such was Hirst's popularity that his benefit match against Lancashire at Headingley in 1904 was attended by 78,792 spectators.

LANCASHIRE v YORKSHIRE
at Old Trafford August 1,2,3, 1910

Yorkshire 103 (Brearley 5-50, Dean 3-25) and 181 (Dean 4-46, Brearley 4-80)
Lancashire 395-5dec (Spooner 200*, Hornby 60*, Sharp 51)
Lancashire won by an innings and 111 runs.

Awarded to Jack Sharp for his benefit match, this Roses game saw Lancashire victorious over Yorkshire for the first time for five years.

In Yorkshire's first innings total of 103, Walter Brearley took five for 50 and would have had better figures if George Hirst, with an innings of 46, had not stood in his way.

Despite losing Hartley without a run on the board, Lancashire ended the first evening 42 runs ahead with eight wickets in hand. Spooner, who had been dropped twice before he had made 14, went on to score 200 not out, the highest individual score so far in Roses matches. The only other chance he offered during his six and a quarter hours at the crease came when he offered a stumping opportunity to Dolphin when on 150. The beneficiary Sharp scored 51 and Hornby, who added 123 in 85 minutes with Spooner, an unbeaten 60.

Lancashire declared at 395 for five, leaving Yorkshire 292 to avoid an innings defeat. The only time they looked like achieving this feat came in the middle of the third afternoon when a heavy shower sent the players scurrying from the field. With only one wicket to fall, and well over a hundred runs to get, nothing but the continuation of the rain could turn defeat into a draw. After three-quarters of an hour huddled in the pavilion, Yorkshire's last pair came out but Dean soon bowled Radcliffe to leave Lancashire the winners by an innings and 111 runs.

REG SPOONER (LANCASHIRE)

Reginald Herbert Spooner will always occupy a distinguished place in Lancashire cricket. He was the epitome of elegance and grace, one of the lovliest stroke players cricket has ever known. Whilst Spooner was at Marlborough, he was rated the school's finest batsman since Allan Steel. In 1899, his last year, he scored 926 runs at an average of 71.23 and topped the batting averages. Naturally enough he was invited to play for the county of his birth and made his first apperarance for Lancashire that year against Middlesex at Lord's. Opening the Lancashire batting with Albert Ward, he scored 44 and 83.

Though he had left school, Spooner, the son of a Liverpool rector, was unable to play for Lancashire between 1900 and 1902 as he was stationed with the militia in Ireland and had served in the Boer War in South Africa. Business commitments restricted drastically the time he could devote to cricket and only in six seasons was he able to play on a regular basis.

The records of many fine innings he played can of course give no indication of the superbly elegant batting he brought to them. In 1910 he scored 200 not out against Yorkshire at Old Trafford, until recently the highest score made by a Lancashire player in the matches between the two counties.

Reg Spooner first played for England in the fourth Test at Old Trafford in 1905 against Australia. He scored 52 in a game the Australians lost by an innings. In the last Test at the Oval he scored 79 in as many minutes, sharing in a stand of 158 with Johnny Tyldesley. In his ten Tests he scored 481 runs at an average of 32.06. That he took part in so little Test cricket when he had so much to offer seems a sad waste of talent.

Spooner played several times in Gentlemen v Players matches and his innings of 114 in 1906 at Lord's is still rated one of the greatest ever played for the Gentlemen in these annual encounters.

For Lancashire between 1899 and 1921 he scored 9,889 runs at an average of 37.17. In all matches he made 13,396 runs. These included 31 centuries, 25 of them for Lancashire. The stark figures cannot conjure up the brilliance of his stroke play or the pleasure it brought to those who were privileged to see it.

As a fieldsman he was rated, at cover, one of the greatest in the game. His fielding had an ease and grace like his batting and his throw was swift, powerful and accurate. He was often compared with the great Vernon Royle, which is high praise indeed.

Spooner was Lancashire's president in 1945 and 1946. At his installation in 1944, he spoke of his readiness to help in whatever way he could with the restoration of the bomb damaged Old Trafford and added almost as an aside, 'Would to God we could put the clock back!'

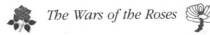

LANCASHIRE v YORKSHIRE
at Old Trafford June 5,6,7, 1911

Yorkshire 199 (Wilson 64, Brearley 7-110) and 376-8dec (Hirst 156, Drake 85)
Lancashire 224 (Makepeace 61, Heap 57, Hirst 6-83) and 192 (Sharp 65, Drake 6-57)
Yorkshire won by 159 runs.

With Walter Brearley again bowling at his best to take seven for 110, Yorkshire were dismissed one run short of 200 - a total that would have been much lower if opening batsman Benny Wilson hadn't scored 64 painstaking runs. By the end of the first day, Lancashire had scored 114 for four.

In the morning the home side, with Heap (57) and Makepeace (61) scoring half-centuries, passed the Yorkshire total with six wickets down. Hirst then took the new ball and claimed the last four wickets of 14 runs so that Lancashire's lead, which at one time looked to be heading for the 100 plus mark, was confined to 25.

Later in the day, Hirst came in to join Alonso Drake after Yorkshire had lost three early wickets and shared in a partnership of 193 for the fourth wicket. Drake, who had been bowled by Brearley without scoring in the first innings, fell to the Lancashire paceman again but this time his hard-hitting had brought him 85 runs. Hirst went on to score 156 as Yorkshire declared their second innings closed at 376 for eight.

Lancashire, who were without J.T.Tyldesley, never looked like making the 352 runs they needed. Sharp battled hard for his 65 and Heap stayed with him for over an hour, but the White Rose county were on top. Drake took six for 57 as Lancashire were bowled out for 192, leaving Yorkshire the winners by 159 runs.

YORKSHIRE v LANCASHIRE
at Bramall Lane August 7,8,9, 1911

Lancashire 167 (Rhodes 4-57, Hirst 4-58) and 364 (McLeod 121, Makepeace 55, Rhodes 4-109)
Yorkshire 281 (Drake 54, Wilson 50, Haigh 50*, Heap 4-38, Brearley 4-119) and 183-6 (Denton 101*)
Match Drawn.

Yorkshire were on top for most of this Roses match and indeed, when stumps were drawn at the end of the second day, appeared fairly certain of victory.

91

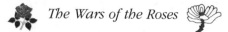

With Hirst and Rhodes, whose benefit match this was, taking four wickets apiece, Lancashire were bowled out for 167. With Wilson (50), Drake (54) and Haigh (50 not out) all scoring half-centuries, Yorkshire scored 281, a lead of 114. At the close of play, Lancashire were just 48 runs ahead with half of their side back in the pavilion.

On the final day, McLeod and Makepeace pulled the game round in remarkable fashion. McLeod, batting for little over two hours, scored 121 with three sixes and fifteen 4's, hitting the Yorkshire bowlers to all parts of the Bramall Lane ground.

Three hours play remained when Yorkshire went in to bat needing 251 to win. Wilson, Rhodes and Drake were out for 45 and though Hirst stayed with Denton for an hour, half the side were out for 111 with nearly an hour left to play. Oldroyd offered some stubborn resistance but when stumps were drawn, Yorkshire had scored 183 for six with David Denton 101 not out - a magnificent innings on a rapidly deteriorating wicket.

YORKSHIRE v LANCASHIRE
at Bradford May 27,28,29, 1912

Yorkshire 226 (Rhodes 107, Huddleston 6-77) and 17-0
Lancashire 76 (Drake 6-33, Hirst 4-28) and 165 (Haigh 5-25)
Yorkshire won by 10 wickets.

Wilfred Rhodes scored his first Roses hundred against some accurate bowling that often turned and bounced awkwardly. Going in first, he batted with exceptional skill and in a stay of three-and-a-quarter hours scored 107, being sixth out at 180. Booth, Haigh and Bates all made useful contributions in a Yorkshire total of 226.

Play on the second day began in bright sunshine but this only made the wicket even more difficult to bat on. With the exception of Tyldesley (43) and Makepeace (20), Lancashire's other nine batsmen had no answer to the bowling of Drake (six for 33) and Hirst (four for 28), managing only ten runs between them!

After failing by one run to avoid the follow-on, Lancashire batted a second time and, though the wicket seemed to play easier after lunch, the visitors were already 37 for three. Jack Sharp batted with great concentration for his 41, whilst lower down the order Bill Huddleston, Lancashire's opening bowler, hit effectively to score 37.

Schofield Haigh took five for 25 off 20 overs as Lancashire were dismissed for 165. Rhodes and Wilson had no trouble in knocking off the 16 runs required to give Yorkshire victory by 10 wickets.

LANCASHIRE v YORKSHIRE
at Old Trafford August 5,6,7, 1912

Lancashire 347 (Spooner 109, Sharp 72, Makepeace 69, Tyldesley 58, Booth 4-23)
Yorkshire 103 (Dean 7-54, Heap 2-23) and 105-7 (Huddleston 5-33, Dean 2-27)
Match Drawn.

Despite the loss of two hours before the game could start, Lancashire, on winning the toss, took advantage of a lifeless wicket to pile up the runs. Spooner and Makepeace (69) gave their side a great start, putting on 181 for the first wicket. Spooner was dismissed by Kilner for 109 just moments before the close of play when Lancashire's score stood at 245 for two. John Tyldesley (56) and Jack Sharp (72) both hit half-centuries the following morning and though Major Booth, Yorkshire's seventh bowler, took four for 23 as the lower order batsmen were ordered to go for quick runs, Lancashire's first innings total was 347.

     With Harry Dean, who was able to bowl medium-fast or slow depending on the state of the wicket, bowling at his best, the visitors were dismissed for 103 in just under three hours play. Dean took seven for 54 off 31.5 overs.

     Heavy rain on the final day prevented any play until half-past three when Yorkshire followed-on 244 runs behind. This time it was Huddleston who did the damage with five for 33, but with David Denton holding his side together with a defiant 48, Yorkshire were 105 for seven when the umpires called time.

LANCASHIRE v YORKSHIRE
at Old Trafford May 12,13,14, 1913

Yorkshire 74 (Heap 6-16, Dean 2-25) and 53 (Heap 5-23, Dean 4-29)
Lancashire 130 (Haigh 5-42)
Lancashire won by an innings and 3 runs.

There were only two-and-a-half hours play on the first day of this Roses match and yet half-an-hour before tea the following day the game was over!

     Yorkshire won the toss, which would have been a good one to lose, and elected to bat. The White Rose county were all out for 74 with slow left-arm bowler James Heap taking six for 16. The visitors' batting was woeful and only Hirst, who hit five boundaries in his innings of 21, stayed at the crease for any length of time. By the time rain stopped play for the day, Lancashire were 34 for one.

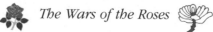

The Wars of the Roses

On the second day it seemed that Lancashire's lead would be no more than a slender one as Haigh (five for 42) and Hirst (three for 37) bowled well. But Huddleston and Whitehead threw caution to the wind for the last wicket, raising Lancashire's total to 130.

In Yorkshire's second innings only David Denton, with 11, managed to get into double figures as Heap (five for 23) and Dean (four for 29) dismissed the visitors for 53. Lancashire's victory by an innings and three runs owed much to the bowling of James Heap, who had match figures of eleven for 39 - a remarkable performance considering that it was said that he couldn't bowl on good wickets and the weather that brought him the bad wickets also gave him lumbago so that he found it difficult to bowl at all!

LANCASHIRE v YORKSHIRE
at Liverpool July 10,11,12, 1913

Yorkshire 177 (Rhodes 58, Dean 9-62) and 73 (Dean 8-29)
Lancashire 92 (Rhodes 5-35) and 159-7 (Hornby 68)
Lancashire won by 3 wickets.

As part of the celebrations for the visit of King George V to Liverpool an extra match between Lancashire and Yorkshire was arranged. Though not a County Championship match, the game was given first-class status and in the end proved an exciting win for Lancashire, who won by three wickets.

So much rain had fallen in the days leading up to the start of the game that the two captains agreed that play shouldn't begin until after lunch. However, the sun shone magnificently and it was found that play could begin much earlier. It was then discovered that Lancashire's Harry Dean, relying on the late start, hadn't arrived and so play got underway without him. Rhodes and Wilson had made a respectable start to the Yorkshire innings but in Dean's first over following his late arrival, he dismissed Wilson. After that, Rhodes suffered a steady loss of partners until he himself was eighth out for a fighting 58. Dean finished with nine for 62 as Yorkshire were all out for 177.

Overnight rain followed by bright sunshine on the second morning made the wicket more treacherous than ever. Lancashire were bowled out for 92 with opening batsman Harry Makepeace the last man out for 48. Yorkshire were dismissed for just 73, with ten of their total being byes. Harry Dean again bowled brilliantly to take eight for 29 and so finish with match figures of seventeen for 91.

In the hour-and-a-half's play that was still possible on the second day, Lancashire soon lost Makepeace and with George Hirst taking a mag-

94

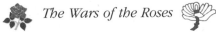

nificent catch to dismiss John Tyldesley, along with two more late dismissals, the home side closed on 61 for four. On the final day, the wicket
played better than at any other time and Hornby (68) and McLeod (30)
added 57 before both were out with the score on 145. Heap too went soon
after but Whitehead struck the winning hit to give Lancashire victory.

HARRY DEAN (LANCASHIRE)

Harry Dean's career spanned the years between 1906
and 1921, during which he took 1,267 wickets for
Lancashire in 256 matches at 18.01 runs apiece.
    Always prepared to bowl his heart out for
his side, he was for some seasons one of the
best bowlers in the country. In 1907, his second season in the Lancashire side, he took
110 wickets with a best of nine for 46 against
Derbyshire at Chesterfield.
    In 1909 his performances in two of the county's
matches stood out above all his other bowling that season. Against Warwickshire at Aigburth, Dean took nine for 31 in their
first innings and followed it up with four for 46 in the second.
Towards the end of the summer he even surpassed this feat with
match figures of fourteen for 77 against Somerset at Old Trafford. The
following season Dean destroyed the Somerset batting again at Bath,
taking nine for 77 in the first innings and seven for 26 in the second.
    The summer of 1911 was Harry Dean's finest as he got through
more overs and took more wickets than any other bowler in the
country. His 179 wickets for Lancashire cost 17.48 runs apiece.
    In 1912 the softer wickets were better suited to his spin than his
swerve and he captured 136 wickets at 12.51 runs each. That summer the Burnley-born bowler made his Test debut for England,
playing against Australia and South Africa in the Triangular
Tournament. He played against Australia at Lord's and the Oval.
The match at Lord's was ruined by rain but at the Oval, he and
Woolley bowled England to victory in the second innings. When
England defeated South Africa at Headingley, Dean had a match
analysis of five for 56.
    In 1913 an extra Roses match was arranged at Aigburth as part
of the celebrations in connection with the visit to Liverpool of King
George V. Dean played a decisive part in Lancashire's three-wicket
win by taking seventeen Yorkshire wickets for 91 runs - nine for 62
in the first innings and eight for 29 in the second.

Had the First World War not taken four seasons from him, it is possible that Harry Dean could have surpassed Johnny Briggs' record of 1,696 wickets for Lancashire. In 1914 he played very little, though apart from his injury he had a difference of opinion with some members of the Lancashire Committee. When cricket did resume in 1919 he had a poor season, taking only 51 wickets at nearly 30 runs each. However, in 1920, his benefit season, he returned to something like his old form and took 124 wickets at 16.16 runs each with a best of eight for 80 against Surrey at Old Trafford.

Though his benefit game against Middlesex was over in two days, it was successful enough financially, making Harry Dean richer by over £2,200. Dean's career was drawing to its close and in 1921, after a season of indifferent form, he faded from the first-class scene. He had always given of his best to Lancashire cricket and of all the bowlers who have served the county, none has had a greater heart than Harry Dean.

YORKSHIRE v LANCASHIRE
at Headingley August 4,5,6, 1913

Lancashire 275 (Heap 90, Makepeace 64, Booth 4-81) and 190 (Sharp 65, Booth 7-77)
Yorkshire 249 (Hirst 78*, Whitehead 5-76) and 220-7 (Haigh 67)
Yorkshire won by 3 wickets.

There was a great finish to this match - the third of the season between Lancashire and Yorkshire - which resulted in the home side winning by three wickets with just eight minutes of the game remaining.

Despite losing early wickets, Lancashire batted for almost all of the first day with Makepeace scoring 64 and Heap 90. The slow left-arm bowler played probably the greatest innings of his career before his last wicket stand with Harry Dean resulted in him being run out ten runs short of his maiden century.

Yorkshire lost two early wickets, including that of night watchman Schofield Haigh, and so the county's captain Sir Archie White went in and it was he, along with Benny Wilson, who got the White Rose county back into the game. However, both were out in quick succession and were soon followed by Booth and Drake. It was then that George Hirst, now 40 years old, took control. Supported by Tom Birtles (40) and some hard hitting by Newstead and Dolphin, Hirst was 78 not out when the last wicket fell, leaving Yorkshire just 26 runs adrift of Lancashire's total.

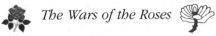

Only Jack Sharp with a fighting innings of 65 seemed comfortable against the bowling of Booth and Drake in Lancashire's second innings. Booth bowled magnificently to take seven for 77 off 38.4 overs but it was Drake who dismissed the dangerous Tyldesley brothers, John and Ernest.

Yorkshire needed 217 to win in a little under two-and-a-half hours but the chances of them reaching this target diminished somewhat when both openers, Rhodes and Kilner, went cheaply. Then Haigh (67) and Wilson (48) put on 108 in fifty minutes and, though three more wickets fell quickly, Yorkshire's captain and Alonso Drake saw their side home.

YORKSHIRE v LANCASHIRE
at Bramall Lane June 1,2,3, 1914

Yorkshire 381 (Kilner 93, Rhodes 53, James Tyldesley 6-129) and 299-4dec
(Birtles 104,
Denton 57, Wilson 55)
Lancashire 370 (Huddleston 88, Hornby 77, James Tyldesley 62*, Booth 6-98)
and 130-2 (Sharp 53*)
Match Drawn.

Both sides made a big first innings score and, though the game was drawn, it was never dull.

Whilst only Rhodes (53) and Kilner (93) made half-centuries, almost every other Yorkshire batsman made a worthwhile contribution in a total of 381. James Tyldesley took six for 129 from 39 overs.

Hornby (77) and Makepeace (47) opened with a first-wicket partnership of 130, but then Major Booth tore through the Lancashire middle-order to leave the Red Rose county on 219 for eight. The follow-on not only seemed a possibility but inevitable. Then James Tyldesley and Bill Huddleston came together and in an hour-and-a-half they thumped 141 runs to all parts of the Bramall Lane ground. With Booth taking six for 98 and Rhodes four for 112, Lancashire were bowled out 11 runs short of Yorkshire's total.

With the wicket still playing well, Birtles was sent in to open with Wilson instead of Rhodes and, in his finest-ever innings for the county, he scored 104. Wilson (55) and Denton (57) also made runs, enabling the White Rose county to declare at 299 for four, leaving Lancashire needing 312 to win.

There was little of the visitors getting that many runs, especially after two quick wickets had fallen. The Home side began to turn the screw but Hornby (45 not out) and Sharp (53 not out) dug in and defended resolutely until stumps were drawn with Lancashire on 130 for two.

LANCASHIRE v YORKSHIRE
at Old Trafford August 3,4,5, 1914

Lancashire 162 (Sharp 53, Hirst 4-31) and 83 (Drake 5-33, Rhodes 4-30)
Yorkshire 190 (Denton 51, Dean 6-75) and 56-0
Yorkshire won by 10 wickets.

In the last Roses game for five years, play didn't get underway until mid-afternoon and even then the wicket was so wet that a fresh one had to be prepared.

For the first couple of hours the wicket played well, allowing Makepeace, J.T.Tyldesley and Sharp to build up a useful start. After that the sun came out and none of the remaining Lancashire batsman had an answer to the bowling of Hirst (four for 31) and Rhodes (three for 56) as the Red Rose side were bowled out for 162.

After the loss of Wilson, Booth and Denton batted well, laying a firm foundation before both were dismissed by Dean. Denton and Rhodes batted very steadily and put on 70 runs in an hour-and-a-quarter and though Harry Dean finished with six for 75, when the visitors' tenth wicket fell they were 28 runs ahead of Lancashire.

When Lancashire batted a second time, they soon lost Spooner out to a magnificent catch on the long-leg boundary by Denton off the bowling of Drake. The Parkgate-born bowler then ran through the upper order to take five for 33 and, with Rhodes taking four for 30, the home side were bowled out for just 83.

Needing just 56 to win, Yorkshire's opening batsmen, Benny Wilson and Major Booth, put them on the board without the slightest problem.

LANCASHIRE v YORKSHIRE
at Old Trafford June 9,10, 1919

Lancashire 319 (Makepeace 105, JamesTyldesley 59* Rhodes 5-74) and 206-9dec
(Makepeace 78, Rhodes 4-49)
Yorkshire 232 (Parkin 6-88) and 153 (Sutcliffe 53, Parkin 8-35)
Lancashire won by 140 runs.

Lancashire's first innings total of 319 owed much to a characteristic century from Harry Makepeace and a fine fighting effort from fast bowler James Tyldesley. Makepeace and J.T.Tyldesley added 80 for the second wicket and Sharp stayed with Makepeace until the score was 161. There was a slight collapse after lunch when the Lancashire score stood at 159

98

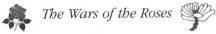

for five but Tyldesley and Parkin, with some lusty blows, gave the total a look of respectability.

Despite good knocks from Holmes and Kilner, both of whom scored 44, Denton had to retire with a badly bruised thumb and Lancashire had a lead of 87 runs that they had hardly expected.

Lancashire's second innings followed the pattern of the first with Makepeace and Tyldesley again being the only performers of note. So well did they bat that Lancashire were able to declare their second innings closed at 206 for nine, leaving their rivals with 294 to get for victory.

The wicket was wearing a little and, after losing five wickets for 65 runs and finding Parkin almost unplayable, they took advantage of some heavy drizzle which put the bowlers at a disadvantage. Sutcliffe, whose concentration had almost carried his side to safety, was brilliantly caught by J.T.Tyldesley off Parkin's bowling with just fifty minutes play remaining.

Three wickets fell to Parkin in quick succession and with less than a quarter-of-an-hour to play, Denton, whose thumb was badly crushed on Monday, walked to the wicket. The partisan Lancashire crowd gave him a loud cheer but five minutes from the close of play, Parkin clean bowled the brave Denton. In fifty minutes, Parkin had dismissed five Yorkshire batsmen for the addition of only 19 runs and Lancashire had won a remarkable game of cricket by 140 runs.

CEC PARKIN (LANCASHIRE)

Cecil Parkin was a native of County Durham and as a young man in 1906 had played for Yorkshire before Lord Hawke (who was not a Yorkshireman by birth himself) discovered that he had first seen the light of day on the wrong side of the border.

He first played for Lancashire in 1914 after a spell as professional with Church, the Lancashire League club. In his first match against Leicestershire at Aigburth, he took fourteen wickets for 99 runs. Unhappily the outbreak of war prevented the development of this early promise and, when the hostilities ended in 1918, Parkin was lured to Rochdale where he was the highest paid professional in the country.

He continued to play for Lancashire, but only on odd occasions. Despite this he was picked to go to Australia in the winter of 1920-21 with Johnny Douglas's team. It was a disastrous tour and England lost all five Test matches. Parkin looked the best bowler in the side. Parkin played for England in all five Tests of the 1921 home series against Australia and in the Old Trafford meeting not only took five for 38 but also achieved the curious distinction, which he shared with Richard Barlow, of opening both the batting and the bowling for England in the same match.

Cecil Parkin was the supreme showman and the crowds loved it. An innings by Parkin was an hilarious experience and if it happened, as it often did, that Dick Tyldesley was the batsman at the other end, no two batsmen could have caused more laughs.

He was 36 when he finally became a full-time first-class cricketer with Lancashire in 1922 and in his first full season he reached 100 wickets ahead of any bowler and finished the campaign with 181. In 1923 he took 184 wickets for Lancashire, 209 in all matches, and again reached 200 in 1924, 196 of them for Lancashire.

His Test career unfortunately ended under a cloud. Criticism of his captain AER Gilligan, under whom he had played in the Test series in South Africa in 1924, appeared in a newspaper article under his name. The article was in fact written by a 'ghost' writer. Parkin was noted for his full and frank comment and very probably he had expressed the opinions mentioned in the article but it seems injudicious of the writer to have put them into print.

In 1926 Parkin took thirty-nine wickets and did not play for Lancashire again after the fourteenth match of the season. In just 157 games he had taken 901 wickets at 16.12 runs apiece. He was an outstanding bowler and if he had spent of all his cricketing life with Lancashire, he could have created records that would still be standing today.

In his later years, Parkin was licensee at an Old Trafford hostelry. There of an evening, after a day at the cricket, he would entertain his friends and customers with his endless stories. When he died in 1943, his ashes, in accordance with his wishes, were scattered on the square at Old Trafford.

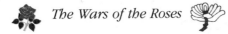 *The Wars of the Roses*

YORKSHIRE v LANCASHIRE
at Bramall Lane August 4,5, 1919

Lancashire 124 (R.Tyldesley 65, Rhodes 4-31, Waddington 4-49) and 271-6dec
(Hallows 102*, E.Tyldesley 82, James Tyldesley 52, Williams 5-67)
Yorkshire 317-5dec (Sutcliffe 132*, Holmes 123)
Match Drawn.

Lancashire made a disastrous start, losing Makepeace and J.T.Tyldesley with only 19 runs on the board before rain drove everybody indoors. There was no further play until after lunch when the Lancashire batting collapsed. Ernest Tyldesley was compelled to look on helplessly as Waddington (four for 49) and Rhodes (four for 31) reaked havoc. Tyldesley's 65 provided more than half of Lancashire's total of 124.

Yorkshire's new opening pair of Holmes and Sutcliffe scored over a hundred before the end of the first day and then went on to put on 253, the highest first-wicket stand ever made in a Roses match, until the same pair passed their own record on the same ground twelve years later with 323.

Early on the second day, Holmes on 57 skied a simple chance to Ernest Tyldesley but he seemed to lose the ball and it dropped yards away from him. During the first half-an-hour, the runs came at the astonishing rate of 90 an hour with very few singles. The two batsmen rattled up the 200 after three hours, Sutcliffe reaching his century in two hours 55 minutes and Holmes thirty minutes later.

Yorkshire declared just after lunch, Lancashire going in 193 behind. They lost Makepeace to Waddington first ball and J.T.Tyldesley with the score on 13. Then Ernest Tyldesley and Charlie Hallows defended stubbornly for two hours before Tyldesley was yorked by Williams for 82, his sixth 50 in successive innings.

There was still over two hours play left but James Tyldesley with 52 provided good support before he too fell to Williams. Heap and Hollins were dismissed cheaply and, though Rhodes took a magnificent catch to send Richard Tyldesley back, the main interest centred around whether young Hallows could find time to get to his century. This he accomplished at 7.15 p.m and stumps were then drawn. Hallows had batted for just over four hours - a superb achievement for a player in his first season.

YORKSHIRE v LANCASHIRE
at Bradford May 22,24,25, 1920

Yorkshire 208 (Holmes 68, Denton 54, R.Tyldesley 5-62, Dean 4-62) and 144
(Dean 7-51)
Lancashire 165 (R.Tyldesley 63) and 165 (Robinson 9-36)
Yorkshire won by 22 runs.

The first day belonged to Yorkshire even though three of their star batsmen made little impact on the scorebook, including Sutcliffe caught by
Hallows off Cook off the eighth ball of the morning. The generations
overlapped in Holmes and Denton but when they were parted, after a
century partnership, no-one apart from Rhodes with 49 could master the
bowling of Richard Tyldesley.

At the close of the first day, Lancashire were 77 for five in reply.
With the exception of Richard Tyldesley, who hammered the Yorkshire
bowling to all parts of the ground in scoring 63 out of 92 in an hour-and-
a-half, the Lancashire batting was indifferent to say the least.

Leading by 43, Yorkshire lost this advantage by lunch when
Sutcliffe was bowled by Richard Tyldesley and Dean completely defeated
Denton with a slower ball. Harry Dean was virtually unplayable and only
Emmott Robinson, who was 37 not out, showed any resistance. Yorkshire
scored 144, leaving Lancashire 188 to win.

There was still over an hour to play and Makepeace and Hallows
put on 44 runs to put Lancashire in the driving seat.

Within a few minutes of the start of the final day, Emmott Robinson
had broken the stand and in a further few minutes three more wickets had
fallen to him. Waddington at the other end was bowling magnificently but
it was Robinson claiming the wickets. Runs came slowly but James
Tyldesley and Sharp took the score to 136 for four.

Then, by inspiration, Burton, the Yorkshire captain, brought
Robinson back and almost immediately he broke the stand. Wickets
began to tumble - Richard Tyldesley, Lol Cook and captain Myles Kenyon
all victims of Emmott Robinson. The only question now was would
Robinson take all ten wickets? Blomley, whose batting average for the season was 2.72, swung wildly at Kilner at the other end and was stumped.
Yorkshire had won a truly remarkable game of cricket by 22 runs.

LANCASHIRE v YORKSHIRE
at Old Trafford July 31, August 2,3, 1920

Yorkshire 253 (Holmes 126, Parkin 5-86) and 216-5dec (Holmes 111*)
Lancashire 179 (Spooner 62, Rhodes 4-60, Waddington 4-62) and 116-4 (Spooner 63)
Match Drawn.

Sutcliffe and Holmes gave Yorkshire a good start, putting on 67 for the first wicket in ninety minutes before lunch. The home side had some success in the first over of the afternoon when Denton was clean bowled by Parkin's slower ball. Six runs later, Kilner tried to hit Parkin over the top but holed out to Johnny Tyldesley. Yorkshire lost Rhodes at 107 and Hirst at 168 before rain fell heavily and 75 minutes play was lost. When Yorkshire resumed their innings they added a further 33 runs for the loss of two wickets to end the first day on 201 for six.

Holmes continued to dominate proceedings and just failed to carry his bat. He was ninth out at 247, his innings of 126 lasting five-and-a-half hours.

By mid-afternoon on the second day, Lancashire were 104 for two but by 5.30 p.m. they were 179 all out. It was only Spooner's innings of 62 that saved the Red Rose county from following-on.

Yorkshire going in a second time increased their lead to 112 without losing a wicket. Holmes was again in fine form and made another century, but it was hardly a match-winning innings.

Lancashire were set 291 to win but lost Heap at 13 bowled by Waddington for two. Rhodes then dismissed Ernest Tyldesley and Sharp to leave Lancashire on 79 for three with just over two hours remaining. The score had reached 98 when Spooner was brilliantly stumped by Dolphin off Rhodes. Mussom and Pewtress defended stubbornly for half-an-hour before rain put an end to the match just before six o'clock.

PERCY HOLMES (YORKSHIRE)

Percy Holmes was an amazingly consistent Yorkshire opening batsman and an outstanding slip fielder whose early career was lost to the First World War.

Holmes arrived at Yorkshire in 1913 via Lindley Zion Sunday School, Golcar Paddock and then Spen Victoria and, though he batted as low as number ten in his first season, an innings of 61 against Middlesex in 1914 confirmed his promise. After the hostilities he began his long and famous association with Herbert Sutcliffe. In that summer of 1919, Holmes scored 1,877 runs, which included a partnership with Sutcliffe of 253 against Lancashire. A year later he was fourth in the national batting averages with 2,254 runs at 50.08. Surprisingly he was not selected for Johnny Douglas's team to tour Australia that following winter but in the following years he passed 2,000 runs on anothert six occasions and made 315 not out against Middlesex at Lord's in 1925.

Holmes only played seven times for England, including against Australia at Trent Bridge in 1921. However, he was not selected again in that series as the selectors decided he had been unsettled by the pace of Gregory and McDonald. It seemed a harsh judgement as Holmes was England's top-scorer with 38. He then toured South Africa under Stanyforth, four times toppping fifty in the five Test series.

Holmes shared 69 century first wicket stands with Herbert Sutcliffe, including eighteen over 250. In 1932 they surpassed the 554 of Tunnicliffe and Brown made against Derbyshire by one run to set a new world record, the occasion being the match at Leyton against Essex. Sutcliffe played on when he had made 313, thereupon Yorkshire captain Sellers declared, only to see the scoreboard move back to 554! However, it was later discovered that a no-ball had been missed and the total was corrected. Holmes was almost 45 years old and troubled with lumbago when he achieved this feat!

Percy Holmes was a great Yorkshire cricketer in one of the most successful periods of the county's history. From 1919, his real baptism in first-class cricket, to his last year of 1933, Yorkshire won the County Championship eight times.

Holmes was a very cheerful and popular cricketer who scored 26,220 runs for Yorkshire at an average of 41.95. He was also the first batsman to score a hundred in each innings of a Roses match when at Old Trafford in 1920 he made 126 and 111 not out.

LANCASHIRE v YORKSHIRE
at Old Trafford May 14,16,17, 1921

Lancashire 239 (Hallows 62, E.Tyldesley 60, Rhodes 7-80) and 178-7dec
(E.Tyldesley 62*)
Yorkshire 154 (Kilner 50, James Tyldesley 4-19) and 116-2 (Holmes 52*)
Match Drawn.

On a showery first day, when only three-and-a-half hours play was possible, Lancashire scored 140 with only Makepeace out. On Whit Monday an amount of moisture on the top layer of a hard wicket allowed Rhodes to cause the odd ball to 'pop' but it was his beautifully controlled flight that allowed him to dismiss Lancashire for less than a hundred more than their overnight total - their last eight wickets falling for 78 runs.

Holmes was run out without scoring but by tea Yorkshire had reached 54 for two. Rhodes and Kilner batted well before the pace of James Tyldesley destroyed the Yorkshire tail, giving Lancashire a lead of 85 runs on first innings.

In Lancashire's second innings, Makepeace and Hallows went cheaply before Ernest Tyldesley with 62 and Richard Tyldesley, who hit 38 in forty minutes, enabled Lancashire to declare.

In the three hours left to play, Yorkshire did not feel justified in going for the 264 runs needed for victory on a wearing pitch. Holmes and Sutcliffe played well for the first hour or so, putting Yorkshire well out of danger. The Yorkshire openers would undoubtedly have made an attempt for the runs if Lancashire had declared a little earlier but the Red Rose county were well aware of the quick-scoring powers of Yorkshire's top-order batsmen.

YORKSHIRE v LANCASHIRE
at Headingley July 30, August 1,2, 1921

Lancashire 153 (Rhodes 3-22, Waddingon 3-38) and 144-3 (E.Tyldesley 51)
Yorkshire 489 (Holmes 132, Macaulay 72, Robinson 59, Burton 52, Cook 6-145)
Match Drawn.

Batting first on a perfect strip, Lancashire were bowled out for a paltry 153 with only Makepeace (39) effectively countering the bowling of Rhodes, Waddington and Wilson.

Yorkshire's innings began at 4.40 p.m. and by the close of play, they had reached 121 for one with Sutcliffe the player out. On the Monday, Percy Holmes gave a holiday treat to nearly 30,000 Yorkshire supporters basking in the sun. Robinson and Burton, the Yorkshire captain, made brisk half-centuries and George Macaulay hit furiously for 72,

105

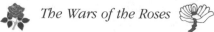

but the leading player was Holmes, who scored 132 out of 232 in three hours and ten minutes. At lunch on the second day, the Yorkshire score was 285 for five wickets, whilst in the afternoon Burton, Robinson, Macaulay, Wilson and Allen cut and drove Lancashire's faltering attack to all parts of the Headingley ground. Even the last wicket added 52 in twenty-five minutes. An oddity of Yorkshire's big total was that Lancashire used only four bowlers, who delivered 140 overs between them.

Lancashire faced an uneasy hour and a quarter at the end of the day, losing Makepeace bowled by Robinson without scoring.

On the final day there was only an hour and three-quarter's play as rain came to Lancashire's aid and just before five o'clock, Yorkshire gave up the struggle against the weather.

YORKSHIRE v LANCASHIRE
at Bramall Lane June 3,5,6, 1922

Lancashire 307 (E.Tyldesley 178, Hallows 66, Robinson 4-68) and 144 (Rhodes 4-28)
Yorkshire 306 (Oldroyd 77, Sutcliffe 65, R.Tyldesley 6-70) and 148-4 (Sutcliffe 73*)
Yorkshire won by 6 wickets.

Harry Makepeace, the hero of so many hard fights for Lancashire, was out early but then Ernest Tyldesley and Hallows took the score to 165 before the second wicket fell. Though Tyldesley stood firm, wickets tumbled at an alarming rate at the other end and by tea Lancashire were 216 for seven with Tyldesley 101 not out. Immediately after tea, Kenyon was caught by Kilner off the bowling of Macaulay. Tyldesley then began to display the powerful batting he had shown in the Old Trafford Test of 1921. He was last out for a magnificent 178. His innings lasted four hours and twenty minutes and after the tea interval he scored 77 runs in an hour out of 87.

The Lancashire attack got its first taste of blood after half-an-hour when Holmes edged Cook into Richard Tyldesley's hands at first slip. Oldroyd and Sutcliffe added 92 runs for the second wicket before the latter was run out for 65. From the first ball after lunch, Roy Kilner was lbw to Richard Tyldesley and further wickets fell at regular intervals until Norman Kilner and Geoffrey Wilson, Yorkshire's captain, batted well so that the White Rose county's innings ended just one run behind Lancashire's.

Lancashire ended the second day on 30 without loss but by three o'clock on the final day, they were all out for 144. Even though they lost two quick wickets, Yorkshire had no trouble in reaching the 146 needed for victory. Kilner and Sutcliffe added 58 runs before the former was stumped for an entertaining innings of 47 as Yorkshire ran out winners by six wickets.

Lancashire - early 1920's

Back Row: Parkinson, Ellis, Parkin, E.Tyldesley, R.Tyldesley, Hallows, Watson
Front row: Makepeace, Barnes, Kenyon, Rhodes, Cook

LANCASHIRE v YORKSHIRE
at Old Trafford August 5,7,8, 1922

Lancashire 118 (Macaulay 3-25, E.Wilson 3-28) and 135 (JamesTyldesley 55*, Macaulay 4-16)
Yorkshire 122 (Cook 3-40) and 129-8 (Parkin 3-28, Norbury 3-36)
Match Drawn.

On a dubious but by no means difficult wicket, Lancashire were bowled out for 118 with only Ernest Tyldesley (45) showing anything like his true form. The home side had an early success when Holmes, so often the thorn in Lancashire's flesh, was brilliantly caught by Richard Tyldesley off the bowling of James Tyldesley off the second ball of Yorkshire's innings. Oldroyd and Kilner soon departed and Yorkshire were 13 for three. Sutcliffe and Rhodes added 53 before Norbury clean bowled the Yorkshire opening batsman and then in his next over trapped Rhodes lbw. It took a fine rearguard action from Macaulay and Robinson to take the Yorkshire total to 122, a lead of four runs.

After heavy overnight rain, conditions were so bad that play on the second day was abandoned.

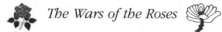

Lancashire's second innings owed much to a fifth wicket stand of 63 at a run a minute between Barnes and James Tyldesley but their last five wickets fell for 35 runs and, with James Tyldesley stranded on 55 not out, the Red Rose county were dismissed for 135.

Needing 132 to win, Yorkshire soon lost Sutcliffe, Oldroyd and Kilner and at tea were 36 for three. In the third over after tea, Holmes was caught at the wicket and Yorkshire, despite a good stand between Rhodes and Robinson, tottered to 126 for eight. This in effect was 126 for nine because Geoffrey Wilson had been rushed to hospital suffering from appendicitis. The last man was Rockley Wilson. Off the next four overs, three runs were scored and Rhodes was left to face the last six deliveries. As each ball came down he played it with the utmost coolness and though Lancashire supporters were hoping he would lose his wicket, the Yorkshire supporters in the crowd hoped he would score the boundary needed to win the game. As it was, both sets of supporters were disappointed that the game ended with Yorkshire still two runs short.

LANCASHIRE v YORKSHIRE
at Old Trafford May 19,21,22, 1923

Lancashire 108 (R.Kilner 5-33)
Yorkshire 126-5 (Parkin 3-32)
Match Drawn.

On the opening day, rain prevented the bowling of a single ball and at five o'clock the match was postponed until the Monday. It meant that the match now fell under the declaration of innings law which operated in a two-day match. A lead of 100 runs would be sufficient to force a follow-on.

Lancashire batted first on a wicket that had dried out and appeared treacherous. When lunch arrived, 48 overs had been bowled and Lancashire were 57 for two. The afternoon saw the mightiest Lancashire landslide of modern times. The last five wickets fell for four runs and a score of 108, whatever the weather, was unlikely to be a winning one.

Sutcliffe and Holmes' run-a-minute partnership took Yorkshire to within 29 of Lancashire's meagre total and another 17 were added before Parkin bowled Oldroyd and the umpires called it a day. On Tuesday, the Old Trafford rain returned and in the few overs that could be bowled, Yorkshire put themselves 18 runs ahead but lost three wickets in getting them. The rain alone was the outright winner.

108

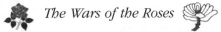

Yorkshire 1923 and 1924
Back row: Leyland, Macaulay, Waddington, N.Kilner, Sutcliffe, Ringrose
Middle row: Dolphin, Rhodes, E.R.Wilson, G.Wilson, Robinson, Holmes
Front: Oldroyd, R.Kilner

YORKSHIRE v LANCASHIRE
at Bradford August 4,6,7, 1923

Lancashire 188 (Kilner 3-21) and 73 (Macaulay 4-32, Kilner 3-17)
Yorkshire 213 (Holmes 80, R.Tyldesley 7-71) and 51-2
Yorkshire won by 8 wickets.

This Roses match had all the usual ingredients - cautious batting, immensely keen bowling and fielding and a ferocious struggle for first innings lead.

By lunch Lancashire had struggled to 58 for four against some very keen Yorkshire bowling. Immediately after lunch, Kilner was allowed to deliver eight consecutive maidens as Lancashire crumbled to 128 for seven. Frank Watson and George Duckworth put their heads down and added 40 runs for the eighth wicket. The last three Lancashire wickets added 65 runs as the visitors totalled 188.

Holmes made light of the struggle in the last hour of the first day and by the end of play, he and Sutcliffe had knocked over fifty off their necessary

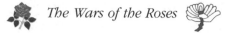

task. On Monday, Sutcliffe was out early on for 30 and although Oldroyd played one of his indomitable bad-wicket innings, two more wickets fell hard on the heels of his dismissal. There was then a fighting stand between Holmes and Kilner but after that, Richard Tyldesley asserted complete mastery over the game, taking seven for 71 as Yorkshire were bowled out for 213.

In Lancashire's second innings, Emmott Robinson bowled eight maidens in eleven overs and took the wicket of Makepeace. George Macaulay got rid of Hallows, Ernest Tyldesley, the defensive Watson and Parkin as Lancashire's batting crumbled - all out for 73!

Play was delayed for over an hour on the final morning because the wicket was very wet.

When Yorkshire began their comfortable task of making 49 runs for victory, the ball turned but not quickly. Parkin and Richard Tyldesley bowled well and took a wicket each before Sutcliffe and Leyland saw the White Rose county safely home.

YORKSHIRE v LANCASHIRE
at Headingley July 7,9,10, 1924

Lancashire 113 (Macaulay 6-40) and 74 (Kilner 4-13, Macaulay 4-19)
Yorkshire 130 (Parkin 5-46, R.Tyldesley 4-69) and 33 (R.Tyldesley 6-18, Parkin 3-15)
Lancashire won by 24 runs.

In one of the most remarkable Roses games ever played, forty wickets fell for 350 runs in two and a quarter days of interrupted cricket played under leaden skies.

At lunch on the first day, Lancashire's total, if that is not too strong a term, was 39 for two. The one substantial partnership of the Lancashire innings was for the third wicket when Watson and Ernest Tyldesley took the score to 64. With the two batsmen nicely set, the rain came and stopped play for 35 minutes. Immediately on the resumption of play, Watson was caught from a mis-hit and Tyldesley was leg-before to a ball from Macaulay which kept low. After another brief interruption for rain, Lancashire lost their last five wickets for 31 runs.

Just before the end of play on the first day, Parkin dismissed Sutcliffe. The first ball bowled by Parkin on the second day pitched outside Holmes's off stump and broke back at least a foot. In his second over, Holmes played for a break that wasn't there and was bowled. Oldroyd and Leyland played each ball on its merit and added 58 runs in an hour for the third wicket. After the dismissals of these two batsmen, Sharp

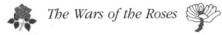

switched Parkin and Tyldesley. It was an ingenious move as the last six Yorkshire wickets fell for 43 runs, Tyldesley capturing the last three wickets for just seven runs.

The wicket was deteriorating fast and, though Watson defended bravely, Lancashire were all out for 74.

When Yorkshire began their second innings at the start of the last day, they needed just 57 runs for victory. By 12.40, they were all out for 33, the fourth smallest Yorkshire score on record and the lowest score against Lancashire.

The third ball of Parkin's second over had Sutcliffe leg before whilst the fifth ball of the next over, bowled by Richard Tyldesley, had Holmes out in the same fashion. In Tyldesley's following over he caught and bowled Leyland - three wickets for three runs! Rhodes was beaten all ends up by a leg break and Oldroyd was clean bowled by Parkin - 13 for five. Robinson was brilliantly run out at 16, the sixth wicket to fall. At 23, Turner was dramatically bowled by Tyldesley and nine runs later, Macaulay was bowled by the best ball of the day. Tyldesley then bowled Waddington and had Dolphin stumped. As the last Yorkshire wicket fell, the Lancashire players jumped for joy after winning their first Roses match since 1919 and ensuring that the club's jubilee year was already assured success.

LANCASHIRE v YORKSHIRE
at Old Trafford August 2,4,5, 1924

Yorkshire 359 (Leyland 133*, Sutcliffe 90)
Lancashire 78-2 (Makepeace 35*)
Match Drawn.

After heavy overnight rain, play on the first day was not possible until 3.20 p.m. The opening three-quarters of an hour was nothing but a duel between Sutcliffe and Lancashire's Australian fast bowler, Ted McDonald. After beating the bat on a number of occasions, McDonald began to lose his line and Sutcliffe powered his way to a splendid fifty. In fact, when Holmes was out at 64, leg-before to Richard Tyldesley, Sutcliffe had scored 52. Oldroyd was run out as a result of Parkin's direct hit, bringing Leyland in to join Sutcliffe. The pair then added 72 runs for the third wicket before Watson had Sutcliffe caught at the wicket, ten runs off his hundred.

Leyland scored his first century and was undefeated at the close of the Yorkshire innings. He batted for almost five hours, watching the ball closely and judging its length quickly. Kilner's innings of 37 lasted only

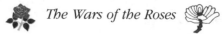

half-an-hour but it was probably the highlight of the day.

Makepeace and Hallows scored 57 for Lancashire's first wicket and after the dismissal of Ernest Tyldesley, the home side ended the second day on 78 for two.

The condition of the Old Trafford pitch was so bad on the third day that the match was abandoned.

LANCASHIRE v YORKSHIRE
at Old Trafford May 30, June 1,2, 1925

Yorkshire 232 (Rhodes 59, Holmes 51, Parkin 4-63) and 186-6 (Rhodes 54*)
Lancashire 265 (Hallows 111*, Kilner 4-67)
Match Drawn.

The game was just about to begin when there was a cloudburst that sent the players scurrying to the pavilion. After a 25 minute delay, play got underway with Holmes and Sutcliffe adding 66 for Yorkshire's first wicket before McDonald removed Sutcliffe's off stump. Holmes, who had played well for his 51, was the next to go, quickly followed by Oldroyd who was bowled by Parkin. Rhodes and Leyland staved off the collapse and added 47 runs for the fourth wicket. Half the Yorkshire side were out for 143 but then a sixth wicket partnership by Rhodes and Robinson lifted the score to 208. Rhodes's fifty was a monumental contribution and Emmott Robinson, with nobody to stop with him for long, was left undefeated on 45 when Yorkshire's last wicket fell at 232.

Duckworth and Hopwood were sent in to combat the few remaining overs of the day but both were dismissed cheaply by Macaulay early on the Monday morning. Makepeace and Hallows stayed together until the last over before lunch, when, with the total on 94, Makepeace was stumped! Lancashire had passed the 150 mark when Ernest Tyldesley hit a ball from Kilner to deep square leg where Waddington took a superb catch. Within the next few minutes, Watson was leg-before and Pewtress ran himself out - Lancashire 176 for six. Rain again interrupted the match but Barnes then stayed with Hallows to add 39 runs for the seventh wicket. Five runs later, Richard Tyldesley was bowled by Robinson. McDonald joined Hallows with Lancashire 13 runs adrift of Yorkshire's total and only two wickets left. Five minutes later, Hallows drove a ball from Robinson to the boundary to complete a magnificent century. He was still there when Lancashire's last wicket fell, on 111 not out.

Yorkshire did not intend Lancashire to obtain full points for a victory and, to that end, the collective skills of Sutcliffe, Leyland and Rhodes were bent. At the end of the day, Yorkshire were 153 ahead with four wickets in hand.

YORKSHIRE v LANCASHIRE
at Bramall Lane August 1,3,4, 1925

Lancashire 320 (Makepeace 90, Hallows 79, Macaulay 4-121) and 74-6 (Kilner 5-14)
Yorkshire 277 (Leyland 80*, Sutcliffe 62, Sibbles 4-60)
Match Drawn.

Makepeace and Hallows struggled in the early stages against some superb Yorkshire bowling, but the batsmen survived between the showers and put on 171 for Lancashire's first wicket, which fell at half-past six. Hallows was the man out, leg-before to Rhodes for 79.

Rain fell in Sheffield at the start of the second day and play did not get underway until noon. In Kilner's second over, Duckworth, who had gone in as nightwatchman, was bowled off his pads. After Makepeace had been dismissed ten runs short of his century, Pewtress began to force the game and drove Macaulay for three fours in succession. At lunch, Lancashire were 243 for four with Watson the last man to be dismissed. Lancashire's last six wickets fell for 79 runs with Herbert Sutcliffe taking the catch of the season. Richard Tyldesley drove a ball high towards the boundary but Sutcliffe, running from long-on and covering some twenty yards, dived full length and with his right hand, held the ball.

Sutcliffe and Holmes replied for Yorkshire and after reaching 50 at a run a minute, lost their first wicket at 86 when Holmes was bowled by McDonald. On the last day, Yorkshire found runs hard to come by against some tight Lancashire bowling. It was Frank Sibbles who made the breakthrough, forcing Sutcliffe to edge to Richard Tyldesley at slip. Three runs later, Sibbles uprooted Oldroyd's off stump and Yorkshire were 117 for three. Rhodes was not happy when facing McDonald and it came as no surprise when he was leg-before to the Australian with the score on 132. Wickets continued to tumble, Yorkshire's innings closing on 277 after Leyland, who finished unbeaten on 80, and wicket-keeper Dolphin had added 41 for the last wicket.

With the first innings points settled, the game could have petered out but it didn't and Kilner took five of the six Lancashire wickets to fall for a cost of only 14 runs.

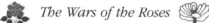

YORKSHIRE v LANCASHIRE
at Bradford May 22,24,25, 1926

Yorkshire 326 (Kilner 85, Oldroyd 64, McDonald 4-110)
Lancashire 159 (E.Tyldesley 52, Rhodes 4-20) and 73 (Kilner 4-19)
Yorkshire won by an innings and 94 runs.

Holmes and Sutcliffe gave Yorkshire their usual steady start but it could have been a different story if Watson had held on to a straightforward chance off Sutcliffe when he had made two. In fact, Lancashire's fielding was deplorable throughout, the costliest miss being Ernest Tyldesley's attempt to hold on to a chance offered by Kilner before he had scored. Kilner, the one cricketer who never took a Roses match seriously, went on to score 85. His innings consisted of two sixes and 10 fours and lasted one hour and fifty minutes. Yorkshire totalled 326 before Lancashire began their innings at noon on the second day.

From the outset, the Yorkshire bowlers were on top. Makepeace, Hallows and Watson, all monuments of stability, left early to leave Lancashire on 49 for three. Ernest Tyldesley stayed to battle it out with Barnes but when these two went the side collapsed.

Following on 167 runs behind, Lancashire had lost three wickets for 20 runs when storm clouds gathered at the end of the day. A wet wicket on the final day prevented any play until half-an-hour after lunch. Only Barnes and Green batted with any patience in a Lancashire innings that ended at 4.15 p.m. when Duckworth was caught by Lupton off the bowling of Waddington. The wickets were amicably shared between Robinson, Macaulay and Kilner, but in all truth, Lancashire's batting display must rank as one of the worst in the history of Roses matches.

LANCASHIRE v YORKSHIRE
at Old Trafford July 31, August 2,3, 1926

Lancashire 509-9 dec (E.Tyldesley 139, Makepeace 126, Watson 92, Rhodes 7-116)
Yorkshire 352 (Holmes 143, Sutcliffe 89)
Match Drawn.

The Old Trafford crowd reveled in the sunshine for once as Lancashire's total of 509 for nine declared, scored in the best part of two days, was their highest Roses total.

In the ninety minutes before lunch on the first day, Makepeace and Hallows took the score to 74 for no wicket. The first wicket fell ten runs

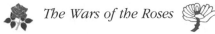

later when Hallows was leg-before to Robinson. Makepeace and Ernest Tyldesley added 169 for the second wicket before Makepeace, attempting a huge drive, was bowled by Rhodes for 126. Batting four hours and fifty minutes and hitting nine boundaries, a more characteristic Makepeace innings one could not wish to see.

Tyldesley went on to score 139, his eighth century of the summer, offering just one chance when on 79 to Leyland on the long-off boundary. Frank Watson, a persevering batsman of the true Lancashire breed, missed a Roses hundred by only eight runs. The only Yorkshire bowler to gain any reward was Wilfred Rhodes, who took seven for 116, his last four wickets costing just 21 runs.

For the rest of the second day, Holmes and Sutcliffe played some beautiful cricket and at the close of play, Yorkshire in reply were 183 for no wicket. Holmes reached his fifty in an hour-and-a-half, easily the quickest half-century of the game.

On the morning of the last day, the Yorkshire openers were within one run of making it a 200 partnership when the immaculate Sutcliffe was out leg-before to Richard Tyldesley. The next batsman, Oldroyd, had scored 12 when he was hit on the back of the head by a short rising ball delivered by McDonald. He was carried from the field unconscious but was even additionally unlucky in that he hit his stumps as he fell.

Holmes was next to go for a magnificent 143, made in five and a half hours. Yorkshire defended stoutly as Green, the Lancashire captain, rang the bowling changes but were eventually all out for 352, seven runs short of saving the follow-on, which could not be followed!

ERNEST TYLDESLEY (LANCASHIRE)

Ernest Tyldesley, sixteen years younger than his brother Johnny, played his first game for Lancashire in 1909 and his last in 1936. In the years between he scored more runs for the county at a better average than any other batsman - 34,222 at 45.20.

His first appearance for the county side was against Warwickshire at Aigburth. He scored 61 and with Archie MacLaren took part in a stand which realised 128 runs in 90 minutes. Despite this early promise, Ernest was much slower in developing than Johnny. In 1913 he hit three centuries and in one remarkable week in June, the two brothers each scored a century at Leicester and went on to the Oval where Johnny made 210 and Ernest 110.

It was not however until cricket was resumed after the war that Ernest Tyldesley's batting ability was adequately revealed.

He did not play for England as often as his great ability warranted. He had the misfortune to be knocking on the door of the England side when there were such fine batsmen as Woolley, Hammond, Hendren, Mead and Sandham competing with him for places. Tyldesley's Test match statistics certainly do not suggest that he was a failure on the occasions when he did play for his country. He played in 14 Tests and scored 990 runs, including three centuries, at an average of 55.00.

On the 1927-28 tour of South Africa, he headed the English batting averages by a considerable margin, scoring more runs than Hammond or Sutcliffe. He did not fail in the Test matches and scored elegant centuries at Johannesburg and Durban. The West Indies visited England in 1928 and Tyldesley scored 122 against them in the Lord's Test match. He went to Australia with Percy Chapman's side in 1928-29 but only played in one Test, scoring 31 and 21. On this tour, Monty Noble, the old Australian captain, wrote of him, 'It seems a pity that knowing this man to be a very fine batsman, the Englishmen did not persevere with him, regardless of a few failures, until he struck form. They lost the services of a class batsman and a great run-getter.'

Sadly, Ernest Tyldesley never played for England again.

For Lancashire his record has not yet been equalled. Of the 102 centuries he made during his career, 90 were made for the county.

He hit five double-centuries, his highest score 256 not out against Warwickshire at Old Trafford in 1930. Twice he made a hundred in each innings of a county match - 165 and 123 not out against Essex at Leyton in 1921 and 109 and 108 not out against Glamorgan at Cardiff in 1930.

In 1926, in a remarkable sequence, Tyldesley scored 1,477 runs in 13 innings between 26 June and 6 August.

Tyldesley was senior professional of the fine Lancashire side that won the County Championship three years in succession in 1926, 1927 and 1928.

He retired from active cricket in 1936 and in his later years he was elected to membership of the committee of the county club. Honour was accorded to him also from Lord's when MCC decided to elect ex-professional cricketers to life membership and the name of Ernest Tyldesley was in the first list of players to be nominated.

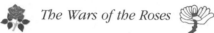

LANCASHIRE v YORKSHIRE
at Old Trafford June 4,6,7, 1927

Yorkshire 166 (Rhodes 44, McDonald 5-68) and 153 (McDonald 6-67)
Lancashire 234 (E.Tyldesley 42, Sibbles 40) and 89-2 (Hallows 43*)
Lancashire won by 8 wickets.

Ted McDonald's first over, pitched short, sent ball after ball flying around the heads of Yorkshire's opening pair, Sutcliffe and Leyland. In his second over he had Sutcliffe lbw before he had scored and, with the score on 10, Leyland edged the Australian to Watson at second slip who took a comfortable catch. Mitchell too fell to McDonald before Oldroyd provided Frank Sibbles with his first victim. Kennie only lasted a few balls and Yorkshire were now 57 for five. Kilner and Rhodes stopped the rot and took the score to 93 before the next wicket fell. Rhodes was the last man out for 44 as Yorkshire totalled 166.

If Yorkshire had progressed slowly, Lancashire were slower still and by the end of the first day were 90 for three. Ernest Tyldesley fell to a dubious stroke in the third over of the second day and Lancashire were 92 for four. Taylor and Sibbles batted well for Lancashire until Yorkshire's score was passed and then Duckworth helped Sibbles in a last wicket stand that took Lancashire 68 runs in front.

Maurice Leyland fell to a brilliant catch by Taylor on the boundary without a run on the board and at 29, Oldroyd provided McDonald with his second wicket. Mitchell went cheaply and then, in the last over of the day, Sutcliffe edged McDonald to Richard Tyldesley at slip and Yorkshire had lost four wickets.

On the last day, McDonald, bowling at his fastest, removed three more Yorkshire batsmen and only a last ditch stand by Rhodes and Robinson delayed a Lancashire victory. Rhodes was tragically run out and this left Lancashire needing 86 to win and though two wickets fell, Hallows and captain Leonard Green hit off the runs to give Lancashire their first win at Old Trafford since Parkin's whirlwind victory over Yorkshire in 1919.

TED McDONALD (LANCASHIRE)

Ted McDonald began his career in his native Tasmania before moving to the mainland to play for Victoria in 1911. Despite some fine bowling after the outbreak of the First World War, McDonald had to wait years for his big opportunity. In 1919 he took eight for 42 against New South Wales on a batsman's wicket at Sydney and after other impressive bowling displays he was chosen to partner Jack

Gregory against England at Adelaide in 1920-21.

When Australia toured England the following summer, McDonald took 27 wickets in the Test series at 24.74 runs apiece and 150 wickets in all matches. After just a year as an international fast bowler, McDonald decided he had had enough, retiring from the Australian team with 43 wickets at 33.28 from his 11 Tests.

McDonald returned to England the following summer to play for Nelson in the Lancashire League but it was 1924 before he first qualified to play for Lancashire. However, he was not fully available and the summer was depressingly wet, circumstances which prevented his achieving his maximum effectiveness. In 1925 he was available throughout the season and he took 182 wickets in Championship games, 205 in all matches, at slightly over 18 runs each, including a hat-trick against Sussex at Hove. In 1926, the first of three Championship years, McDonald's wickets numbered 175 in county matches (including another hat-trick against Kent at Dover) and he distinguished himself in the Middlesex game at Old Trafford with a hard-hit undefeated hundred, his only century in first-class cricket.

McDonald utilised spin much more on the wet pitches of the following season and took 150 wickets that summer, his best performance being eight for 73 against Northamptonshire.

McDonald's best season was 1928 when, at 36-years-of-age, he played in all the thirty Championship games and maintained his form and speed magnificently to take 178 wickets at 19 runs apiece.

At 36, his remaining years as a fast bowler were obviously limited; even he, lion-hearted as he was, could not go on forever. In 1929 he took 140 wickets; in 1930, 108 (including the third hat-trick of his first-class career at Edgbaston and to his own great delight, the wicket of Don Bradman at Aigburth).

He had a serious loss of form in 1931 and at the end of a summer in which he could not produce his own pace, his contract was terminated by mutual agreement. McDonald, who had taken 1,053 wickets at 20.96 runs apiece, then returned to play in the leagues with Bacup and Blackpool.

He was manager of the Raikes Park Hotel in Blackpool and was returning home in the small hours of the morning after playing in a benefit match at Manchester when his car was in collision with another vehicle at Blackrod and crashed through a fence and into a field. Unhurt, he climbed from his car and was walking back along the road to offer assistance to the other driver when he was hit by another car and killed.

YORKSHIRE v LANCASHIRE
at Headingley July 30, August 1,2, 1927

Yorkshire 157 (Sutcliffe 95, Sibbles 4-54) and 314 (Sutcliffe 135, Macaulay 61*)
Lancashire 360-9dec (E.Tyldesley 165, Iddon 77)
Match Drawn.

There were two batting heroes in this game, Sutcliffe for Yorkshire and Ernest Tyldesley for Lancashire.

Ted McDonald bowled exceedingly fast in his opening spell and took the first three wickets to fall, all of them with the score on 35. Kilner went for 11 and then Rhodes joined Sutcliffe and they produced the biggest stand of the Yorkshire innings - 59 in 43 minutes for the fifth wicket before Rhodes fell to a brilliant one-handed catch by Richard Tyldesley off the bowling of Frank Sibbles. Yorkshire's last five wickets fell for 26 runs with Herbert Sutcliffe last but one out for 95.

Ernest Tyldesley defended vigilantly until Lancashire had passed Yorkshire's total of 157, then with Jack Iddon he began to hit out. The Yorkshire bowling was bludgeoned to the extent of 164 for the seventh wicket in two hours and forty minutes. After Oldroyd had caught Tyldesley off the bowling of Rhodes for 165, Iddon tried to force the pace but soon lost his wicket. After Richard Tyldesley had hit one enormous six, Green declared the Lancashire innings closed, 203 runs ahead.

Yorkshire lost Holmes before the close of play but on the final day, Sutcliffe produced an innings that was even more impressive than his first innings 95. Rhodes joined Sutcliffe with Yorkshire needing 128 to save themselves from an innings defeat and only six wickets left. The two batsmen added 126 runs with Sutcliffe scoring 100 of them. The danger of an innings defeat had been averted and Sutcliffe was eventually dismissed for 135 before Robinson and Macaulay, in an unbeaten century stand, hammered the Lancashire attack to all parts of the ground.

YORKSHIRE v LANCASHIRE
at Bramall Lane May 26,28,29, 1928

Lancashire 385 (Iddon 87, Taylor 66, Hallows 58, Green 52, Rhodes 4-56) and
80-1
Yorkshire 473 (Sutcliffe 140, Holmes 79, Mitchell 74)
Match Drawn.

Yorkshire were saddened by the death of the well-loved Roy Kilner at the

120

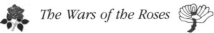

age of 37 by enteric fever after a winter engagement in India - it seemed as if Roses matches would never be the same again.

Lancashire won the toss and batted first on what looked a good wicket. Watson had hit three fours in quick succession when he glanced a ball from Jacques down the leg-side where wicket-keeper Wood dived to his left and held a magnificent catch. Hallows and Ernest Tyldesley took the score to 71 before Rhodes had Tyldesley caught by Worsley. Makepeace batted seventy minutes for nine runs and Hallows three-and-a-quarter hours for 58. The brightest batting came from Taylor and Iddon, who put on 112 for the fifth wicket in a little under two hours, Iddon lifting Rhodes high into the pavilion for six. At the end of the first day, Lancashire were 289 for six.

On the Monday morning, Lancashire's captain Green hit out, as did Richard Tyldesley, with the result that Yorkshire had to face a total of 385, laboriously compiled in seven-and-a-half hours.

Holmes and Sutcliffe scored 142 at over a run a minute before Holmes was bowled for 79. Mitchell and Sutcliffe took the score to 200 in as many minutes before on the final day, Booth had Sutcliffe caught at the wicket for 140. Leyland and Mitchell added 73 runs in 80 minutes and at lunch Yorkshire needed only 39 for the first innings lead with seven wickets in hand. But within forty minutes of the afternoon session they were 374 for seven. Then Emmott Robinson and Arthur Wood attacked the Lancashire bowling and the Yorkshire innings ended 88 runs ahead.

Lancashire's second innings saw them score 80 for one off a tolerant Yorkshire attack, which included overs by Holmes, Sutcliffe and Mitchell.

LANCASHIRE v YORKSHIRE
at Old Trafford August 4,6,7, 1928

Yorkshire 352 (Sutcliffe 126, Holmes 54, McDonald 6-144)
Lancashire 244-3 (Watson 110, Makepeace 81*)
Match Drawn.

The Lancashire team took to the field without Richard Tyldesley, who had hurt a bowling finger on the Friday in the cause of charity. The Red Rose county certainly missed his services as Holmes and Sutcliffe took the Yorkshire score to 115 for 0 at lunch on the opening day.

The first Yorkshire wicket fell on 134 as Holmes snicked McDonald into Duckworth's gloves. The opener had made 54 in two-and-a-quarter hours. McDonald then accounted for Mitchell in similar fashion and at 161, Maurice Leyland was run out by a direct hit from Hopwood. Duckworth then caught Barber before Sutcliffe reached his hundred in three hours and forty minutes.

The great man eventually went for 126, brilliantly caught low down by Watson off the bowling of Sibbles. The last two hours' play saw Yorkshire score 137 and end the day on 338 for eight.

Lancashire soon removed Yorkshire's last two wickets and had done well to get the old enemy all out for 352 on a good wicket.

There was a sensational start to the Lancashire innings as three fours were scored off the first four balls before Hallows played across a ball from Macaulay and was bowled. By lunch Lancashire had scored 75 for one but, early in the afternoon, Ernest Tyldesley pushed a ball from Rhodes into the hands of Robinson at first slip.

Frank Watson then began to change his game and in the next two hours, only scored 33 runs. After tea, Makepeace reached his fifty after two hours and twenty minutes at the crease, whilst Watson brought up his hundred with the Lancashire score on exactly 200. The two Lancashire batsmen added 153 for the third wicket before Watson was bowled by a good length ball by Macaulay.

Lancashire ended the second day on 244 for three and looked set to crawl in search of first innings points the whole of the last day. However, fate decided that enough was enough and heavy rain prevented any play whatsoever on what was one of the wettest days of the year.

LANCASHIRE v YORKSHIRE
at Old Trafford May 18,20,21, 1929

Lancashire 305 (Hallows 152*, Duckworth 55) and 127-3 (E.Tyldesley 54*)
Yorkshire 347 (Sutcliffe 69, Turner 69*, Leyland 65, Oldroyd 51, McDonald 5-119)
Match Drawn.

After Hallows had taken a single off the first ball of the day, Watson snicked Robinson's second delivery to Macaulay at first slip. Ernest Tyldesley and Len Hopwood didn't last long and Lancashire were soon 14 for three. Iddon scored 33 in two-and-a-half hours at the crease but after his dismissal, the home side lost three wickets for the addition of just seven runs. When Duckworth walked to the middle to join Hallows, Lancashire were 123 for seven. The wicket-keeper and Hallows added 128 for the eighth wicket, during which time Hallows reached his century in ten minutes under six hours. Duckworth fell leg-before to Rhodes for a fighting 55.

Lancashire's innings ended just before lunch on the Monday, but not before Ted McDonald had hit a beautiful straight six off Rhodes. Charlie Hallows was unbeaten throughout for 152, having dominated the

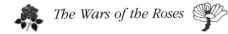

Yorkshire attack.

The start made by Yorkshire was almost as catastrophic. With just 20 runs on the board, Holmes and Mitchell were out to lightning deliveries from McDonald. Leyland and Sutcliffe added 124 for the third wicket in just over two hours before Richard Tyldesley clean bowled Leyland. With the Yorkshire score on 173, Sutcliffe was beaten for pace by McDonald and lost his off stump. Robinson soon went and at the close of play on the second day, the decision for first innings points was hanging in the balance.

On the last day, Yorkshire lost three wickets for the addition of just 26 runs before a stand of 91 between Turner and Rhodes for the ninth wicket gave Yorkshire the first innings points. Their innings ended at 347 when Duckworth stumped last man Worsley off the bowling of Richard Tyldesley.

Lancashire batted again on a lovely afternoon and ended the game on 127 for three as Yorkshire's main bowlers were rested.

CHARLIE HALLOWS (LANCASHIRE)

Charlie Hallows first played for Lancashire in 1914 as a left-arm slow bowler, but it was as a batsman, and for a short time one of the best in England, that he made his mark in Lancashire cricket.

Playing his last match in 1932, Hallows scored 20,142 runs for the county with 52 centuries at an average of 39.72. His record includes three double centuries and two occasions on which he made a century in each innings of a county match, curiously enough both away from Old Trafford.

For eleven seasons from 1919 to 1930, he exceeded a thousand runs and in 1925, 1927 and 1928 he made over two thousand. In 1928, the best year of his cricketing career, he scored 2,564 runs for the county at an average of 65.74 and achieved an honoured place in cricket records when he became one of the select group of three batsmen (Grace and Hammond were the others) who have scored a thousand runs in the month of May, as distinct from the others who scored the thousand before the end of May. Hallows scored his runs at a better average (125.00) than Grace (112) or Hammond (74) but it should be mentioned that both Grace and Hammond had slightly higher aggregates than Hallows and each reached their thousand in 22 days, whereas Hallows took 27 days to reach his.

Unfortunately, Charlie Hallows never reproduced the splendid form of that golden summer. He scored only six more hundreds between then and his retirement in 1932, though in the following season he achieved the distinction of carrying his bat through the Lancashire innings of the Roses match at Old Trafford. It was an innings of monumental patience which lasted over seven hours.

Opening the innings with Harry Makepeace in his early years played a large part in Charlie Hallows' success. But his partnerships with Frank Watson were more prolific and in that summer of 1928, they shared in twelve stands worth more than 100, five of them double centuries.

He was very unfortunate to be chosen to play in only two Test matches, one against Australia in 1921 and the other against the West Indies in 1928, but his two competitors for a place were Kent's Frank Woolley and Yorkshire's Maurice Leyland and Hallows lacked the all-round ability of both these fine cricketers.

Hallows was, however, a fine county batsman. He played a significant part in Lancashire's three successive Championship victories of 1926, 1927, and 1928 and of course he will always be remebered for the trail of glory he blazed in that memorable summer when he scored his thousand runs in May.

When his county career was over, Hallows went into the leagues and held professional engagements in all four home countries before becoming a coach. After a successful term at Worcestershire, during which they won the County Championship, he returned to Old Trafford as chief coach. He could not command the same success as he had achieved at New Road but the young players he had under his charge in due time, under the captaincy of Jack Bond, restored lost glories to Lancashire cricket after a long spell in the doldrums.

YORKSHIRE v LANCASHIRE
at Bradford August 3,5,6, 1929

Lancashire 192 (Makepeace 68, Leyland 7-52)
Yorkshire 285-7 (Sutcliffe 106, R.Tyldesley 4-112)
Match Drawn.

This was the first Roses match that Wilfred Rhodes had not taken part in since 1898 and, in fact, it did not look like a Roses match with Rhodes not there!

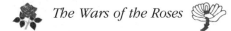

Hallows and Watson began Lancashire's innings dubiously and just before lunch, Hallows was caught at mid-on by Bowes off the bowling of Robinson. After lunch, Ernest Tyldesley was defeated by Leyalnd's flight and offered a simple chance to Barber at cover. Iddon went cheaply and Watson for 44 before Hopwood played down the wrong line and was leg-before to Leyland. Soon after, Macaulay uprooted Eckersley's middle stump and this brought in the resolute Duckworth to join Makepeace. In just over an hour, these two batsmen added 67 runs for the sixth wicket before Makepeace was caught by Barber off the bowling of Leyland. Duckworth was then run out without any addition to the score before Leyland wrapped up the tail to finish with seven for 52.

Holmes and Sutcliffe added fifty in the first hour of Yorkshire's innings before Holmes gave a simple catch to Watson at slip. This was followed by two more admirable partnerships from Sutcliffe and Oldroyd and from Sutcliffe and Leyland. The first partnership added 79 in an hour-and-a-half before Oldroyd was caught by Hopwood off the bowling of Iddon. The second added 64 in forty minutes with Leyland scoring 42 of them before he was caught by Lancashire's substitute fielder off the bowling of Frank Watson.

Sutcliffe went on to score 106 and, when he was out at 242, Yorkshire were already 50 ahead. Barber and Robinson added another 43 before rain swept the rest of the match away.

YORKSHIRE v LANCASHIRE
at Headingley June 7,9,10, 1930

Yorkshire 417-9dec (Leyland 211*, Oldroyd 49) and 11-1
Lancashire 305 (Hopwood 107*, Leyland 4-49)
Match Drawn.

Herbert Sutcliffe, for once, scored only 40 and took two hours to make them. This was well below his personal standard in Roses games, because his last six innings in the series had brought him 95, 135, 140, 126, 69 and 106.

Yorkshire had to depend on Maurice Leyland, who hit 211 not out, the highest individual score in a Roses match, mainly obtained by powerful pulling and driving.

At the end of the first day, Yorkshire finished on 360 for eight and when Rhodes was bowled by McDonald early on the second day, Leyland was still six runs short of his double hundred. Yorkshire's last man, Bill Bowes, stayed with Leyland and with the two batsmen still at the crease, Yorkshire declared at 417 for nine.

By lunch on the second day, Lancashire had reached 42 without loss but shortly afterwards they lost two wickets in two balls - Hallows bowled by Robinson for 33 and Ernest Tyldesley caught by Barber off the same bowler from the first ball he faced. Watson was the next to go for 36, scored in five minutes short of two hours. Lancashire's fourth wicket went down at 127 when Wood stumped Iddon off the bowling of Rhodes. Hopwood, who could have been out first ball, went on to score an unbeaten 107 but when last man McDonald walked to the crease, Lancashire still needed 16 to save the follow-on. The last pair added 53 with many of the runs coming off the edge of McDonald's bat.

Rain prevented Yorkshire's second innings from starting on time but when play did get underway, Sibbles accounted for Sutcliffe, beautifully caught by McDonald in the slips, before the rain returned, this time heavily and decisively.

MAURICE LEYLAND (YORKSHIRE)

The son of a former league professional who became groundsman at Headingley, Maurice Leyland graduated to the Yorkshire team via the Lancashire League, war-time Army service and three seasons as professional to his home-town team, Harrogate.

Leyland's progress with the White Rose county was slow but the club felt there was potential and they were rewarded when this cheerful and pugnacious Yorkshireman gradually blossomed into one of the country's most outstanding middle-order batsman between the two World Wars.

He made a thousand runs a season from 1923 to 1939, including 2,000 on three occasions, and in August 1932 scored 1,013 runs.

Robustly built, he was a powerful strokeplayer with a high grip and a splay-footed stance. There were times when many of the old Yorkshire professionals thought some of his shots, especially the cut, were a little risky. Leyland, however, relished a scrap and at the Scarborough Festival of 1928 hit Wilfred Rhodes for three sixes and a four in one over! In 1934 he scored hundreds in three successive innings, whilst two years later he hit the highest score of his career, 263 against Essex at Hull, one of five double centuries he scored for the county.

Had Yorkshire needed the services of his bowling more often, then he would have been remembered as an all-rounder. Even though he was only an occasional performer, he took 409 wickets for the county at 27.08, including a hat-trick against Surrey and a best of seven for 52 against Lancashire.

He had to wait eight years for his Test cap but then remained an automatic choice for a similar period, a sequence ended prematurely by war when he was 39.

Leyland possessed a magnificent temperament and scored 137 on his debut against Australia at Melbourne in 1929. He averaged over 40 on each of his three tours of Australia and was described by cricket writers Down Under as the 'English Clem Hill'.

In the 1934 series against Australia, he scored three centuries and on his final appearance against them at the Oval in 1938, he scored 187 before being run out. Leyland, who played in 41 Tests, scored 2,764 runs at an average of 46.06.

After the Second World War, Leyland played a full season, helping Yorkshire to the twelfth Championship of his career and taking his total of runs for the county to 26,180 at an average of 41.03.

For most of two decades, Maurice Leyland represented all that was good in the cricket of Yorkshire and England and it was his pride to wear the Yorkshire cap when he batted for his country. On retirement he became the county's good humoured and much loved coach, his career being commemorated by a set of gates at the Harrogate ground.

127

LANCASHIRE v YORKSHIRE
at Old Trafford August 2,4,5, 1930

Lancashire 284-6dec(E.Tyldesley 107, Iddon 70, Watson 50)
Yorkshire 125 (McDonald 7-58)
Match Drawn.

Except for a showery interval or two, Watson, Tyldesley and Iddon batted all through Saturday, painstakingly building up a defensive structure of 218 for two.

Makepeace went early, caught behind off Bowes for 14, but at lunch, after one hundred minutes of dour cricket, Lancashire were 57 for one. Lancashire's second wicket fell at 113 when Watson was caught at square-leg from a long hop bowled by Leyland. Tyldesley and Iddon then began to attack the Yorkshire bowlers and added a further 105 runs before close of play.

There was no play at all on the Monday due to heavy overnight rain and on the Tuesday, Lancashire did not declare until they had safely added another 66 runs for the loss of a further four wickets. This at least allowed Ernest Tyldesley to complete a stubborn century and set Yorkshire the awkward task of getting ahead in four hours.

Holmes and Sutcliffe reached 33 with deceptive ease but then five wickets fell with just another 12 runs added. Ted McDonald and Len Hopwood were bowling well in tandem, but by tea Yorkshire had reached 69 for five with Mitchell and Robinson defending well. Mitchell was dismissed by McDonald in the first over after tea with the score on 70. Arthur Wood began to hit out with a view to spoiling the magnificent bowling of Ted McDonald, who ended up with seven for 58. Richard Tyldesley was brought back into the attack to tame him, but by the time he was out, Yorkshire were 159 behind. However, there was no time for Lancashire to put them in again.

LANCASHIRE v YORKSHIRE
at Old Trafford May 23,25,26, 1931

Yorkshire 231 (Sutcliffe 75, Oldroyd 55) and 76-2
Lancashire 128 (Verity 5-54, Robinson 4-29)
Match Drawn.

Holmes and Sutcliffe made a steady start during the period of well under two hours that rain allowed on the Saturday and scored 53 before Holmes was bowled by Hopwood.

128

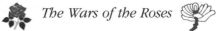

The sun shone at the start of play on the second day and Sutcliffe and Oldroyd made the most of it. After lunch, Yorkshire lost three quick wickets to be 170 for five before a series of heavy showers had the players running for shelter. When play was finally resumed, the Lancashire bowlers quickly finished off their work, the White Rose county's last eight wickets falling for 65 runs.

In the hour's play that remained on the second day, the Lancashire batsmen had a nightmare. Watson was run out going for an impossible single and Verity dismissed both Ernest Tyldesley and Iddon within the space of four balls to leave the home side 26 for three. With Verity and Emmott Robinson bowling well on the final day, Yorkshire dismissed their rivals for 128. With Lancashire having saved the follow-on, Yorkshire batted a second time and had reached 76 for two when stumps were drawn.

YORKSHIRE v LANCASHIRE
at Bramall Lane August 1,3,4, 1931

Yorkshire 484-7dec (Sutcliffe 195, Holmes 125, Mitchell 58)
Lancashire 221 (Verity 4-57) and 165-2 (Paynter 87*)
Match Drawn.

Though McDonald bowled with plenty of fire in his opening spell, he couldn't break through the defences of Holmes and Sutcliffe and at lunch,Yorkshire were 123 for 0. Sutcliffe went on to make 100 out of 165 in two-and-a-half hours and at tea, Yorkshire were 280 for 0, with Sutcliffe 171 and Holmes 95. In an hour and three-quarters since lunch, the Sheffield crowd had seen 157 runs - 91 made by Sutcliffe and 57 by Holmes.

Sutcliffe and Holmes easily broke the stand of 280 achieved in 1887 by Louis Hall and Frank Lee against Lancashire at Bradford. At 286, Holmes was dropped behind the wicket by Duckworth but at 323 the first wicket fell. Sutcliffe pulled a ball from Hopwood towards the deep mid-on boundary where Paynter took a magnificent catch inches from the ground and then fell over in a double somersault but still kept his grip on the ball. Holmes then began to hit out and was caught at mid-off with the score on 351. Leyland was bowled by Iddon and at the close of play Yorkshire were 391 for three.

Greenwood kept Yorkshire batting on Monday morning until 94 quick runs had been added for the loss of four more wickets.

Lancashire lost Hopwood at 42 and should have also lost Hallows next ball as he pulled a half-volley from Robinson straight into the hands of Holmes at mid-on, who dropped this relatively simple chance.

Verity replaced Bowes, who had bowled well without much luck, and with his first ball forced Ernest Tyldesley into giving a simple return catch.

129

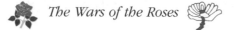

Hallows and Iddon defended well but Lancashire's best batsman was Paynter who was 45 not out when Lancashire's last wicket, that of McDonald, fell.

Following on 263 behind, Tyldesley and Paynter mastered the Yorkshire bowling and the game ended with Lancashire on 165 for two with Paynter having scored 132 runs in his two innings without once being out.

HERBERT SUTCLIFFE (YORKSHIRE)

Herbert Sutcliffe was an outstanding opening batsman whose remarkable technique and temperament enabled him to play long innings on the most difficult of pitches. Sutcliffe was born at Summerbridge near Harrogate but, while he was still a baby, the family moved to Pudsey where his father, who had Yorkshire trials, played for St Lawrence. Herbert played for the other Pudsey club, Britannia, making his debut at the age of fourteen. Sadly he lost both parents whilst still young and was brought up by his three aunts. At the age of twenty, whilst playing for Pudsey St Lawrence, Sutcliffe broke a Bradford League batting record, scoring 715 runs at an average of 47.00. During the First World War he served with the Ordnance Corps and then the Sherwood Foresters. Before the hostilities ended he was commissioned into the Green Howards and was playing for the West of Scotland. He was twenty-four when he first played for Yorkshire, ending his first season with five centuries in a total of 1,839 runs. It was the largest first-class aggregate ever achieved by a batsman in his first season and he went on to score at least 1,000 runs in every season between the wars. In fourteen consecutive summers (1922-1935) he exceeded 2,000 runs.

Sutcliffe also established a first-wicket partnership with Percy Holmes and for fourteen years these two batsmen opened the innings for Yorkshire, putting on a hundred on 74 occasions.

At Test level, Sutcliffe's association with Jack Hobbs became the most accomplished of all opening partnerships and against Australia at Melbourne in 1925 they became the first and only English pair to bat throughout a full day's Test match play. Their stand of 283 in 289 minutes remains the longest for the first wicket in this series. Sutcliffe was also the first to score 100 in each innings of a Test against Australia and the first Englishman to score three successive hundreds in Test cricket. When he scored 194 against Australia at Sydney in 1932 he overtook Jack Hobbs' world record of 15 Test hundreds. Sutcliffe went on to play in 54 Tests, scoring 4,555 runs at an average of 60.73.

130

Matches against Lancashire stirred him to make nine centuries and though his defensive patience and skill became a byword, he could certainly hit when the need arose. Against Northants at Kettering in 1933 he met spin on a sticky wicket with an innings of 113 that contained 10 sixes. At Scarborough against the fast bowling of Franes and Nichols of Essex, he took his score from 100 to 194 in just forty minutes. His 100th first-class century was the 132 he hit in less than two hours at Bradford when Yorkshire were hurrying to beat Gloucestershire.

Sutcliffe scored 112 centuries for Yorkshire and 149 in his career with a highest score of 313 against Essex at Leyton in 1932 as he and Percy Holmes shared in a then world record first wicket stand of 555 in 455 minutes. As well as holding the Yorkshire record for the most centuries, Sutcliffe holds the career record for the most runs (38,561), most instances of 1,000 runs in a season (21) as well as records for the most runs (2,883) and hundreds (12) in a season (1932).

He made his final appearance in 1945 before concentrating his mind with equal success on business. For three seasons (1959-1961) he made a welcome return in the guise of an England selector. He died at the age of 84 in Keighley, having lived long enough to see both Len Hutton and Geoff Boycott join him as scorers of more than a hundred centuries.

YORKSHIRE v LANCASHIRE
at Bradford May 14,16,17, 1932

Lancashire 263 (Paynter 152, Verity 8-107)
Yorkshire 46 (Sibbles 7-10) and 167 (Sutcliffe 61, Sibbles 5-58)
Lancashire won by an innings and 50 runs.

Watson and Paynter scored 67 for Lancashire's first wicket in ninety minutes before Watson pulled a full-toss from Verity straight into Holmes'
hands at square-leg. Ernest Tyldesley hooked Verity for four first ball and
then went on the defence as Paynter ran amok.

He hit two sixes off Verity into the football stand and two more
over the stand on to the football pitch itself. Maurice Leyland then came
on at the other end, genially offering Paynter a pint of beer after the match
for every six he hit. He only hit one more, but it hurtled high over the
square-leg boundary before striking the stone wall between the ground
and the adjoining park. Shortly after this delivery, Verity had him stumped
as he chased a widish ball. In his innings of 152, made out of 209 in three
-and-a-half hours on a bowler's wicket, he had hit five sixes and 17 fours.
Verity ended up with eight for 107 as Lancashire's innings ended at 263.

Heavy rain prevented any play until mid-afternoon on the Monday.

The very first ball bowled by Sibbles accounted for Holmes who
chopped a catch to Tyldesley at backward point. Mitchell was bowled
three balls later before Sutcliffe and Leyland added twenty runs to ease
the tension. Sutcliffe went on to make 27 in an hour and a quarter, the
next highest contributor being Leyland with six. Yorkshire were all out,
routed for 46, without one single boundary being scored. Sibbles did not
send down a single loose ball, his figures of: 20.4 -13-10-7 were awe-
inspiring.

Yorkshire began their second innings at 5.00 p.m. 217 runs behind.
Parkin's first ball of the match, for he didn't bowl in the first innings, got
Holmes lbw, but Sutcliffe was batting with confidence and reached his
fifty after an hour at the crease. The Yorkshire and England opener was
caught in the first over of the final day and, with nobody but Leyalnd (43)
showing any resistance, the side slowly faded away to be all out for 167
at a quarter-past one.

Lancashire had won by an innings and 50 runs with Frank Sibbles
having match figures of twelve for 68.

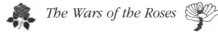

EDDIE PAYNTER (LANCASHIRE)

Eddie Paynter started work at 12 as a part-timer in a cotton mill and later moved into a brickyard in Accrington. He was brought up on Lancashire League cricket with Enfield, first went to Old Trafford in 1921 and joined the staff in 1926.

He was 28 years of age before he played his first game in the county side, for Lancashire in those days had a powerful batting line-up. Even though he played in half the games in 1930, he was in some doubt at the end of the summer whether or not he could retain his place, so much that he had decided to leave Old Trafford. Before the new season had started, he had changed his mind. In that season he opened England's innings at Old Trafford with Herbert Sutcliffe and though he only scored three, it was the first of twenty appearances for his country.

It is fair to say that but for the war, Paynter would have gained many more than twenty caps, for the tragedy about the career of this wonderful little character was that six years were lost at the beginning and six at the end of it. His first-class cricket was compressed into ten seasons and his record is the more remarkable for the shortness of the span.

His 16,555 runs for Lancashire at an average of 41.59, and the even more impressive figures of 1,540 runs at 59.23 in his twenty appearances at Test level, are ample proof of his standing in the game.

Paynter won everlasting fame with his performance in the fourth Test at Brisbane during the acrimonious 'body-line' tour of Australia in 1932-33. Paynter developed tonsilitis but discharged himself from a sick bed and, though still ill and weak, played a superb innings of 83 which guided England into a first innings lead. He also achieved the distinction later on of making the winning hit which enabled the Ashes to be regained.

In the 1938 series in England, Paynter was second in the averages to Len Hutton, who made 364 at the Oval, both having averages of over 100. At Trent Bridge in the first Test of that summer Paynter scored 216 not out, whilst he was unlucky to be dismissed one short of his century in the second Test at Lord's. In the 1938-39 series in South Africa he hit 653 runs at an average of 81.62, which remains the highest aggregate for a series between the two countries in South Africa, including hundreds in each innings of the Johannesburg Test and 243 in the third Test at Durban.

For Lancashire, Paynter hit 36 hundreds including four double centuries and a highest score of 322 against Sussex at Hove in 1937.

Roses matches always brought the best out of Eddie Paynter and the match at Bradford in 1932 will always be associated with him. On a bad wicket he made 152 of Lancashire's total of 263 in a three-and-a-half hour stay at the crease.

After the Second World War, Eddie did not return to Old Trafford but did appear in representative matches and in 1947 scored centuries against the South and for the Rest against Leyland's XI, both at Harrogate. But at that time he was a league cricket professional, playing in the Bradford League with Keighley for nine years and starting an association with Yorkshire that saw him live the rest of his life in that county.

LANCASHIRE v YORKSHIRE
at Old Trafford July 30, August 1,2, 1932

Lancashire 170 (E.Tyldesley 50, Bowes 4-57, Verity 4-71) and 187 (E.Tyldesley 56, Verity 5-35)
Yorkshire 362-9dec (Sutcliffe 135, Leyland 91, Mitchell 56*)
Yorkshire won by an innings and 5 runs.

Lancashire had to fight for every run on a fairly difficult wicket and at lunch were 64 for two with Watson and Hopwood back in the pavilion, courtesy of Bill Bowes. It was the gangling bespectacled Bowes who uprooted Iddon's off stump to leave the home side on 83 for three. Only Ernest Tyldesley seemed capable of dealing with the Yorkshire bowlers but when he was dismissed for 50, half the side were out with 105 on the board. Sibbles and Booth batted adventurously for the eighth wicket, Booth hitting Verity into the pavilion for six. With the score on 153, he was bowled, aiming for another huge hit. Lancashire were all out for 170, not a large total but one that every run had been fought for.

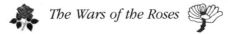

Yorkshire lost Holmes and Barber fairly cheaply but then Sutcliffe and Leyland added 141 runs for the third wicket in an hour and three-quarters. Sutcliffe scored a glorious 135 to register his seventh Roses century whilst Leyland missed his hundred by just nine runs. Later, Mitchell hit an unbeaten 56, enabling Sellers to declare at 362 for nine.

Though 192 behind, Lancashire had a good chance of saving the game. Tyldesley and Hopwood batted well and at lunch on the final day, Lancashire were 118 for one with Watson the man out.

However, soon after lunch, Verity broke the partnership and from then on, Lancashire's batsmen lacked confidence, whether they were facing the bounce and pace of Bowes or the deceptive slows of Verity. Tyldesley was out at 121, Iddon at 122 and Paynter at 124. In an attempt to stave off an innings defeat, Hodgson, Lancashire's last man, went to hit the ball for a six but was stumped and Yorkshire had gained their first Roses victory for five years.

LANCASHIRE v YORKSHIRE
at Old Trafford June 3,5,6, 1933

Yorkshire 341 (Mitchell 123, Barber 62, Iddon 4-60)
Lancashire 93 (Macaulay 7-28) and 92 (Macaulay 5-21)
Yorkshire won by an innings and 156 runs.

Yorkshire won the toss and elected to bat and though they lost Holmes, Sutcliffe and Leyland early on, Mitchell, with help from Barber and Sellers, pulled the game round Yorkshire's way. At the end of the first day, Yorkshire were 287 for five with Mitchell unbeaten on 116.

A crowd of almost 15,000 watched the end of Yorkshire's innings and then saw Lancashire lose five wickets in an hour and a quarter for just 54 runs.

Watson went before lunch, pulling a widish delivery from Macaulay into the hands of Leyland at square-leg. At 36, Tyldesley played on to a ball from Bowes and one run later, Iddon was bowled by Macaulay. Hopwood and Paynter added 20 runs before Hopwood was leg-before to Macaulay. Paynter and Parkinson attacked the bowling and took the score to 90 before Paynter was caught at backward point for 17. Bennett was bowled first ball and Eckersley caught at slip. Parkinson, who top-scored with 24, was the next man out - four wickets down in six balls. Duckworth was leg-before first ball - Macaulay had performed the hat-trick, dismissing Paynter and Bennett with his fifth and sixth balls of one over and Duckworth with the first of his next over. He then bowled Booth to take four wickets in five balls - Lancashire 93 all out.

135

When the Red Rose county followed-on, Watson had to retire hurt after being hit on the head by a rising ball from Bowes. Verity and Macaulay were bowling well in tandem and by tea, Lancashire had crawled to 48 for four. With the wicket crumbling, only Paynter, who was unbeaten on 29, and last man Hodgson with 18, including a mighty six off Verity, showed any resistance. Lancashire were all out for 92 - twenty-four wickets had fallen in the day for 239 runs - and George Macaulay had match figures of twelve for 49 as Yorkshire won by an innings and 156 runs.

GEORGE MACAULAY (YORKSHIRE)

George Macaulay was a 23-year-old right-arm fast bowler when he first appeared at the Headingley nets, but after Hirst and Rhodes

had persuaded him to reduce his pace to around medium and concentrate on length, swing and spin, his career really took off. Macaulay gave up his banking job and in that summer of 1921 took 101 wickets, including an inspired spell of six Derbyshire wickets for just three runs.

Mixing late swing with sharp off-breaks, he was quite unplayable at times. He was exceptionally accurate and would open the attack off a short bustling run before switching to his vast off-breaks, usually from around the wicket.

In fifteen seasons as a regular member of the Yorkshire side, he took 1,773 wickets for the county at 17.08 runs apiece and altogether in first-class cricket 1,838 at 17.64. His best season was 1925, when in County Championship matches he claimed 176 wickets at 15.21.

Macaulay performed the hat-trick on four occasions - against Warwickshire at Edgbaston in 1923, against Leicestershire at Hull in 1930, against Glamorgan at Cardiff in 1933 and against Lancashire at Old Trafford in 1933 when he actually took four wickets in five balls!

Macaulay could also keep batsmen on the defensive for long periods of time and such an instance occurred against Northamptonshire at Kettering in 1933 when he bowled 14 overs for nine runs and dismissed seven batsmen!

Macaulay played for England on eight occasions and took a wicket with his first ball in Test cricket against South Africa in Cape Town in 1922, then in a sensational finish to the match, he made the stroke which brought England victory by one wicket. In his only match for England against Australia, he did little with the ball but, joining George Geary, he scored 76 in a ninth wicket partnership of 108 which helped England to save the match.

Macaulay frequently gave useful help with the bat for Yorkshire, hitting three centuries in a total of 5,579 runs at 18.11.

It was no coincidence that during his fifteen complete seasons, Yorkshire won the County Championship eight times.

He was still at the peak of his career when in the match against Leicestershire at Headingley in 1934 an injury to his spinning finger from an attempted return catch compelled his retirement to league cricket.

Educated at Barnard Castle, Macaulay regularly brought an XI of noted players to meet his old school in the years following his retirement. In the First World War he served in the Royal Field Artillery but sadly died on active service in the Second World War soon after being commissioned as an RAF Pilot Officer.

YORKSHIRE v LANCASHIRE
at Headingley August 5,7,8, 1933

Yorkshire 296 (Barber 81) and 153-3 (Leyland 53)
Lancashire 431 (Hopwood 120, Hawkwood 113, Parkinson 69*, Bowes 4-109)
Match Drawn.

Yorkshire were all out for 296 in their first innings with Wilf Barber, who scored 81, being their only adventurous batsman. The home side's total would have been considerably less if Lancashire had held all their catches. Five were dropped including Holmes before he had scored, Mitchell when 15 and Barber when only 22.

By lunch on the second day, Lancashire were 50 for three with all three batsmen caught by Macaulay in the slips. But when Hawkwood, a young member of the Old Trafford staff, joined Hopwood, Lancashire's resistance grew. The two had added 200 for the fourth wicket in 175 minutes when Macaulay clean bowled Hawkwood for 113. The young Lancastrain had hit 15 fours in his first Roses innings.

Hopwood eventually went leg-before to Leyland for 120 before Sibbles and Parkinson hit the Yorkshire bowling to all parts of the Headingley ground, adding 79 runs in less than an hour.

Finishing 135 runs ahead, Lancashire only needed to take eight wickets for victory in three-and-a-half hours that remained. However, Yorkshire, aided by some defiant batting from Leyland and Mitchell, had no difficulty in saving the game.

YORKSHIRE v LANCASHIRE
at Bramall Lane May 19,21,22, 1934

Yorkshire 346-5dec (Mitchell 121, Sutcliffe 73, Leyland 73*)
Lancashire 111 (Verity 5-25) and 232 (Iddon 62, Bowes 4-60)
Yorkshire won by an innings and 3 runs.

Sutcliffe and Mitchell scored 143 for Yorkshire's first wicket in two hours and forty minutes. Yet in the second over of the morning, Sutcliffe was bowled by Booth, but it was a no-ball. Later in the day, Sutcliffe was caught from a 'skier' but that too was a no-ball! Eventually he went for 73, caught by Sibbles at square-leg off the bowling of Booth.

Barber was the next to go, his innings of 44 being scored in less than an hour. At the end of the first day, Yorkshire were 293 for two, yet in mid-afternoon they had been 200 for one.

Play didn't begin until after lunch on the second day because of heavy overnight rain. Yorkshire added 53 in forty-five minutes before declaring. Mitchell's 121 had taken him almost five hours to compile.

The rain followed by bright sunshine had turned the Sheffield wicket into a batsman's nightmare.

Watson and Hopwood defended stubbornly for seventy-five minutes but when Hopwood was deceived by Verity into giving an easy catch to Sellers at silly point, the wickets began to tumble. At the end of the day, Lancashire were 93 for seven. Their innings was polished off in a further twenty-five minutes play on the final day and they had to follow-on, 235 runs behind.

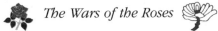

The first wicket went down at 25 when Bowes yorked Frank Watson. Hopwood went at 51, bowled by Verity, and then Tyldesley, who had defended well with Iddon was caught by Mitchell at backward point for 27. Paynter was dismissed for 16 and Lancashire were 121 for four. Iddon was adjudged lbw to Turner for 62 and with all the recognised batsmen out, the tea interval was claimed for play by the Yorkshire captain.

Despite one or two lusty blows by Booth, Lancashire were all out for 232 with just twenty-five minutes play remaining.

ARTHUR MITCHELL (YORKSHIRE)

Arthur Mitchell was a very steady and determined batsman whose long playing career with Yorkshire was virtually terminated by the Second World War.

Although he made his debut in 1922, so strong was the Yorkshire batting that he did not command a regular place for another six seasons, although an innings of 189 against Northamptonshire in 1926 revealed his possibilities. In 1930, he was one of five Yorkshire batsmen who averaged over 50. After Percy Holmes retired in 1933, he was promoted to open the innings and enjoyed his most prolific season. He scored 2,100 runs, ending with a purple patch of four successive hundreds and an aggregate of 508 for once out. Also that season, he and Herbert Sutcliffe scored 105 in 55 minutes against Surrey at Bradford after Hutton had been dismissed when Yorkshire needed 199 to win against the clock.

If he was often content to accumulate with on-side strokes, he could suddenly change mood and indulge in a spasm of off-drives and cuts. In 1934, Mitchell made his only appearance for the Players against the Gentlemen at Lord's. He took two hours and five minutes over his first 50 and an hour later was out for 120.

As a member of the MCC side in India in 1932-33, he played in three Test matches but met with only moderate success.

Mitchell was summoned from his garden at the last minute to take the place of his Yorkshire team-mate Maurice Leyland, stricken by lumbago, for the third Test against South Africa at Headingley in 1935. He took over three hours to compile a valuable 58 in the first innings but in the second, sent in first with Denis Smith, he made 72 in under two hours in an opening stand of 128. In the final Test of that series at the Oval, after again going in first, he made 40 in a little over three hours.

For Yorkshire, he scored 18,034 runs at 37.64, including 39 centuries.

In his early Bradford League days, Arthur Mitchell had been a very limited fielder but by sheer determination and hard work he became one of the best close catchers in the world, whether fielding on the leg or the off.

He was also one of the most talkative, his constant chatter earning him the nickname 'Ticker'.

He continued to play regularly up to the outbreak of the Second World War but in 1945 he became the county's coach, a post he held until 1970. He died aged seventy-four in a Bradford hospital on Christmas Day 1976. He was, said Wisden, 'a wonderful man in a crisis. No match was ever lost until the opposition had got him out.'

LANCASHIRE v YORKSHIRE
at Old Trafford August 4,6,7, 1934

Yorkshire 291-6dec (Sutcliffe 66, Sellers 54)
Lancashire 273 (Iddon 142* Bowes 4-73)
Match Drawn.

Yorkshire's first wicket fell when the score was 111 as Mitchell was adjudged leg-before to Hopwood. But shortly after lunch, Sutcliffe left the field suffering from dizziness to be replaced by Barber. The number three batsman should have been out first ball but Duckworth fumbled the chance of a stumping.

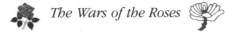

Leyland was bowled by Iddon with a ball that turned viciously and then Barber was cleverly caught at the wicket off Booth almost before Leyland had taken off his pads and at tea Yorkshire were 186 for three. Sellers batted well to score 54 and on his departure, Sutcliffe returned to complete his fifty. Yorkshire ended the opening day's play on 291 for six.

Torrential rain on the Monday meant that there was no play all day.

Sellers declared at once and Lancashire set off at a brisk rate in an attempt to secure first innings points. Watson and Hopwood began Lancashire's reply with a terrific fusillade of boundaries but both were back in the pavilion in half-an-hour with Lancashire 51 for two. Iddon and Tyldesley batted throughout most of the afternoon to put on 142 runs in as many minutes. Tyldesley fell four runs short of his half-century and, though wickets fell quickly, Iddon reached his hundred.

With just five minutes left to play, Leyland bowled a maiden to Iddon who was on 142 and this enabled Bowes to bowl the last over the match to last man Dick Pollard. He promptly removed his middle stump to give Yorkshire the first innings victory in this drawn match.

LANCASHIRE v YORKSHIRE
at Old Trafford June 8,10,11, 1935

Lancashire 153 (Bowes 4-53) and 80-0
Yorkshire 140 (Pollard 6-56)
Match Drawn.

Rain prevented any play on the Saturday but on the Monday there was, as the year before, a dour struggle for first innings lead.

Hawkwood, the Lancashire opener was bowled from the last ball of Bowes' first over with just one run on the board. Iddon and Hopwood took the score to 67 before a good length ball from Smailes removed Iddon's off stump. Eddie Paynter scored 43, the highest score of the match but it was slow, taking the normally aggressive left-hander, two-and-three-quarter hours.

At tea, Lancashire were 129 for six but were all out for 153 shortly afterwards.

Sutcliffe and Hutton opened the Yorkshire innings but both were soon back in the pavilion. Sutcliffe edged Pollard to Iddon at slip and Hutton was bowled off his pads by the Westhoughton-born bowler. Pollard also accounted for Mitchell leg-before and Booth dismissed both Leyland and Sellers to leave Yorkshire 53 for five.

Pollard continued his good work in the first few overs of the final day, dismissing Wood and Verity. Barber and Smailes then added 44 for

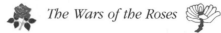

the eighth wicket before Smailes provided Pollard with his sixth wicket. Barber was out for 41, bowled by Parkinson. Yorkshire's last pair, Macaulay and Bowes, added 25 for the tenth wicket before Bowes was run out with the visitors score on 140.

With the issue of first innings lead settled, Lancashire's openers, Hopwood and Hawkwood, put on 80 without being separated until a final thunderstorm in mid-afternoon sent the players scurrying into the pavilion.

YORKSHIRE v LANCASHIRE
at Bradford August 3,5,6, 1935

Yorkshire 225 (Leyland 58, Turner 57, Sibbles 5-56) and 181-3 (Mitchell 69*, Barber 57)
Lancashire 53 (Bowes 6-16) and 352 (Watson 141, Washbrook 85, Bowes 6-83)
Yorkshire won by 7 wickets.

Yorkshire struggled on a pitch which every now and then kicked viciously. By lunch they had scored 75 for three. The first to depart was Mitchell, caught in the deep by Washbrook one-handed as the ball was sailing over his head for six. Barber was leg-before to Sibbles and Sutcliffe was run out by a wonderfully quick return by Oldfield.

Only Leyland and Cyril Turner batted with any sense of purpose. Leyland, who hit 58 in an hour, played all through with a heavily bandaged wrist after suffering some damaging blows from Sibbles. Yorkshire's last wicket fell at 225 and when Lancashire went out to bat at half-past five, the light was dim and only one ball bowled before the players came off the field. However, that was not the end of play for fifteen minutes later, with most of the crowd having departed, play resumed. The first ball Bowes bowled after play restarted uprooted Hopwood's middle stump. Then Paynter was run out and Watson brilliantly caught at cover by Sellers. Verity then held on to a catch at slip to help dismiss Ernest Tyldesley and with just minutes to go to the end of the day, Washbrook was caught at the wicket - Lancashire 26 for five!

The remaining five wickets were taken inside three-quarters of an hour on the second day and Lancashire were all out for 53 with only Eckersley reaching double figures.

Most spectators expected another Lancashire collapse in the second innings but Bowes was not given the chance to repeat his first innings figures of six for 16. While Watson and Washbrook were together, there even seemed to be a chance of Lancashire turning the tables on Yorkshire altogether. Watson scored 141, including 25 determined fours, and Washbrook 85, an

142

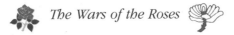
innings of attractive stroke play. A last wicket stand of 39 between Washbrook and Sibbles took Lancashire's total to 352, leaving Yorkshire 181 to win.

The wicket on the final day seemed easier for the batsmen than at any other time and with Mitchell and Barber leading the way, Yorkshire reached their goal for the loss of three wickets - Lancashire's resolute recovery had been in vain.

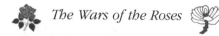

BILL BOWES (YORKSHIRE)

Bill Bowes was a gangling, bespecatcled fast bowler, who, in tandem with Hedley Verity's left-arm spin, provided the basis of a Yorkshire attack which claimed seven County Championship titles in the 1930s.

The young Bowes performed the hat-trick for West Leeds High School and, though his mother wanted him to be a teacher, when he left school, he started work in an estate agent's office. He became secretary and bowler for the Armley Wesleyan Sunday School Club and on one Easter Monday he was invited to play in an impromptu match in a Leeds park where his performance led to him receiving a further invitation to play for Kirkstall Educational Second XI against Leeds City Gas Works. Bowes was later offered five pounds a week to turn professional in league cricket but his friends persuaded him to write to Warwickshire for a trial. However, MCC were seeking to enlarge their groundstaff and so, after a trial at Lord's, he was offered a season's contract. In his first season he performed the hat-trick against Cambridge University and won a year's extension to his contract.

Meanwhile, Yorkshire had been alerted to his talent and agreed with MCC that the 22-year-old Bowes should be made available to the county when not required by that club.

Bowling right-arm at a fast-medium pace from a ten-yard run, he swung the ball either way, had a sharp break back and memorised the technical defects of his opponents. He took 100 wickets or more in eight of the next nine seasons in an era of batsman's pitches. In 1932 he bowled 40 overs in three and a half hours under a burning sun at Scarborough to take nine for 121 against Essex. When wickets did help him, he was deadly; in four successive matches in 1935 he took 40 wickets for 321 runs and in August of that same season took 34 wickets in successive games. Included in that sequence were figures of sixteen for 35 against Northamptonshire at Kettering (eight for 18 and eight for 17). For Yorkshire, Bowes took 1,351 wickets at 15.71 runs apiece.

Bowes was a late selection behind Larwood, Allen and Tate for Douglas Jardine's 'body-line' tour of 1932-33 and although he only played in one Test and took one wicket, that wicket was Don Bradman's, dismissed first ball! In the Oval Test of 1934, he and

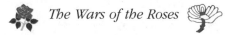

Hedley Verity shared nineteen Australian wickets though England did lose by 562 runs!

Bowes did not play until the last two Tests of the 1938 series against the Australians but headed the bowling averages with 10 wickets at 18.80 each.

Converted into a wartime army officer and captured at Tobruk, he spent three years in Italy with his fellow Prisoner-of-War Freddie Brown and when he returned to England, he was four and a half stones lighter than he had been in 1939.

Though he bowled at a much reduced pace he served Yorkshire for two more years, helping them win another County Championship in 1946. Bowes, who enjoyed mathematics and conjuring tricks and was a member of the Magic Circle, later turned his attention to forty years of notable cricket writing.

YORKSHIRE v LANCASHIRE
at Headingley May 30, June 1, 2, 1936

Yorkshire 175-7dec (Sutcliffe 89, Hopwood 4-53)
Lancashire 16-3 (Verity 3-2)
No Result.

The whole of this Roses game lasted just five hours, none of them on Saturday due to the heavy rain.

Play was only just possible on the Monday morning but Sutcliffe and Mitchell added 114 for the first wicket in three hours. Warburton accounted for Mitchell, caught by Lister, and then had Sellers leg-before without scoring. When rain and bad light put an end to the second day's play, Yorkshire were 134 for two.

A heavy thunderstorm just before the final day's play was due to begin was followed by blazing sunshine, making the wicket quite treacherous. Hutton was caught at the wicket first ball and after Leyland had hit five fours in his unbeaten innings of 21, Sellers declared.

His declaration was justified as Verity took two wickets in his first over and got rid of Paynter in his third. At lunch, Lancashire were 16 for three but then the heavens opened and there was no further play.

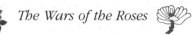

LANCASHIRE v YORKSHIRE
at Old Trafford August 1,3,4, 1936

Lancashire 202 (Paynter 92, Smailes 4-46, Hutton 4-49) and 174 (Hopwood 61,
Bowes 4-17, Smailes 4-58)
Yorkshire 246-9dec (Hutton 46) and 10-0
Match Drawn.

On a slow, easy wicket, Lancashire struggled throughout the first day to end on 190 for six with Eddie Paynter the top-scorer with 92. He struggled over two hours for his fifty but then the remainder of his runs came at a run a minute.

Lancashire were all out for 202 within half-an-hour of the start of the second day as Hutton and Smailes finished off the tail. Only Hopwood and Oldfield, who both scored 31, contributed totals to support Paynter's innings.

Sutcliffe went early in Yorkshire's innings and it was left to a young Len Hutton to hold the innings together. He top-scored with 46 and at tea, Yorkshire were 153 for four. However, wickets began to fall and with only three wickets in hand, Yorkshire wanted 19 runs to win the first innings points. Verity and Wood settled the issue and Yorkshire closed their innings at 246 for nine.

Lancashire started their second innings with a fine partnership between Washbrook and Hopwood, who added 89 for the first wicket. Iddon soon followed Hopwood, who had been bowled by Leyland for 61, and with Lancashire only 72 ahead there was time for a Lancashire collapse and a Yorkshire victory.

Even though Bowes and Smailes bundled out the later batsmen, Paynter held firm until the proceedings had become a formality. Yorkshire needed 131 for victory but there was only time for four overs to be bowled!

LANCASHIRE v YORKSHIRE
at Old Trafford May 15,17,18, 1937

Lancashire 106 (Verity 6-32) and 197 (Paynter 86, Watson 56, Verity 4-43)
Yorkshire 270 (Mitchell 77) and 35-0
Yorkshire won by 10 wickets.

The Lancashire batsmen could make nothing of Hedley Verity's flight and six of them fell to him for 32 runs. They were all out for 106 in an hour and a half's laborious batting, with Iddon top-scoring on 25. In fact, if Pollard and Booth hadn't retrieved the innings with some lusty blows for the last wicket, the Lancashire total seemed certain to fall below a hundred.

146

Sutcliffe and Hutton opened for Yorkshire, the latter being bowled for 13 with the score at 49 after playing back to a ball from Sibbles. Leyland was aggressive but he too lost his off stump to Sibbles after hitting seven boundaries in his innings of 30. Mitchell, who top-scored with 77, came out of his shell and scored at a brisk rate. Yorkshire were all out at half-past two on the second day and had a lead of 164 runs.

Lancashire soon lost Hopwood and Iddon but then Paynter and Watson knocked off half the arrears before a storm put an end to play just after tea.

Once Watson had been dismissed on the final day, there was nobody capable of staying with Paynter, who went on to score 86. When Verity had the last man caught by Mitchell, his match figures were ten for 75.

Sutcliffe and Hutton then knocked off the 35 runs required for victory to give Yorkshire a ten wicket win.

YORKSHIRE v LANCASHIRE
at Bramall Lane July 31, August 1,2, 1937

Yorkshire 246 (Sutcliffe 122, Mitchell 71, Pollard 5-59) and 168 (Iddon 9-42)
Lancashire 324 (Oldfield 51, Phillipson 50*) and 91- 5 (Verity 3-26)
Lancashire won by 5 wickets.

Lancashire had an early success when Hutton edged the first ball of Phillipson's second over to Pollard at first slip. Pollard missed the catch with one hand, then caught it with the other. Sutcliffe, too, should have gone when he'd scored three but Hopwood failed to accept the chance off the bowling of Sibbles.

After lunch, Pollard wrecked the Yorkshire innings, taking five wickets in 12 overs with four of his victims being clean bowled. Sutcliffe however continued on his way to his eighth Roses century, adding 142 for the second wicket with Mitchell. There was some fierce hitting by Wood towards the end of the Yorkshire innings which totalled 246.

When Lancashire batted, the Yorkshire spin bowlers could not take advantage of the worn patches and only two batsmen failed to score double figures. Six Lancashire batsmen scored over 30 with both Oldfield and Phillipson hitting stylish half-centuries. Eventually Lancashire were all out for 324, a lead of 78, most of which was made by the last two wickets.

By the time Yorkshire had knocked off the arrears, they had lost Sutcliffe and Hutton. When the partnership between Hutton and Mitchell was broken, Iddon began to exploit a worn patch and the later Yorkshire batsmen were less and less able to deal with him. He achieved the bowling performance of his life - nine for 42, five for seven in 17 balls!

Only needing 91 to win, Washbrook and Paynter took the score to 70 before Washbrook was dismissed by Verity. It was now Verity's turn to find the 'spot' and before the target was reached, five Lancashire wickets went down.

In one of the most exciting of Roses matches, Lancashire had gained their first victory at Bramall Lane since 1899.

JACK IDDON (LANCASHIRE)

Jack Iddon was born at Mawdesley near Ormskirk in 1902, the son of a professional cricketer. When he was in his teens, he played many good innings and took plenty of wickets for both Nelson and Leyland Motors cricket clubs.

He was a right-hand batsman and left-arm spin-bowler and played for Lancashire from 1924 until 1945, except for the years of the Second World War when no cricket was possible. He was a highly-valued member of five Championship winning teams and for many years batted at number four immediately after Ernest Tyldesley.

After a modest start to his county career, Iddon became a regular in the Lancashire side and in 1928, the third successive year of the county's Championship success, he had his best season to date when he scored 1,353 runs at an average of 52 and took 63 wickets at a cost of 25 runs apiece. That was the start of twelve successive seasons up to the outbreak of war when he scored 1,000 runs.

Iddon's best season was 1934 when he scored 2,381 runs at an average of 53, his form earning him a place in the MCC team in the West Indies where he played in four Tests. He played once more for England against South Africa in 1935, completing his Test career with two half-centuries and a batting average of 28.33.

Roses games always seemed to bring the best out of him. He played a wonderfully defiant innings of 142 not out at Old Trafford in 1934 when the Yorkshire bowlers were on the rampage and turned in a match-winning bowling performance of nine for 42 at Sheffield in 1937 on a wearing pitch which Hedley Verity had not been able to exploit.

During the war, Jack Iddon turned his attention to business. However, he did not neglect his cricket. He organised games on behalf of war charities and travelled miles to give relief to workers and keep the game of cricket alive despite the difficulties imposed by the war.

Iddon sacrificed his leisure time to play cricket, even if the Sabbath was not his own - for during the war this was the only time war workers were free. He saw to it that they had good cricket to watch and the British Red Cross Association benefitted from the proceeds taken at these matches.

When the war was over, Jack Iddon was 43 years of age. He decided to play in the 1946 season as an amateur and it is possible that he might have captained the county side, bringing to it an experience - 21,975 runs at 37.05 and 533 wickets at 26.66 runs apiece - that would have been extremely valuable at that difficult period, but this was not to be. Before the season began he was tragically killed in a motoring accident and another fine cricketer was lost to the game he had adorned.

YORKSHIRE v LANCASHIRE
at Bradford June 4,6,7, 1938

Lancashire 232 (Hopwood 70) and 138 (Iddon 66, Verity 6-49)
Yorkshire 273 (Turner 69, Sellers 50) and 98-2
Yorkshire won by 8 wickets.

Lancashire batted for almost all of the first day but with Washbrook not playing, and the loss of Place and Paynter with only 20 on the board, the run-rate was very poor. Hopwood's innings of 70 was completed in two hours, whilst Nutter laboured two-and-a-half hours over his 45.

Verity opened the batting for Yorkshire but was out without scoring, treading on his own wickets as he tried to pull a short ball from Pollard. Len Hutton, fast developing as one of the country's most accomplished batsmen, played well for his 44 but shortly after lunch, Yorkshire were 106 for six. Turner and Sellers then transformed the Yorkshire innings, taking the score to 202 before Sellers was leg-before to Phillipson. There was yet another little gem of an innings from wicket-keeper Wood which enabled Yorkshire to finish with a lead of 41.

Lancashire appeared to be saving the game with ease when Hutton, with one of his innocently cunning leg-breaks, made the breakthrough. He was only given three overs but in these, at a cost of only four runs, he took the vital wicket of Jack Iddon.

There then followed one of the worst collapses of Lancashire batting in Roses history as six wickets fell for 18 runs in 45 minutes after lunch. They were all out for 138, leaving Yorkshire 98 for victory, which they achieved for the loss of two wickets.

149

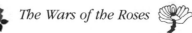 *The Wars of the Roses*

LANCASHIRE v YORKSHIRE
at Old Trafford July 30, August 1, 2, 1938

Lancashire 133 (Robinson 5-57) and 120 (Paynter 58, Verity 5-21)
Yorkshire 453 (Leyland 135, Sellers 82*, Gibb 78, Nutter 5-68)
Yorkshire won by an innings and 200 runs.

Lancashire gave a poor batting display on the opening day of this Roses match. Only a brave knock from Hopwood, who scored 45, prolonged their innings until four o'clock. Yorkshire replied confidently and, despite losing Mitchell in the third over, Sutcliffe and Gibb saw them safely through to the close of play.

The two Yorkshire batsmen were both out to lbw decisions in the morning session before Leyland and Barber took the score to 232 for three at lunch. Barber and Yardley were given out lbw in the afternoon session and at 285 for five, Sellers joined Leyland. The two batsmen scored 108 for the sixth wicket in an hour-and-a-half before Leyland was bowled by Nutter for a magnificent 135. Sellers let the innings run its course, Yorkshire being all out for 453, a lead of 320.

Washbrook and Paynter saw Lancashire safely through to the close of play but by half-past twelve on the final day, Lancashire were all out for 120. Only the first three batsmen reached double figures - Washbrook 30, Paynter 58 and Iddon 14 - as Verity bowled at his best, aided by some magnificent close to the wicket catches.

LANCASHIRE v YORKSHIRE
at Old Trafford May 27, 29, 30, 1939

Lancashire 300 (Nutter 85, Pollard 54) and 185 (Oldfield 66, Paynter 60, Bowes 6-43)
Yorkshire 528-8dec (Sutcliffe 165, Mitchell 136, Wood 65, Sellers 53*,
Wilkinson 4-168)
Yorkshire won by an innings and 43 runs.

After winning the toss and electing to bat, Lancashire lost a number of early wickets but by lunch had recovered somewhat to be 130 for four. There then came an excellent stand in mid-innings by Hopwood and Nutter before the innings collapsed again to leave Lancashire on 188 for eight. Then Pollard and Nutter laid about the Yorkshire bowling to the extent that 106 runs were added for the ninth wicket in 75 minutes.

Hutton was bowled off his pads by Wilkinson before the close of play but then Sutcliffe, with 165, and Mitchell, with 136, added 288 for the

150

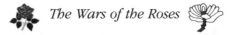

second wicket in four-and-a-half hours. That wicket fell at 329 when Mitchell was caught by Phillipson off Nutter. Next over Sutcliffe was clean bowled by Phillipson and without any addition to the score, Yardley lost his middle stump to Nutter - Yorkshire 329 for four. Sellers and Wood added a century stand and at 528 for eight, the Yorkshire captain declared.

Washbrook and Iddon soon departed but Paynter and Oldfield contributed a fighting stand of 103 towards the 228 that formed the deficit. Bowes bowled Oldfield shortly after lunch with the Lancashire score on 131 but from then on the wickets tumbled. Oldfield had batted brilliantly for his 66 and though Paynter went for 60, Lancashire collapsed and were all out for 185, leaving Yorkshire to win their third consecutive Roses match by an innings and 43 runs.

YORKSHIRE v LANCASHIRE
at Headingley August 5,7,8, 1939

Lancashire 217 (Oldfield 77, Robinson 5-80) and 92 (Robinson 8-35)
Yorkshire 163 (Barber 52, Garlick 4-52) and 147-5 (Hutton 105*)
Yorkshire won by 5 wickets.

The Roses game at Headingley is remembered not only because it was the last match between the two counties for six years, but because it ended in a thunderstorm.

Ellis Robinson took Lancashire's first four wickets for 34 runs and though Oldfield batted beautifully for 77 before being caught by Mitchell in Verity's close-wicket trap, the other batsmen did little and Lancashire were all out for 217.

Yorkshire went in to bat two overs before lunch on the second day and hit up 14 runs. However, after lunch Garlick bowled some superb inswingers and clean bowled Hutton with only 21 runs on the board. Only Barber, with a fighting innings of 52, showed any resistance and Yorkshire were bowled out for 163, some 54 runs behind.

Once the opening stand of Paynter and Washbrook had been broken by Verity, Ellis Robinson was irresistible. Hitting the stumps again and again, he took five of the last six wickets to fall for just a handful of runs, capturing in all eight for 35. His combined match figures were thirteen for 115 as Lancashire were all out for a paltry 92.

Yorkshire needed 147 for victory and were made to struggle by Lancashire. They were dependent wholly on one batsman, Len Hutton, then aged 23 and destined to become one of the greatest batsman and most successful England captain of his age. As wickets fell around him, Hutton scored

151

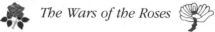

a magnificent unbeaten 105 to lead Yorkshire to a five wicket victory.

The winning hit was made from a missed and difficult chance; three minutes later, the Headingley ground was flooded. Had the catch been held by Washbrook, there would have been no more play and Yorkshire, one run short of victory, would most certainly have been cheated!

LANCASHIRE v YORKSHIRE
at Old Trafford July 2,3, 1945

Lancashire 116 (Coxon 5-48) and 155 (Barron 64, Booth 8-54)
Yorkshire 172 (Pollard 4-58) and 82-5
Match Drawn.

After Yorkshire's Alex Coxon had removed both Paynter and Place with very few runs on the board, it was left to Washbrook (29) and Iddon (34) to repair the early damage. However, the only other Lancashire batsman to reach double figures was Higson, and, with Coxon, assisted by some outstanding fielding, taking five for 48, the home side were bowled out for 116.

Although Pollard and the left-arm swing bowler Chadwick bowled well, Yorkshire through Hutton (37) and Leyland (36) built up a lead of 56 runs.

Lancashire lost three wickets in clearing off the arrears before Arthur Booth, spinning and flighting the ball with marked skill began to take wickets. At one point, he took six wickets for 25 runs but a fighting innings of 64 by Bill Barron, a knock that included a six and 9 fours, spoiled his figures. Lancashire rallied to 155 all out with Booth taking eight for 54 from 29.2 overs.

Yorkshire needed 100 to win in as many minutes and almost made it, finishing on 82 for five.

YORKSHIRE v LANCASHIRE
at Bradford August 13,14,15, 1945

Lancashire 239 (Washbrook 97, Rae 74, Bowes 4-22) 107-3
Yorkshire 259 (Barber 88, Nutter 5-7)
Match Drawn.

Known as the 'Hedley Verity Memorial Match' this Roses game was played in aid of his family and raised around 3,000 pounds.

Lancashire batted first and, with Cyril Washbrook in fine form, reached 239. The Red Rose county's opening batsman fell three runs short of a century, dismissed by Arthur Booth, the scourge of Lancashire in that summer's pre-

152

vious contest. Washbrook was well supported by Bobby Rae who scored 74.

Bill Bowes, who had been a Prisoner of War in Italy, was only a shadow of his former self, though he was still Yorkshire's best bowler, taking four for 22 off 18 overs.

All Yorkshire's top-order batsmen scored runs freely but Wilf Barber and Brian Sellers shared in a brisk partnership which took the home side 20 runs ahead of Lancashire on the first innings.

Barber was eventually dismissed for 88, caught by Nutter off the bowling of Pollard.

Though not a vintage Roses game, at least the weather, which held up play for most of the last day, reminded us that rain is almost an essential element in Lancashire v Yorkshire matches.

YORKSHIRE v LANCASHIRE
at Bramall Lane June 8,10,11, 1946

Yorkshire 171-3dec (Gibb72*)
Lancashire 127-4 (Place 68*)
No Result.

Already in June, it was clear that Lancashire or Yorkshire were the most likely county champions and the huge crowd that assembled at Bramall Lane showed that cricket had lost none of its appeal after the hostilities.

Yorkshire won the toss and made the most of batting on a dead, unresponsive pitch. Hutton was in fine form, but at 36 he was leg-before to a swinging ball from Pollard. Barber helped Gibb take the score into the eighties by lunch-time but early in the afternoon session, he was bowled by Pollard's in-swinger. There was just time for Gibb to hit two fours through mid-wicket before the rain came down and put an end to the first day's play.

Rain also prevented any play on the Monday and on the last morning, the two captains came to a surprising arrangement. Yorkshire were to bat for another half-hour, then Lancashire could try for first innings lead. If they gained this, they would declare at once and the time remaining was to be equally divided by the two sides. The emphasis on going all out for a win was obvious. As it happened, rain prevented any result. Yorkshire hit hard in the morning and kept their side of the bargain but the pitch was now beginning to turn and Booth and Robinson bowled well as Lancashire fought hard to avoid collapse. Three men were dismissed cheaply but Winston Place batted for over three hours to save his side.

The game was not so much a cricket match, more a semi-aquatic exercise!

LANCASHIRE v YORKSHIRE
at Old Trafford August 3,5,6, 1946

Yorkshire 180 (Smailes 61, Roberts 5-56) and 220-5 (Sellers 53*)
Lancashire 396 (King 122, Place 107, Coxon 4-120)
Match Drawn.

This match was really the key to the 1946 County Championship. By the beginning of August it was felt that Yorkshire were firm favourites for the title, but if Lancashire could win this Bank Holiday match at Old Trafford, they might just turn the scales.

The weather on the Saturday was fine and the crowds so enormous that many thousands were locked outside the gates.

Yorkshire began shakily, and never really recovered though that admirable all-rounder Frank Smailes, along with captain Brian Sellers, did their utmost to master the Lancashire attack. Even so, Yorkshire could only total 180.

Lancashire began equally unimpressively, for after Washbrook and Ikin had failed, Place and Wharton had to fight hard to play out time.

On the Monday, this pair gave Lancashire a distinct advantage. Place not only reached his century but put his county ahead. He and Wharton had shared a century stand and immediately afterwards the young Wharton was awarded his county cap. King, formerly of Worcestershire, hit a solid century. There was a feeling amongst the Lancashire members that Fallows should have declared at the tea interval when Lancashire were nearly 200 ahead. As it was, he lost 40 minutes play by letting the innings run its full course. However, Phillipson captured the wickets of Hutton and Barber before the close of play and the home side looked set for a victory that would bring the championship within their grasp.

Things continued to go well for Lancashire right up to lunch on the final day, for though Willie Watson defended stubbornly, three more wickets fell and it seemed impossible that Yorkshire would avoid defeat. There then followed an unbroken partnership between Maurice Leyland and Sellers, who batted for two-and-three-quarter hours to save the game for Yorkshire. Leyland weathered two violent attacks by Pollard and some unnecessary barracking and though he had lost his old attacking strokes, he was the very essence of Yorkshire cricket.

154

LANCASHIRE v YORKSHIRE
at Old Trafford May 24,26,27, 1947

Lancashire 327 (Phillipson 52, Bowes 4-44) and 176-7dec (Ikin 69*, Bowes 4-50)
Yorkshire 209 (Hutton 95, Roberts 4-16) and 251-5 (Hutton 86, Watson 57)
Match Drawn.

The first Roses game of the summer provided one of those exciting struggles which swayed first one way and then the other.

In Lancashire's first innings, only Eddie Phillipson with scored a half-century, but eight batsmen made over 20 and this enabled the home side to reach 327.

Hutton and Watson got Yorkshire off to a flying start with a century opening partnership, Hutton eventually being dismissed five runs short of his century. The rest of the Yorkshire side failed and the result was a deficit of 118 runs.

In Lancashire's second innings, wickets fell quickly as the Red Rose county's batsmen tried to increase the scoring rate and thus make the visitors struggle in the game's fourth innings. However, Jack Ikin did bat aggressively and scored an unbeaten 69, enabling Lancashire's new captain Ken Cranston to declare.

Set 295 to win, Yorkshire accepted the challenge. Hutton (86) and Watson (57) batted with great determination, as did Norman Yardley. Jakeman ran himself out going for a quick single and when stumps were drawn, Sellers and Smailes were at the wicket with Yorkshire 44 runs short of their target and five wickets still in hand.

YORKSHIRE v LANCASHIRE
at Bramall Lane August 2,4,5, 1947

Yorkshire 310-8dec (Smithson 98, Sellers 80)
Lancashire 160 (Washbrook 63, Robinson 5-61) and 180-7 (Wardle 4-40)
Match Drawn.

Lancashire saved the return game this summer by sheer refusal to give in. When newcomer Gerald Smithson went in after the first Yorkshire wicket had fallen, just 12 runs were on the board. He began a delightful innings by hitting 4 fours and a three in the first over he faced! When he was caught two runs short of his hundred, he had hit a five and 13 fours. In spite of his fine innings, he still received a ticking off from Emmott Robinson, who though long retired was still a regular visitor to Roses matches. At the end of his conversation, Emmott was seen to shake his

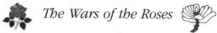

head and heard to mutter, 'We'll never learn that lad'.

Yorkshire's captain Brian Sellers also played well and scored 80 in his side's total of 310 for eight declared.

There was no play before lunch on the Monday but when it was possible to make a start, the Lancashire batsmen found that the wicket had begun to deteriorate.

Though Cyril Washbrook batted well for 63, Lancashire failed by one run to avoid the follow-on. It was the bowling of Ellis Robinson with five for 61 which did the damage.

When they went in again, Johnny Wardle took three quick wickets but Ken Cranston and Alan Wharton dug in and, aided by some light showers which made the ball greasy for the bowlers to hold, held Yorkshire's attack at bay and though the extra half-hour was claimed, stumps were drawn ten minutes into this period.

YORKSHIRE v LANCASHIRE
at Headingley May 15,17,18, 1948

Lancashire 450 (Washbrook 170, Edrich 121, Cranston 73, Smailes 4-55, Aspinall 4-125)
Yorkshire 256 (Hutton 100, Halliday 60, Pollard 5-58) and 177-5 (Wilson 51,
Roberts 4-44)
Match Drawn.

Lancashire lost three early wickets but once Eric Edrich joined Washbrook, a large total on this flat Headingley wicket was never in doubt. Washbrook (170), in his impertinent approach to any bowling, and Edrich (121), in the solid, hard-hitting style that charcaterised his family of Norfolk brothers, added 150 before captain Ken Cranston hit hard for 73 to enable Lancashire to reach 450.

But it had taken the Red Rose county quite a time to amass that total and when Yorkshire's Pudsey-born openers Hutton (100) and Halliday (60) started with a first wicket partnership of 153, an evenly balanced draw looked the only outcome. However, by the Tuesday morning, the wicket had deteriorated and Pollard polished off the tail to finish with five for 58 and leave Yorkshire 194 runs behind and having to follow-on.

It was Bill Roberts who did the damage as Yorkshire batted for a second time, taking four wickets with the home side still 100 runs in arrears. Then Vic Wilson was joined by Ron Aspinall and the two batsmen stayed together for almost two hours. When Wilson was caught and bowled on reaching his half-century, Yorkshire were still 20 runs behind but play ended a few minutes later and the White Rose side, after looking like succumbing to an innings defeat, had secured an honourable draw.

CYRIL WASHBROOK (LANCASHIRE)

At school, both at Barrow near Blackburn and at Bridgnorth in Shropshire where the family moved, Cyril Washbrook was considered something of a cricketing prodigy. Scouts from Lancashire, Warwickshire and Worcestershire became interested in his performances and at the age of 16 he was offered terms to join the respective groundstaffs. After choosing Lancashire he reported to Old Trafford where he came under the shrewd eye of Harry Makepeace. His first Minor Counties game as a member of the groundstaff was in a testing match with Yorkshire 2nd XI at Bradford in 1933. He distinguished himself by scoring an unbeaten double-century. Playing in the same game was a young Yorkshireman some eighteen months younger, named Leonard Hutton. More than a decade and a world war later, the two men were to open the England innings together.

After scoring 40 against Sussex at Old Trafford in his first County Championship match, his next first-class game was against Surrey, also at Old Trafford. Alf Gover was the fastest bowler he had faced to that time, redoubtable, perseving and accurate. In a remarkable innings, the young Washbrook scored 152 and went on to his first county century with four successive boundaries. In 1935 he scored 228 out of 431 against Oxford University and in the match against Worcestershire, facing Perks at his quickest and batting first on a lively wicket, he carried his bat through both Lancashire innings and was awarded his county cap.

157

In six matches in 1937 he scored 670 runs and his run of success gained him a place in the Oval Test match against New Zealand, when Eddie Paynter, who had originally been selected, was obliged to withdraw through injury. In the two seasons immediately pre-ceeding the Second World War, Washbrook consolidated his place in the Lancashire team. He hit five centuries in 1938, including an unbeaten double-century against Gloucestershire at Bristol, but was not invited to play in any of the representative games.

During war service with the RAF, Washbrook played all the cricket he could and in 1945 he took part in the 'Victory Tests'.

County cricket started in earnest again in 1946 and in that sea-son Washbrook scored 2,400 runs in all matches at an average of over 68. These runs included nine centuries, earned him a recall into the England side and earned him selection as one of Wisden's 'Five Cricketers of the Year.' He was chosen to tour Australia and New Zealand in 1946-47. Hutton and Washbrook opened the innings in all five Tests, this series marking the beginning of their association as England's first-wicket pair. Back in England in 1947, Washbrook was soon amongst the runs, scoring over 2,600 at an average of 68. His eleven hundreds included unbeaten double-cen-turies against Surrey and Sussex.

Over the next few seasons, runs flowed prolifically from Washbrook's bat. In 1948 he played in four of the five Tests against Australia. At Headingley he scored 143 in the first innings and 65 in the second and he shared with Hutton a century opening stand in each innings, a performance which established a new world record for the feat had never before been accomplished twice by the same batsmen. The two batsmen set up a new record for an opening partnership with 359 against South Africa in the second Test of the 1948-49 tour at Johannesburg. Washbrook was last selected for England at the age of 42 when he was Lancashire's cap-tain and a Test selector! Persuaded to play at Headingley, England were 17 for three when Washbrook walked to the wicket. He pro-ceeded to make 98 before succumbing inevitably to a forcing shot.

He played his last game for Lancashire in 1959. A master bats-man, he scored 27,863 runs for the county at an average of 42.15.

He later sought refuge on the Lancashire committee before in 1988 being elected President, only the second professional player after Len Hopwood to be so honoured.

158

The Wars of the Roses

LANCASHIRE v YORKSHIRE
at Old Trafford July 31, August 2,3, 1948

Yorkshire 359 (Lester 125*, Hutton 104, Greenwood 6-68) and 241-5 (Lester 132)
Lancashire 361-5dec (Washbrook 156, Ikin 106)
Match Drawn.

Not so often at Old Trafford does the bat completely defeat the ball. This Bank Holiday, however, the bat was supreme. The match was memorable for the feat of Ted Lester, who equalled the 28-year-old record of Percy Holmes by scoring a century in each innings of a Roses game.

Altogether this encounter produced five three-figure scores. Lester's first innings display was rather overshadowed by the brilliance of Len Hutton, who made 104 out of 184 before a fierce thunderstorm flooded the ground. Lester batted three-and-a-quarter hours for his 125 and hit 18 fours. Greenwood bowled extremely well for Lancashire to record figures of six for 68 from 22.4 overs.

When Lancashire went in to bat, they lost Place and Edrich both to Smailes with just 12 on the scoreboard but Washbrook hit a six and 21 fours during his innings of 156 in just over three hours. Ikin scored 106, helping Washbrook put on 244 for the third wicket. Lancashire passed Yorkshire's total with just five wickets down and immediately declared.

Lester's second hundred, made in 110 minutes, was marked by superb driving and quite vigorous pulls. Norman Yardley, the Yorkshire captain, decided that the White Rose county should continue batting rather than declare and the match petered out into a draw.

TED LESTER (YORKSHIRE)

One of the most unorthodox batsmen ever to play for Yorkshire, Scarborough-born Ted Lester forced himself to the attention of the Yorkshire committee by some prolific scoring on the flat batting tracks of the North Marine Road and in 1939 he was invited to play in a Colts trial at York. Throughout the war years his achievements for Scarborough kept him in the public eye and in 1945 he appeared for Yorkshire in a number of two-day friendly matches under the captaincy of Maurice Leyland.

Lester first played in the County Championship for Yorkshire in 1947 when, after making 127 against Derbyshire, he hit two centuries, 126 and 142, in the next match against Northamptonshire.

159

He ended the season ahead of Hutton in the batting averages with an extraordinary high figure of 73. In 1948, Lester passed 1,000 runs for the first time and in the match aaginst Lancashire at Old Trafford again scored a century in each innings with knocks of 125 not out and 132.

Especially strong on the leg-side, Lester's fast scoring, which was based on an extremely quick eye and fine co-ordination, made him an extremely dangerous batsman once set. In the summer of 1949, he made what was his highest score for Yorkshire, 186 against Warwickshire.

Lester's best season in terms of runs scored was 1952 when his total of 1,786 contained centuries in each of the matches against Nottinghamshire and a fine knock of 110 not out against the touring Indians.

His last good season was 1954 when he hit four centuries in a total of 1,330 runs, the last being 142 against Surrey. He was by now having increasing difficulty because of a foot problem from appearing regularly in three-day cricket and at the end of that season, Lester, who had scored 10,616 runs at an average of 34.02, decided to retire from first-class cricket.

A qualified MCC coach, Ted Lester became the Colts' senior professional and captain before beginning a second career as Yorkshire's scorer, a position he held for over twenty-five years. During this time, he was a great friend and counsellor to a long line of Yorkshire captains who rarely made an important decision without consulting him.

Despite all the travelling involved with his job as the county scorer, Ted Lester continued to live in his beloved Scarborough and it was only when he reached the age of sixty-five in 1988 that he ceased to attend all Yorkshire's away games.

LANCASHIRE v YORKSHIRE
at Old Trafford June 4,6,7, 1949

Yorkshire   326-7dec (Hutton 201, Halliday 69) and 168-3dec (Hutton 91*)
Lancashire 177 (Mason 4-46) and 227-5 (Wharton 73*, Grieves 69)
Match Drawn.

Len Hutton, by scoring a double century in Yorkshire's first innings, equalled the feats of Leyland and Spooner, the only others at this time to accomplish this performance in a Roses match. He batted faultlessly for ten minutes short of seven hours, hitting 3 sixes, a five and 19 fours. Nobody else but Halliday, who shared in an opening stand of 163, did anything of note and when Yardley declared at 326 for seven, Lancashire had to struggle hard to avoid the follow-on.

They made indifferent progress after losing Washbrook for 17 against the bowling of Close, Mason and Hutton. In fact, until Grieves and Greenwood came together for the sixth wicket, they did not look like avoiding the follow-on. Eventually, Lancashire were all out 149 behind, but that one run made all the difference.

In Yorkshire's second innings, Hutton again batted in a masterly fashion for 91 not out before Yardley declared for a second time, setting Lancashire 318 to win. There seemed a good chance of a Yorkshire victory when Lancashire lost their first four wickets for 65 runs but Wharton and Grieves came together, playing each ball on its merit. Anything loose was severely punished and Grieves in his 69 hit 4 sixes and 8 fours. When Close finally bowled him, the chance of a positive finish had slipped away.

LEN HUTTON (YORKSHIRE)

Born into a cricketing family, Len Hutton passed rapidly through the Yorkshire ranks and began his first-class career just before his 18th birthday, registering a duck against Cambridge University. Before that initial season was out he had shown his worth with an innings of 196 at Worcester and though 1935 and 1936 brought him only one century each, by 1937 he was ready for an England cap. Opening with Jim Parks senior against New Zealand three days after his 21st birthday, he was bowled for a duck and despite only scoring 1 in the second innings kept his place for the second Test at Old Trafford where he made 100.

His debut against Australia came at Trent Bridge in 1938 where he scored 100 again, posting 219 for England's first wicket with Charlie Barnett. In the final Test of that summer at the Oval, Len Hutton made 364, a then world record score, in 13 hours and 17 minutes.

Now a national hero, Hutton swept all before him. In 1939 he exceeded his 10 centuries of 1937 with 12 and raised his highest score for Yorkshire from 271 not out against Derbyshire to 280 not out against Hampshire at Bramall Lane. That summer against the West Indies, he made 196 at Lord's and 165 not out at the Oval.

Though the war brutally derailed his career, he scored a century in the Lord's 'Victory' Test of 1945. He went with MCC to Australia in 1946-47 and scored centuries at Melbourne, Adelaide and Sydney. In 1947, Hutton went past 2,500 runs for the third time, averaging 64 with 11 centuries and scoring 270 not out against Hampshire, this time at Bournemouth. A quiet Test summer was illuminated by his first Test appearance on his home ground at Headingley and he responded by hitting a century against the South Africans.

In 1948 he made nine centuries for Yorkshire and one for the Players against the Gentlemen at Lord's, launching him to South Africa that winter where he added two more Test centuries in a successful campaign - his 158 at Johannesburg being part of a record opening stand of 359 for the first wicket with Cyril Washbrook. In 1949 he scored another 12 centuries, two of them - one a double - in the New Zealand Tests and 3,429 runs in all.

He crowned a quieter summer in 1950 with 202 not out against the West Indies at the Oval, carrying his bat through an innings of 344 and holding at bay the spin of Ramadhin and Valentine. In 1951, Hutton became the 13th batsman to make 100 centuries, narrowly missing the mark in the Old Trafford Test (98 not out) but making certain with 151 against Surrey at the Oval.

Appointed captain of England he led the country to an Ashes victory in 1953 and then helped them retain them in Australia in 1954-55. He played in two more Tests against New Zealand and then retired from the international arena with a bad back, having scored 6,971 runs at an average of 56.67.

In June 1955, he stroked his last first-class hundred, 194 against Nottinghamshire at Trent Bridge, the last 94 coming in little more than an hour. For Yorkshire he scored 24,807 runs at an average of 53.34 and hit 85 centuries.

His knighthood, conferred in 1956, was only the second, after Sir Jack Hobbs, to go to a professional cricketer. In 1975 he became an England selector but resigned a year later saying that the modern players didn't find it easy to relate to him. Len Hutton died on 6 September 1990 after surgeons at Kingston Hospital in Surrey had fought to save him from a ruptured heart artery.

YORKSHIRE v LANCASHIRE
at Headingley July 30, August 1,2, 1949

Yorkshire 301-8dec (Halliday 96, Lester 55) and 8-2
Lancashire 356 (Ikin 107, Washbrook 70, G.Edrich 71, Wharton 52, Close 6-130)
Match Drawn.

Lancashire made a good start to the game as Yorkshire's opening batsman Len Hutton, who had scored 292 runs in the summer's first Roses encounter, was run out off the third ball before a run had been scored.

However, defiant innings from Halliday (96), Lester (55) and Lowson (46) helped Yorkshire to declare at 301 for eight.

A century by Jack Ikin and a polished 70 by Cyril Washbrook helped Lancashire get off to a good start. The Red Rose county overtook Yorkshire's total with only three wickets down but then the Headingley wicket began to play tricks and the fast-emerging Brian Close took five for 15 in 7.2 overs.

Yorkshire lost two wickets for eight runs but the visitors were left to regret the loss of three hours play earlier on the last day.

YORKSHIRE v LANCASHIRE
at Bramall Lane May 27,29,30, 1950

Lancashire 257 (Wharton 93, G.Edrich 70) and 117 (Grieves 52, Wardle 6-44)
Yorkshire 193-8 dec (Lowson 49) and 167 (Yardley 51, Tattersall 5-60)
Lancashire won by 14 runs.

There have been few more exciting Roses games than the 1950 game at Bramall Lane in which Lancashire, after a prodigious struggle, snatched victory by 14 runs.

Lancashire's first innings total of 257 owed almost everything to a fighting stand by Wharton (93) and Edrich (70). Yorkshire's batting started with an admirable partnership between Hutton and Lowson but as the pitch deteriorated, wickets fell at regular intervals and Yardley the Yorkshire captain calculated that it would pay him to get Lancashire in and out in these conditions, even though it meant declaring 64 runs behind.

Yardley's judgement was sound, because Wardle and Close played havoc with the Lancashire batting and only Grieves, with a battling 52, resisted their wiles. The first three wickets had gone for 35 when he came to the crease but he scored his runs out of the next 76 in well under the hour.

When Yorkshire went in a second time, they needed 182 for victory but the pitch had deteriorated even more and Frank Lowson, Halliday, Lester and Vic Wilson all went quickly to Berry and Tattersall. Then Yardley joined Hutton and the White Rose county appeared to be fighting their way to victory when Ikin took a marvellous catch close in to dismiss Hutton off Tattersall. When Wardle joined Yardley, Yorkshire only had 125 on the board with just Brennan and Trueman to bat. The two batsmen added 27 in a quarter-of-an-hour before Wardle drove Berry hard off the meat of the bat straight back to the bowler who clung safely to the ball. With 30 runs still needed, Brennan snicked a four before Yardley monop-

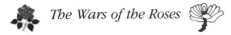

The Wars of the Roses

olised the situation. His half-century arrived to a crescendo of cheering and then Brennan swung at Tattersall's off-break and Wharton held a good catch at short mid-wicket.

Now it was Yardley or no one. He refused to take singles to each of the first three balls of Bob Berry's next over but then lobbed the fourth round the corner to Ikin and Lancashire had beaten their enemies for the first time since on the same ground Iddon's fine bowling had won the day 13 years before.

LANCASHIRE v YORKSHIRE
at Old Trafford August 5,7,8, 1950

Yorkshire 226 (Yardley 119, Statham 5-52) and 282-7dec
(Hutton 91, Watson 73*, Tattersall 6-67)
Lancashire 233 (Washbrook 88, Wardle 5-73, Coxon 5-78) and 160-3 (Washbrook 74)
Match Drawn.

A bowler by the name of Brian Statham made his Roses debut and shot down Yorkshire's first three wickets for 13 runs and saw half the side out for under 50. Then Yardley, with Halliday, stemmed the tide in a defiant century stand before Statham in his second spell dismissed Halliday. Norman Yardley went on hitting and made 119, a classic Roses innings, and with Wardle making some lusty blows, Yorkshire totalled 226. Statham finished with five for 52.

The battle for first innings lead was fought every inch of the way with Washbrook hitting 15 fours in his innings of 88 before he was brilliantly caught on the boundary by Leadbeater. His knock was as vital to Lancashire as Yardley's had been to Yorkshire. The ninth wicket fell with Lancashire still behind their rivals' total but though Statham was dropped twice, the Red Rose county eventually ended seven runs ahead.

Yorkshire needed to score quickly in their second innings to make a reasonable declaration. Yet despite the Lancashire attack making things difficult for the Yorkshire batsmen, Hutton played brilliantly and missed his hundred by only nine runs. The left-handed Watson hit 73 as the visitors declared at 282 for seven.

It was too late for Lancashire to seriously go for the 275 runs needed for victory. As it was, Washbrook scored 74 out of a first wicket partnership of 102 but after that, the match slowly faded away, Lancashire finishing on 160 for three.

165

LANCASHIRE v YORKSHIRE
at Old Trafford May 12,14,15, 1951

Yorkshire 313 (Wardle 79, Wilson 64) and 172 (M.Hilton 5-33)
Lancashire 289 (Place 67, Washbrook 51) and 111-4
Match Drawn.

Yorkshire's first innings total of 313 had, as its backbone, a solid innings of 64 by Vic Wilson and a quick-fire 79 by Johnny Wardle. The left-handed spinner hit 6 sixes and 7 fours in just 75 minutes at the wicket after the first five batsmen had been dismissed with 165 runs on the board.

Lancashire's reply started briskly with Ikin and Washbrook, who in the absence of Nigel Howard captained the side, putting on 71 for the first wicket. When Grieves joined Place at the fall of the third wicket, they rattled up a similar total in less than an hour. After they were dismissed, only Greenwood caused the visitors any trouble as Wardle and Leadbeater finished off the innings to give Yorkshire first innings points with a lead of 24 runs.

Yorkshire had to score quickly to set their rivals a challenging target. Yet in attempting this, half the side fell to Malcolm Hilton's leg-breaks. He finished with five for 33 as Yorkshire were bowled out for 172 in just two-and-a-half hours.

Lancashire were left to score 197 runs for victory in 145 minutes. The early loss of Washbrook, Edrich, Grieves and Ikin for 74 runs made the task impossible and the game ended in a draw.

YORKSHIRE v LANCASHIRE
at Bramall Lane August 4,6,7, 1951

Lancashire 215 (Washbrook 68, Place 62, Yardley 4-14)
Yorkshire 34-2
No Result.

On a thoroughly wet wicket, Yorkshire captain Norman Yardley had no hesitation in asking Lancashire to bat. He must have had grave doubts about his decision as Cyril Washbrook gave one of his most dazzling displays of batting. He hit a six and 11 fours in 68 out of a total of 91 in 100 minutes. The majority of his runs came from his favourite hook shot or square-cut. The defiant Place and his partner Geoff Edrich carried the score to 102 at lunch but only a further 88 runs were scored before tea for the loss of three more wickets. The last five Lancashire wickets fell in just over half-an-hour after tea for 23 runs. Yardley, who dismissed Wharton and Tattersall in successive deliveries, claimed four of them in 22

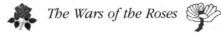

balls to finish with figures of four for 14.

At the end of the first day, Tattersall struck two quick blows for Lancashire to dismiss Lowson and Wilson but unfortunately for all concerned, it rained for the next two days.

YORKSHIRE v LANCASHIRE
at Headingley May 31, June 2,3, 1952

Yorkshire 347-2dec (Hutton 152, Lowson 120, Wilson 51*) and 145-8dec
Lancashire 260-9dec (Washbrook 63) and 146-8 (Lomax 52, Close 5-36)
Match Drawn.

Yorkshire won the toss and elected to bat first on a damp wicket. Though play was interrupted several times on the first day, the home side's opening pair of Len Hutton and Frank Lowson were still there at the close of play as Yorkshire reached 170 for 0. They continued their first wicket partnership on the Monday morning until Hutton was caught by Tattersall off the bowling of Statham for 152 with the score on 245. After his dismissal, Lowson, who went on to score 120, and Vic Wilson, with a hard-hit unbeaten 51, attacked the bowling and added 87 in an hour. This enabled Yorkshire captain Norman Yardley to declare at lunch.

Washbrook and Ikin then began to make light of a Yorkshire attack that contained Trueman, Wardle and Close. Washbrook was the county's top-scorer with 63 but there were useful contributions from Ikin, Edrich and Hilton. Lancashire captain Nigel Howard issued the White Rose county a challenge, declaring his side's innings closed although 87 runs behind.

Yorkshire accepted the challenge and lost wickets in going for the runs. They declarted at 145 for eight, asking Lancashire to score 233 to win two-and-a-half hours.

They were handicapped by Washbrook having a badly bruised thumb but despite losing Ikin's wicket early, Edrich and Lowson looked set. Then Yardley brought on Brian Close and he created such havoc that the next seven wickets fell for 28 runs. At this point, Washbrook, with thumb heavily strapped, walked to the wicket. Yorkshire claimed the extra half-hour. The last over was bowled in deadly silence but Washbrook and Wilson survived it. The wicket-keeper's score of 11 not out, which was the second highest score of his first-class career, robbed Yorkshire of eight precious points.

LANCASHIRE v YORKSHIRE
at Old Trafford August 2,4,5, 1952

Yorkshire 200 (Hutton 57, Berry 6-52) and 163-8dec (Close 61)
Lancashire 65 (Trueman 5-16, Burgin 5-20) and 166-9
Match Drawn.

Seldom has there been such an exciting finish to a Roses match. Yet those present on the Saturday were given little indication of the excitement to follow, for after rain prevented play until four o'clock, Hutton and Lowson were content to occupy the crease.

On the Monday, Bob Berry perplexed the batsmen on a drying pitch, taking six wickets for 52 runs, but Yorkshire's struggle in scoring 200 was nothing with that of Lancashire, who were dismissed for their lowest total ever against Yorkshire at Old Trafford since 1909.

Eric Burgin, playing in his first ever Roses match, bowled accurate in-swingers to take five for 20 whilst Fred Trueman took five for 16, Lancashire's last four wickets falling for one run.

Had Yorkshire been able to enforce the follow-on, victory would have been almost certain. As it was, holding a 135-run lead, they threw everything into a quick-scoring second innings and were able to declare with eight wickets down. The declaration left Lancashire to score 299 in three and three-quarter hours.

They never appeared likely to get the runs but for a long time, danger of defeat looked equally remote. Then batsmen attempted suicidal strokes and at 157 for seven, the game swung in Yorkshire's favour.

There was still half-an-hour to play as Trueman took the new ball. He clean bowled Statham and Tattersall and ten minutes remained when last man Bob Berry joined Frank Parr. Amid tremendous enthusiasm, the two Lancashire batsmen defied all efforts to dislodge them. Parr, having stayed gallantly for an hour, was 9 not out. Not long after this match, Parr left the game and made something of a name for himself as a jazz musician!

LANCASHIRE v YORKSHIRE
at Old Trafford May 23,25,26, 1953

Lancashire 173 (Wardle 4-53) and 186-7 (Washbrook 65*, Wardle 6-78)
Yorkshire 249-9dec (Sutcliffe 82, Halliday 76, Tattersall 5-56)
Match Drawn.

After losing openers Washbrook and Place cheaply, Lancashire reached 84 for two at lunch-time but in the afternoon session, slumped badly and at

168

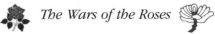

tea were 146 for eight. Only Malcolm Hilton, who scored 44, stood firm against the pace of Trueman and the spin of Wardle in the home side's total of 173.

With Billy Sutcliffe scoring 82 and Halliday 76, Yorkshire had passed the Lancashire total soon after lunch on the second day for the loss of only two wickets when a thunderstorm cleared the ground and play was abandoned.

Play started on time on the third day and as the Yorkshire batsmen threw the bat in an attempt to force the win, Tattersall picked up some cheap wickets, finishing with five for 56. Yardley declared at noon, 66 runs ahead but with Cyril Washbrook scoring 65 not out, well supported by Ken Grieves with 46, Lancashire had no trouble in saving the match. For Yorkshire, Johnny Wardle took six for 78, giving him match figures of ten for 131.

YORKSHIRE v LANCASHIRE
at Bramall Lane August 1,3,4, 1953

Lancashire 373 (G.Edrich 65, Howard 62, Ikin 54, Marner 52, Trueman 6-109)
and 159-7dec (G.Edrich 92)
Yorkshire 177 and 200-6 (Wilson 98)
Match Drawn.

Lancashire took full advantage of winning the toss for despite a period in the afternoon when the scoring rate was pegged down by some accurate bowling by Wardle and Illingworth and some astute field setting, they had reached 360 for eight by the close of play. Top-scorer was Geoff Edrich with 65 though Howard (62) Ikin (54) and Marner (52) all scored half-centuries. For Yorkshire. Fred Trueman produced his best figures in a Roses atch, taking six for 109.

After being bowled out for 373, Lancashire produced some excellent all-round cricket and with Roy Tattersall taking four for 25 and Brian Statham three for 60, Yorkshire were dismissed by tea on the second day, 196 runs behind.

With only three regular bowlers available, Lancashire captain Nigel Howard decided that to enforce the follow-on would prove too great a risk on what was a good wicket opted to bat again. Runs didn't come as quickly as he had hoped and by the close of play, Lancashire were 132 for six, a lead of 328. Once Geoff Edrich had been dismissed eight runs short of his century, Howard declared, leaving Yorkshire 355 runs to win.

With their score at 180 for four, Vic Wilson having made 98, the White Rose county looked to be in a good position. Sadly for both sides, the weather worsened and after three stoppages for rain, the home side abandoned their attempt and what would have been a great match ended as a draw.

YORKSHIRE v LANCASHIRE
at Headingley June 5,7,8, 1954

Yorkshire 348-7dec (Wilson 90, Yardley 78. Watson 52, Close 52*)
No Result.

Whilst it is in the nature of Roses matches to be hampered by the weather, few have been completely restricted to one day.

Hutton made 26 out of the first 27 scored and Wilson and Watson put on 129 for the third wicket, whilst Yardley and Close took toll of the tiring bowlers with another hundred partnership for the sixth wicket. Statham and Tattersall bowled well, but at the end of the day Yorkshire were 348 for seven. Twenty thousand frustrated Yorkshire spectators hung about on the Monday hoping for the rain to stop but neither then nor on the Tuesday would it oblige them!

LANCASHIRE v YORKSHIRE
at Old Trafford July 31, August 2,3, 1954

Yorkshire 248 (Wilson 130*, Yardley 67, Statham 6-76)
Lancashire 73 (Wardle 9-25) and 137 (Appleyard 7-33, Wardle 3-60)
Yorkshire won by an innings and 38 runs.

Yorkshire gained their first post-war victory, beating Lancashire by an innings and 38 runs, yet before Norman Yardley joined Vic Wilson, four wickets were down for 34. When Yardley was out, 170 runs, some of them lucky ones, had been added. The last wicket fell at 248 but Wilson had carried his bat for 130 not out.

On the Monday, only two-and-a-half hours play was possible but in that time, Yorkshire conceived a position of overwhelming advantage over Lancashire. From their weekend's 30 for two, Lancashire collapsed to 73 all out and, following on, scored 17 for no wicket, thus leaving themselves in need of another 158 runs to avoid an innings defeat.

Bowling unchanged through the remainder of the Lancashire first innings, Wardle's figures were 21.2-12-25-9 - it was an achievement of some distinction, even though as the pitch began to dry, the conditions ideally suited the slow left-arm bowler.

The only batsman in double figures was Alan Wharton with 41, more than half Lancashire's total.

170

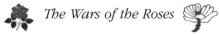
When Lancashire followed-on, they collapsed again, only this time the destroyer was Bob Appleyard, who bowled his medium right-hand deliveries with bewildering variations of pace. He captured seven wickets for 33 runs and though the tail-enders threw the bat, the side were still 38 runs in arrears when the final wicket was taken.

JOHNNY WARDLE (YORKSHIRE)

One of cricket's more colourful characters, Johnny Wardle was a unique slow left-arm leg-break bowler who developed the googly and Chinaman so well that he could bowl it with the same degree of accuracy.

Wardle first demonstrated outstanding ability at Wath Grammar School where, despite topping the batting and bowling averages for the school 1st XI, he was not awarded his school cap!

On leaving schhol, he became an apprentice fitter at Hickleton Main where he could fit in his sporting engagements into a colliery life. In four of five wartime seasons, Wardle won the Yorkshire Council junior bowling prize and in 1940, whilst playing for Brampton, took all ten Rockingham wickets for 36 runs. By 1944 he had moved to play for Denaby and had taken 113 wickets at 7.85 runs apiece when he was given a chance by Yorkshire.

In 1946 he took 70 wickets in the Championship at an average of 23 and was awarded his county cap. After falling out of favour with the Yorkshire committee in 1949, he returned to first team action the following summer with 172 wickets with a best of eight for 26 against Middlesex.

Wardle, who had played the first of his 28 Tests back in 1948 against the West Indies at Port-of-Spain, had taken four for 7 when the Australians collapsed to 35 for eight at Old Trafford in 1953, yet the selectors preferred Tony Lock on English pitches and Wardle's only complete home series was against Pakistan in 1954. In that series, Wardle took 20 wickets at a cost of 8.30 runs each and a best of seven for 56 at the Oval.

Also in that summer of 1954, Wardle had match figures of sixteen for 110 (nine for 48 and seven for 62) against Sussex at Hove before producing his best ever figures of nine for 25 in the Roses match at Old Trafford.

Once he had fine tuned his unorthodox armoury, Wardle became an automatic requirement for the harder surfaces overseas and in 1956-57 he toured South Africa with England. He took twenty-six Test wickets at an average of 13 and headed the tour averages with ninety at 12. His twelve for 89 at Cape Town was regarded by many of his colleagues as the finest spin bowling they had ever seen.

When Wardle returned to Yorkshire, he found a newly elected captain in Ronnie Burnet called up from the Bradford League. Wardle, who was at the peak of his career, was expected to take orders from a 39-year-old with no experience of first-class cricket and so a confrontation was inevitable.

After his selection for the 1958-59 tour of Australia, he was told that he would not be re-engaged for the following season. When he put his name to a number of newspaper articles criticising his county captain and colleagues, he was sacked by Yorkshire and his tour invitation was withdrawn by MCC. The latter decision consdierably weakened the balance of the England side on Australian pitches.

Wardle, who had taken 1,539 wickets at a cost of 18.13 runs apiece, finished his playing days with Cambridgeshire (1963-1969) and in the Lancashire League.

LANCASHIRE v YORKSHIRE
at Old Trafford May 28,30,31, 1955

Lancashire 204 (Washbrook 70) and 230 (Grieves 83*, Close 4-53)
Yorkshire 271 (Watson 94, Tattersall 5-91) and 168-5 (Lowson 63)
Yorkshire won by 5 wickets.

In warm sunny weather, Lancashire, on winning the toss, elected to bat first. Ikin and Place gave the Red Rose county a good start but when Place was bowled by Cowan, Edrich soon followed without scoring. Ikin and Washbrook took the score to 113 before the former was out, after which the middle-order collapsed. Washbrook top-scored with 70 whilst Jordan and Statham batted sensibly, adding 56 in 75 minutes for the ninth wicket.

Len Hutton, who had captained England in the Ashes' winning tour of Australia, was bowled for two by Leeds University student Ken Standring and though four wickets went down for 68, Watson, with the aid of Close, Yardley, Booth and Trueman, pulled the batting together. Watson scored 94 and was extremely unlucky not to reach his hundred. Tattersall was the pick of the Lancashire bowlers, taking five for 91 as Yorkshire were dismissed for 271, a lead of 67 runs.

Batting for a second time Lancashire lost early wickets, and if a simple catch offered by Ken Grieves before he had scored been accepted, Yorkshire would have won with ease. As it was, Grieves, well supported by Hilton and Statham, added 57 and 42 for the eighth and ninth wickets respectively. Eventually he ran out of partners and was 83 not out when Lancashire's tenth wicket fell.

Chasing 164 for victory, Yorkshire began very slowly and by three o'clock had reached 68 for three. Willie Watson, the hero of the first innings, arrived at the crease and, with Lowson, soon dispelled any hopes Lancashire had of winning by hitting 46 in 50 minutes to give the visitors victory by five wickets.

YORKSHIRE v LANCASHIRE
at Bramall Lane July 30, August 1,2, 1955

Yorkshire 312 (Watson 174, ILlingworth 53)
Lancashire 139 and 203-7 (Washbrook 66)
Match Drawn.

Lancashire began magnificently with Brian Statham and Alan Wharton and a rather fortunate run out reducing Yorkshire to 60 for five on a near-per-

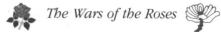

fect batting strip. Willie Watson, so often a thorn in the Lancashire side, was joined by Ray Illingworth and the two of them added 188 for the sixth wicket before Illingworth became Statham's fourth victim when he had scored 53. Next man in Wardle curiously failed to respond to Watson's call, and so ended one of the finest innings of the England football international's career as he was run out for 174.

Lancashire could not cope with the Yorkshire attack and in particular the pace of left-arm Mike Cowan. The visitors were reduced to 60 for seven before Ken Grieves and Malcolm Hilton added 51 in an hour. However, the follow-on was inevitable and though Cowan, who had taken four for 44 in the first innings, struck two early blows, Ikin and Washbrook looked to have retrieved the situation as Lancashire ended the second day on 85 for two.

On the final day Yorkshire, in the shape of Wardle and Close, kept up the pressure and by lunch Lancashire were only 14 runs ahead with just three wickets to fall. Bad light which gave way to rain meant it was 4.30 p.m. before the game could be re-started, and though Yorkshire captain Yardley claimed the extra half-hour, Edrich and Jordan were still there when the last ball was bowled.

WILLIE WATSON (YORKSHIRE)

Despite ducks in his first three innings for Yorkshire Second XI, Willie Watson made his first appearance for Yorkshire in 1939 when he was only nineteen. He had played in three Championship matches before the war and one after it when he was picked for the Rest of England in the second of the 1946 Trial matches for the Australian tour. He made 61, the highest score but one for the Rest's second innings, but he was not given a regular place in the Yorkshire side and was not picked for the tour of Australia!

It was 1947, following Maurice Leyland's retirement, when Watson gained a regular place in the Yorkshire side, scoring 1,331 runs in that glorious summer. Yet he exceeded that the following season when the climate was much damper!

Watson, who was the son of the famous Huddersfield Town and England wing-half Billy Watson, followed in his father's footsteps and after beginning his career with the then Leeds Road club he won four full caps for England, for whom he played in the 1950 World Cup. During his later football career, Watson played for Sunderland and Halifax Town.

When he returned to Yorkshire after his World Cup exploits, he showed a great enthusiasm for cricket and in the few remaining weeks

of the season scored three centuries and finished with an average of more than 70.

In 1951 he became that rarity, a double international, when he played in his first Test against South Africa at Trent Bridge.

When he made his debut against Australia at Lord's in June 1953, Willie Watson played one of the most memorable innings in cricket history. On the last day of this second Test, Watson, who had come in the previous evening with England 12 for three needing an improbable 331 to win, wrote his name indelibly in the game's chronicles for his part in saving the match. First with Denis Compton, and then with Trevor Bailey, Watson batted for five-and-three-quarter hours to save England from defeat and make his first Test century - England went on to win the series and regain the Ashes after 19 years.

After that epic performance, Watson might have been expected to occupy one of the highest places in English cricket, yet he only played in 23 Test matches, scoring 879 runs at an average of 25.85.

For Yorkshire, Watson scored 14,049 runs at an average of 38.28 and a highest score of 214 not out against Warwickshire in 1955.

He left Yorkshire to captain Leicestershire in 1957 and in his four seasons with his adopted county topped the batting averages each summer with a best of 2,212 in 1959. He later became assistant secretary of his new county and a Test selector before emigrating to South Africa in 1968 to become coach to the Wanderers club in Johannesburg.

175

YORKSHIRE v LANCASHIRE
at Headingley May 19,21,22, 1956

Lancashire 214 (Grieves 60) and 217 (Grieves 57)
Yorkshire 134 (Tattersall 6-47) and 144 (Tattersall 8-43)
Lancashire won by 153 runs.

Despite winning the toss and electing to bat, Lancashire lost their first six wickets for 85 runs on a wicket that was at its best on the first day. The turning point was a seventh wicket stand of 42 in an hour between Grieves and Hilton and this was followed by an even more profitable one between Grieves and Jordan which added 52 runs. When Grieves was dismissed by Trueman for 60, the last wicket pair of Jordan and Tattersall put on 35.

Yorkshire started well with Lowson, Padgett and Vic Wilson all reaching their twenties, but they too collapsed and half the side were out for 81. Yorkshire captain Sutcliffe batted very stubbornly but ran out of partners as Bolton-born spinner Roy Tattersall took six for 47 to give Lancashire a surprising lead of 80.

Lancashire's second innings was similar to their first, both in total and the fact that it was Grieves (57) who held it together.

Yorkshire's task of scoring 298 for victory at 70 runs an hour was formidable but with the first 50 on the board, they were ahead of the clock. At 57, Lowson trod on his own wicket whilst attempting a hook shot and though all the Yorkshire batsmen tried to keep up the scoring rate, five wickets were down for 108 with Doug Padgett out for 47. The rest of the side could only add another 36 runs and the triumphant Tattersall had taken eight for 43, the last six of his wickets in 16 overs for 18 runs!

It was quite definitely Roy Tattesall's match as he finished with a match analysis of fourteen for 90.

ROY TATTERSALL (LANCASHIRE)

After playing with Tonge and Bradshaw in the Bolton League, Roy Tattersall joined Lancashire for a career which effectively spanned only nine seasons during which he took 1,168 wickets for the county. His county bowling average of 17.39 is lower than that of Jim Laker, lower indeed than any post-war off-spinner who took more than 1,000 wickets and only George Macaulay, the Yorkshire off-spinner between the wars, took his wickets more cheaply.

176

The Wars of the Roses

Between 1951 and 1954 Tattersall played 16 times for England, taking 58 wickets at 26.18 runs apiece; many better known bowlers have produced much less.

When Tattersall joined the county at the comparitively advanced age of 25, Lancashire's main priority was to find new-ball bowlers and the tall Tattersall's ability to swing the ball away at medium-pace gave him possibilities in this area. After two seasons of mediocre performances, Tattersall decided to forsake seam-up for spin. He started 1950 quietly, but his six for 69 at Edgbaston had much to do with Lancashire's victory. In the next match at Sheffield his five for 60 in Yorkshire's second innings enabled Lancashire to squeeze home by 14 runs. From that point, the season became a personal triumph. He took 163 wickets in the Championship alone and his total haul of 193 wickets at 13.59 runs apiece put him comfortably at the top of the national bowling averages.

Tatt's Test debut came when, in the company of the youthful Statham, he flew out to Australia to reinforce Freddie Brown's beleagured troops in 1950-51. In the summer of 1951 he played in all five Tests against South Africa, taking 21 wickets at 20.90. A rain damaged wicket at Lord's gave him an opportunity which he did not spurn; he took seven for 52 and five for 49 and bowled England to victory by 10 wickets. He was a key member of the England party which toured India in 1951-52. In the drawn series he bowled nearly twice as many overs as anyone elese, taking 21 wickets at 28.33 on unresponsive pitches. Strangely, this excellent performance effectively marked the end of his Test career.

In 1952 Tattersall took 145 wickets at 17.70 runs each but was not selected for any of the Tests. In the following season he took 164 wickets including the remarkable match analysis of fourteen for 73, including the hat-trick against Nottinghamshire at Old Trafford. Another good season in 1954, when he took 117 wickets at less than 17 runs apiece, earned him one Test against Pakistan but it was to be his last appearance for England.

He continued to be an integral part of Lancashire's attack and in the 1956 Whitsun match against Yorkshire at Headingley, he took fourteen for 90, bowling Lancashire to victory by 153 runs. By mid-July, Lancashire were hot on Surrey's heels; Tattersall had taken 91 wickets, lay third in the national averages and had a chance of being first to 100 wickets. At this point, the committee in their wisdom decided to omit Tattersall for the next seven games. Lancashire failed to force victory in four of these games and though he was recalled for the vital game against Surrey at the Oval, where he took six for 32, rain washed out the last two days after the home side had been bowled out for 96.

Over the next four seasons, Tattersall was left out of the side on a number of occasions and one increasingly gained the impression that his career at Old Trafford was over, and so it proved when at the end of the 1960 season, he was not re-engaged.

LANCASHIRE v YORKSHIRE
at Old Trafford August 4,6,7, 1956

Yorkshire 145 and 214-4dec (Padgett 56*, Wilson 54)
Lancashire 157 (Wardle 5-37, Illingworth 5-48) and 132-9
(Washbrook 70, Wardle 5-67)
Match Drawn.

There was no play before lunch on the first day but when the game eventually got underway, the cricket was desperately slow. Yorkshire, who had won the toss and elected to bat, scored just 47 runs for the loss of Lowson's wicket in the two hours leading up to tea. Close and Sutcliffe later put bat to ball but the White Rose county could only muster 145.

Lancashire gained a 12 run lead, mainly through the steady batting of the left-handed Wharton and a typical fast bowler's innings from Cambridge Blue Colin Smith. There was some good bowling by Illingworth and Wardle, who took five wickets apiece.

In their second innings, Yorkshire, in the face of some hostile bowling by Statham, made much better progress with Padgett (56 not out) and

178

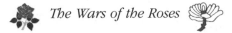

Vic Wilson (54) scoring half-centuries. They were able to declare and set the home side a target of 203 to win at just 48 runs an hour.

Lancashire made a tremendous start with Wharton and Washbrook hitting 102 in 67 minutes before Washbrook mis-hit Wardle and was out for 70, having hit 3 sixes and 7 fours. As so often happens, Wharton was out soon afterwards and from 100 for none, the score crumbled to 128 for nine. When last man Statham joined Hilton, Lancashire were 75 short of victory with 15 minutes play remaining. Hilton snicked a four but runs mattered little. The last over came with Trueman to bowl to Hilton. He beat the bat on a couple of occasions and hit Hilton in the ribs but at the end of play, Lancashire's last two were still there.

LANCASHIRE v YORKSHIRE
at Old Trafford June 8,10,11, 1957

Yorkshire 153 (Wilson 54) and 183 (Illingworth 53, Tattersall 5-51)
Lancashire 113 and 175-9 (Grieves 50)
Match Drawn.

Yorkshire's innings started late because of heavy rain but when it did, only Vic Wilson with a fighting 54 and Bryan Stott (44) provided any resistance. Malcolm Hilton had the remarkable figures of five for 6 from five overs but owed his success to a number of careless strokes from the Yorkshire middle-order.

Lancashire's effort was similar to that of their rivals and when Pullar joined Washbrook, the home side were 46 for four. By good, sensible cricket, the two added 63 for the fifth wicket before Wardle finished off Lancashire's innings in even more dramatic fashion than Hilton had previously done and the Red Rose county were all out for 113.

By the end of the second day, Yorkshire were 87 for four, a lead of 127. Illingworth, who hit a splendid half-century was out early the following morning as was Bryan Stott, who played another useful innings. Trueman and Binks then bludgeoned 45 runs for the ninth wicket before the wicket-keeper was dismissed by Tattersall, who finished with five for 51. Trueman remained unbeaten on 40 as the Yorkshire innings ended at 183.

With only three hours to score the 224 runs needed for victory, Lancashire required a solid start. After Trueman had removed Wharton and Ikin, Ken Grieves came in to hit 50 in 36 minutes, with a six and 9 fours. Cyril Washbrook (41) looked to be leading Lancashire to victory but Wardle and Illingworth got among the ickets. When Trueman trapped Jordan leg-before, nine wickets were down and Yorkshire claimed the extra half-hour.

179

Statham and Tattersall were beaten time and time again but Yorkshire couldn't prize either batsman out and Lancashire clung on for a draw.

YORKSHIRE v LANCASHIRE
at Bramall Lane August 3,5,6, 1957

Lancashire 351 (Wharton 102, Grieves 68, Trueman 5-75)
Yorkshire 151 and 86-5
Match Drawn.

Alan Wharton and Colin Smith gave Lancashire a fine start, putting on 136 for the first wicket. Aided by some unintentionally friendly fielding, Wharton scored the county's first century in a Roses match for eight years. His innings of 102 contained 16 fours, whilst Smith made a striking debut as an opening bat with 42. There were also good knocks from Washbrook, who hit 6 fours and a six before he fell to Pickles for 49, and Ken Grieves, who scored 68 before he too was dismissed by the Yorkshire paceman. Dyson and Greenhough added useful runs as Lancashire's innings ended at 351. Fred Trueman on a fairly flat Sheffield wicket took five for 75 - an heroic effort.

With the exception of Vic Wilson who batted for three hours before being run out for 45, the home side's top-order batsmen had no answer to the bowling of Statham and Smith. Trueman later hit 4 fours and a six before falling, last out to Tattersall. Lancashire, with a first innings lead of exactly 200, enforced the follow-on and after reducing Yorkshire to 32 for three at the end of the second day, it seemed only a matter of time before victory was theirs.

However, heavy rain prevented any play before 3.45 p.m. and by then the wicket was much too wet to offer any assistance to the bowlers. Despite this, Smith and Greenhough picked up a wicket apiece and Washbrook claimed the extra half-hour. Illingworth and Sutcliffe dug in and Yorkshire ended on 86 for five, still 114 runs short of making Lancashire bat again.

YORKSHIRE v LANCASHIRE
at Headingley May 24,26,27, 1958

Yorkshire 64-9dec (Statham 6-16) and 144 (Wilson 54)
Lancashire 138 (Washbrook 51) and 71-2
Lancashire won by 8 wickets.

On one of the coldest days that Roses cricket has ever been played, Yorkshire, captained by Johnny Wardle, won the toss and elected to bat. But

180

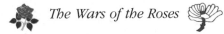

before a ball could be bowled, rain fell and play did not get underway until 4.30 p.m. With the wicket quickly drying, the Yorkshire batsmen had no answer to the speed and accuracy of Brian Statham. Only Ray Illingworth appeared to be able to cope with the Lancashire and England paceman who took six for 16 from 14 overs. In the hope of seizing a quick wicket before bad light stopped play, Wardle optimistically declared at 64 for nine.

Whit Monday was the only fine day of the three but Lancashire, who held out without losing a wicket overnight, were made to struggle. Wardle greeted the sunshine by bowling Barber and Wharton. Then Pickles bowled Pullar and Lancashire were 17 for three. Then Washbrook (51) and Grieves (35) added 87 runs for the fourth wicket, the only two batsmen to reach double figures in a Lancashire total of 138.

Statham again made early inroads into the Yorkshire batting and with both Hilton and Tattersall bowling with great accuracy, the home side were 94 for five. Trueman, Wardle and Appleyard battled hard and between them added another fifty runs to the total.

The wicket was now playing the easiest it had all through the match and Lancashire had little trouble in reaching their target of 71 for victory soon after lunch on the third day.

BRIAN STATHAM (LANCASHIRE)

Brian Statham first played for Lancashire in 1950 and in nineteen seasons and nine MCC tours between then and his retirement in 1968, he took 2,259 wickets in all matches at 16.35 runs each. For Lancashire he took 1,816 wickets at 15.12. No other bowler has taken more wickets for the county.

In his 70 Test matches, home and overseas, Statham claimed 252 wickets at 24.87 runs each.

Somewhat surprisingly, he became a cricketer almost by accident. As a boy he was not particularly interested in cricket and preferred to play soccer or tennis. He played some cricket at school but his interest seems to have ended there.

It was whilst he was serving with the RAF that he first turned his attention seriously to cricket. His unit sports NCO was impressed by the airman's bowling ability and wrote to the Lancashire authorities suggesting they give him a trial. This they did but as it rained, Statham didn't bother to turn up. The following spring he received an invitation from Harry Makepeace asking him to report to Old Trafford. He made his county debut against Kent on his twentieth birthday but it was in the Yorkshire match at Old Trafford in August that Statham first gave notice to the cricket world that a new and exciting fast bowling prospect had arrived.

In his first taste of Roses cricket he found himself bowling to the great Len Hutton. Twice in his first three balls he fell flat on the ground as he ran up to bowl on the slippery surface. Though he did not take Hutton's wicket he finished with five for 52 in his first meeting with the old enemy.

In 1951, his first full season in county cricket, he took 97 wickets at 15 runs apiece, topping Lancashire's bowling averages. He was to remain at the top for the next fifteen seasons.

He stamped himself beyond question as a first-choice Test bowler in the West Indies in 1953-54, then in 1954-55 with Frank Tyson he formed one of the immortal fast-bowling combinations. Though Tyson took most wickets, it was Statham who bowled with sustained fire giving the Australian batsmen no rest. At Lord's in the 1955 Test series against South Africa, Tyson couldn't play and it was Statham who demolished the visitors in their second innings with seven for 39 to give England victory by 71 runs.

Statham's splendid career in county and Test cricket continued through the years, playing his last Test match in 1965 against South Africa when he was recalled for one game at the age of 35. In that one Test he took seven for 145 to prove that on the international scene he was still a force to reckon with.

Statham captained the Lancashire side for three years from 1965 to 1967. He had intended to continue to play until the end of June 1968 but he postponed his final appearance for Lancashire so that he could take part in the Roses match at Old Trafford in August. Statham took the Yorkshire batting by the scruff of the neck to take six for 34 as the White Rose county were bowled out for 61.

After his retirement from first-class cricket, Statham received offers from league clubs, but refused them all, taking the view that he would not be happy bowling flat out against youngsters starting out on their cricketing careers.

Awarded the CBE in 1966 for his services to cricket, Brian Statham is one of the all-time greats.

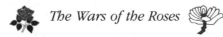

LANCASHIRE v YORKSHIRE
at Old Trafford August 2,4,5, 1958

Yorkshire 166 (Close 61) and 36-0
Lancashire 193 (Washbrook 58*)
Match Drawn.

Cyril Washbrook returned after injury to captain Lancashire in a game that amid interruptions for rain and bad light on each of the three days ended in a draw.

Yorkshire won the toss but only Taylor, Padgett and Close were able to cope successfully with the keen Lancashire attack. Close made a solid 61 in the White Rose county's overnight total of 155 for six. The visitors lost their remaining four wickets for just 11 runs early on the second day.

Lancashire in reply started well with Barber and Wharton putting on 47 for the first wicket but by the time stumps were drawn on the second day, the home side had slumped to 64 for three.

The morning's play on the final day was dominated by Marner (44) and Washbrook (58 not out), both of whom played splendidly. Following the dismissal of Marner, Trueman took three quick wickets to leave Lancashire on 121 for seven but Statham joined Washbrook and the two added 41 to virtually make certain of both first innings and bonus points.

There was little time for Yorkshire to reply but in their second innings they had scored 36 without loss when the game ended.

LANCASHIRE v YORKSHIRE
at Old Trafford May 16,18,19, 1959

Lancashire 282-9dec (Pullar 78, Washbrook 55) and 230-5dec (Pullar 105, Barber 95)
Yorkshire 188 (Padgett 100) and 145 (Padgett 57)
Lancashire won by 179 runs.

With the sun shining brightly, Pullar and Washbrook, who was in his last year of captaincy, laid the foundations of a good Lancashire first innings score of 282 for nine declared.

Yorkshire collapsed against the bowling of Statham and Higgs and when captain Ronnie Burnet joined Doug Padgett, the visitors were 41 for five. The two Yorkshire batsmen added 44 for the sixth wicket with the captain hitting 3 sixes. Padgett went on to play a splendid innings of 100, adding 56 for the last wicket with Mel Ryan who was 12 not out.

183

Ken Higgs was Lancashire's most successful bowler, taking four for 31 as the Red Rose county led by 94 runs on first innings.

After Wharton had been dismissed by Trueman without scoring, Pullar and Barber put on 158 for the second wicket before Don Wilson trapped the former batsman for 105. Barber went on to score 95 but with Lancashire's lead being 324, Washbrook declared the county's second innings closed.

The visitors needed to score at 86 runs an hour and though Bryan Stott launched a few brave hits, he was eventually bowled neck and crop by Statham. Realising that the task was too much for them, the batting turned to the defensive, but even then no-one could stay with Padgett until Illingworth came along. The two added 82 for the fifth wicket before Ken Higgs took two quick wickets, enabling Washbrook to claim the extra half-hour. Yorkshire were 190 runs behind with eight wickets down but five minutes into that final period, the ninth wicket fell. The last pair stayed together for a further twenty minutes but with just five minutes to play, Don Wilson was caught by Grieves off the bowling of Dyson to give Lancashire victory by 179 runs.

GEOFF PULLAR (LANCASHIRE)

Geoff Pullar arrived at Old Trafford in 1954 still an apprentice watchmaker at Samuels and was invited by Lancashire coach Stan Worthington to play in the Second XI. On only his second appearance he hit a big hundred and followed it the next day with a half-century at St Helens in the match against Northamptonshire, for whom a certain Frank Tyson was playing.

Despite making his first-class debut against Surrey in 1954, it was 1957 before he passed a thousand runs for the first time, yet at times his fielding seemed so casual. At one point in 1958, his county captain Cyril Washbrook - one of the earliest and most convinced appreciators of his talent - sent him back from the Oval in the Championship match against Surrey for a spell in the second team. It was characteristic of Pullar that, without argument or resentment, he buckled down to the task of justifying himself. He made 199 runs in three innings (two of them not out) and within a week he was back in the first team, a conscientious if not brilliant fieldsman!

184

It was during that summer of 1958 that Geoff Pullar acquired the nickname of 'Noddy' when Lancashire's Australian all-rounder Ken Grieves found Pullar in rapt attention to the television with the cartoon programme 'Noddy' showing!

Pullar began the 1959 season by playing seven consecutive innings of over fifty. That attracted the Test selectors who chose him for the third Test against India at Headingley. Opening the innings with Gilbert Parkhouse, Pullar scored 75 out of 146, the highest first wicket partnership for England for 26 Tests.

On 23 July 1959, he became the first Lancashire cricketer to score a century in a Test at Old Trafford. His innings of 131 was a truly remarkable score bringing back memories of the prowess of Eddie Paynter, Archie MacLaren, Cyril Washbrook and the Tyldesley brothers. His sudden rise to eminence earned him the position of England's opening batsman on the 1959-60 winter tour of the Caribbean. He amassed a highly creditable 385 runs at an average of 42.77. As England's established opening batsman he made a career-best 175 against South Africa at the Oval in 1960. He scored over a thousand runs on the 1961-62 tour of India and Pakistan, including innings of 119 and 89 in India and 165 in Pakistan. His Test career came to an end when playing against Australia. He strained his groin and simultaneously tore a cartilage while throwing the ball in. He had played in 28 Tests, scoring 1,974 runs at an average of 43.86

He had to miss the whole of the 1963 season but five years later, after scoring 16,853 runs at an average of 35.18 for Lancashire, he followed David Green to Gloucestershire. He joined an exciting West Country side and with Pullar opening the batting they almost won the Championship in his first season. In 1970 his knee problem flared up again and after taking medical advice, he retired.

YORKSHIRE v LANCASHIRE
at Middlesbrough June 3,4,5, 1959

Yorkshire 348 (Stott 110, Close 71, M.Hilton 6-124)
Lancashire 180 (Birkenshaw 5-39) and 151 (Grieves 92)
Yorkshire won by an innings and 17 runs.

In between the two Championship matches, a first-class friendly game was staged at Middlesbrough for cricket followerrs in the north-east.

Lancashire, who didn't arrive at Middlesbrough until the early hours of the morning, were forced to field first. Stott, who scored 110, and Close

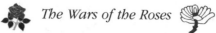

(71) added 117 for Yorkshire's third wicket and helped to build a total of 348. When Lancashire went in to bat they found the wicket taking spin and with Jack Birkenshaw taking five for 39 with his cleverly flighted off-breaks, the Red Rose county were dismissed for 180. Wicket-keeper Geoff Clayton, who was making his Lancashire debut, was the county's top-scorer with 43.

Following-on 168 behind, Lancashire lost their first three wickets for eight runs before Ken Grieves and Noel Cooke added 93 for the fourth wicket. Grieves was the county's top-scorer, falling eight runs short of a deserved century, but the only support he received lower down the order came from young Clayton as Yorkshire ran out winners by an innings and 17 runs with a day to spare.

YORKSHIRE v LANCASHIRE
at Bramall Lane August 1,3,4, 1959

Lancashire 343 (Pullar 109, Greives 63, Booth 62, Dyson 53) and 102-4 (Grieves 56)
Yorkshire 361 (Close 128, Illingworth 74, Higgs 6-85)
Match Drawn.

On an easy-paced Bramall Lane pitch, there was never much chance of an outright result.

Geoff Pullar, with a fine innings of 109, hit his second century of the season in a Roses match whilst Ken Grieves with a hard-hit 63 helped him add 154 for the third wicket. Though Trueman (three for 89) and Platt (four for 82) bowled well, both Booth (62) and Dyson (53) scored half-centuries to help Lancashire to total 343.

Yorkshire struggled against the bowling of Statham and Higgs and their first 50 took two hours. Brian Close then changed the entire course of the game with a magnificent fighting innings. Batting for over five hours, he scored 128, adding 159 for the fifth wicket with Ray Illingworth, who scored 74. With Ronnie Burnet throwing caution to the wind, Yorkshire's first innings lead was 18.

With Yorkshire using seven bowlers, Lancashire, for whom Ken Grieves made 56, were 102 for four when stumps were drawn.

186

YORKSHIRE v LANCASHIRE
at Headingley June 4,6,7, 1960

Yorkshire 96 (Greenhough 4-17) and 117 (Dyson 4-30)
Lancashire 210 (Pullar 121, Wilson 5-49, ILlingworth 5-55) and 5-0
Lancashire won by 10 wickets.

Yorkshire had not beaten Lancashire in Yorkshire since the war.

The home side opted to bat first on a dry and dusty wicket and were all out by three o' clock, completely baffled by the leg-breaks and googlies of Greenhough and Barber. Only Ken Taylor made any headway against the Lancashire spinners.

Lancashire would probably have gone the same way if it hadn't been for a superb innings from Geoff Pullar. The Lancashire and England opener rose to the occasion and hit his third successive Roses century. His innings of 121 was considerably more than half of Lancashire's total and gave his side a lead of 114 runs.

Yorkshire again made a wretched showing in their second innings with only Bryan Stott and Ray Illingworth, who had bowled well in Lancashire's innings, showing any resistance. Again it was Tommy Greenhough who led the way for Lancashire, ending with match figures of eight for 61 as Yorkshire were bowled out for 117.

This left Lancashire with only five runs to make to secure a ten wicket win, the game ending in the middle of the second afternoon.

LANCASHIRE v YORKSHIRE
at Old Trafford July 30, August 1,2, 1960

Yorkshire 154 (Close 63, Statham 5-43) and 149 (Statham 4-23)
Lancashire 226 (Wharton 83, Barber 71) and 81-8 (Ryan 5-50)
Lancashire won by 2 wickets.

Splendid bowling by Statham and Higgs dismissed Yorkshire for a moderate total despite a sound innings of 63 by Brian Close. Lancashire took the lead with only one wicket down due to a second wicket stand of 121 by Barber and Wharton but Yorkshire were so keen in the field that Lancashire were denied bonus points. Lively bowling by Trueman and Ryan slowed matters and they were only 33 in front when the fourth wicket fell.

A heavy storm broke early on the Monday afternoon and when play resumed, Trueman and Ryan rattled out the rest of the side for 39 runs more, 28 of which were made by wicket-keeper Geoff Clayton.

187

Statham again troubled Yorkshire when they went in to bat for a second time and only Phil Sharpe with 46 and the two Wilsons resisted effectively as the White Rose county were dismissed for 149.

Lancashire were left 125 minutes to score 78 but sustained hostility from Trueman and Ryan made the task far from easy. A brilliant return by Padgett ran Barber out with the score on 16 and eleven runs later Wharton was bowled by a devastating ball from Ryan. Ten minutes later, Pullar was well caught by Padgett and so it went on. Marner went for a duck; Collins 11 runs and thirteen minutes later went for two; Statham was caught at the wicket for another duck.

Ken Grieves was joined by Clayton at 43 for six and the two of them added 29 runs in 25 minutes. Grieves was the next man out, caught behind off Ryan. Lancashire had seven wickets down and needed six more runs off the last over of the match bowled by Fred Trueman.

Off the first ball, Clayton pushed a single; the second bowled Greenhough; the third went away off Dyson's pads and the batsmen ran two; the fourth Dyson played into his feet but Clayton scampered a single; Clayton scored another single behind the wicket off the fifth and then Trueman bowled the last ball which Dyson turned away to the boundary for four runs; Lancashire had won by two wickets and completed their first Roses 'double' since 1893.

LANCASHIRE v YORKSHIRE
at Old Trafford May 20,22,23, 1961

Lancashire 216 (Bond 68, Collins 61, Taylor 6-75) and 102 (Illingworth 8-50)
Yorkshire 301 (Close 111, Illingworth 61) and 20-0
Yorkshire won by 10 wickets.

Yorkshire took to the field without Trueman and Platt, their main opening bowlers who were both absent owing to injury. It was Cowan and Taylor who bowled Lancashire out for the modest score of 216, with Taylor, normally a batsman rather than an all-rounder, taking six for 75 with his harmless looking deliveries.

Bond and Collins, both of whom were awarded their county caps on the first day, added 96 for the sixth wicket after early disasters.

On the second day, Yorkshire went ahead with five wickets in hand. Brian Close hit a six and 18 fours, completing his century in 152 minutes and scoring 97 runs to Ray Illingworth's 20 in a sixth wicket stand of 117.

Lancashire started the third day on 37 for 0 but allowed ten maiden overs to be bowled before the first run was scored. From 75 for three, Lancashire collapsed against the off-breaks of Illingworth who took the

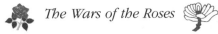 *The Wars of the Roses*

final wicket early in the afternoon to finish with eight for 50 as Lancashire were all out for 102.

Yorkshire did not lose a wicket in scoring the 18 runs needed for victory.

RAY ILLINGWORTH (YORKSHIRE)

Ray Illingworth played his early cricket for Farsley and by the age of fifteen was playing in their first team in the Bradford League. An innings of 148 not out made over several evenings, and attracting a record crowd, brought him more than local attention.

Illingworth spent his National Service at RAF Dishforth where he was given plenty of time to further his cricket career with Farsley, Yorkshire Colts and RAF and Combined Services. He made his debut for Yorkshire in August 1951, scoring 56 against Hampshire at Headingley. He still had another year of his National Service to do and so only played in a handful of matches in 1952, but the following summer he was an important member of the Yorkshire side and scored his maiden century, 146 not out against Essex at Hull. However, as a bowler he had to bide his time behind Appleyard and Wardle and it wasn't until the appointment of Ronnie Burnet as captain and the departure of the two great spinners that Illingworth came into his own. It was a similar situation at Test level, Illingworth having to wait until 1958 before making his debut against New Zealand at Old Trafford.

In 1957 he produced his best bowling figures for the county, taking nine for 42 against Worcestershire at New Road. In 1959, Illingworth made his highest score for Yorkshire, hitting 162 against the Indian tourists. He was a vital member of a team which ended Surrey's domination and gained Yorkshire its last seven Championships. Then, following a dispute over his contract, he moved to Leicestershire as captain. Within a few weeks, Colin Cowdrey had torn an Achilles tendon and he found himself captain of England. Although his tenure was meant to be temporary, he revealed such admirable leadership qualities that he held the post for 31 Tests. His tally of 12 wins and five defeats included a sequence of 19 matches before his first defeat and under his careful direction the Ashes were regained and successfully defended.

By the time he retired from county cricket in his 47th year, Illingworth had led Leicestershire for ten seasons and gained their first Championship in 1975, the Benson and Hedges Cup twice and

189

the Sunday League twice.Yorkshire had achieved little during his absence and in 1979 he was invited back as manager. He did take the White Rose county to a Benson and Hedges semi-final against Essex, but the match was marred by a public dispute between the manager and the senior professional, Geoffrey Boycott, over Boycott's fitness. Boycott didn't play and Yorkshire lost the match! Fifteen days after Illingworth's fiftieth birthday in 1982, the Yorkshire committee sacked Chris Old from the captaincy and handed it to Illingworth, who became the county's oldest appointed captain. His last eighteen months in first-class cricket saw Yorkshire win a trophy for the first time in fourteen years when the White Rose county won the Sunday League Championship.

Illingworth, who had scored 14,986 runs at 27.90 and captured 1,431 wickets at 18.73 runs apiece, left Yorkshire to become a radio and TV commentator and newspaper correspondent before later becoming the England team manager.

YORKSHIRE v LANCASHIRE
at Bramall Lane August 5,7,8, 1961

Lancashire 173 (Ryan 5-58) and 1-0
Yorkshire 174-8dec (Trueman 54*, Higgs 5-47)
Match Drawn.

Heavy rain limited play on the first day to just three-and-a-half hours and in that time Lancashire scored 132 for five, mainly through the resolute concentration of Pullar and Grieves. The England opener scored 46 in two hours whilst the Australian-born all-rounder scored 40 in an hour-and-a-half.

On the second day it took Lancashire 75 minutes to add another 41 runs to their total with Ryan taking five for 58. Jimmy Binks, the Yorkshire wicket-keeper, was in splendid form and took five catches in a row.

Statham and Higgs bowled tightly and the Yorkshire batsmen found it difficult to score runs. Their five leading batsmen were out for 52 nd their first signs of resistance came when Vic Wilson joined Illingworth. It had taken Yorkshire 195 minutes to reach 106 for six when Fred Trueman arrived to enliven the proceedings. He hit an unbeaten 54 out of 68 in just over an hour.

A declaration with Yorkshire just one run ahead gave Lancashire two overs to face before the close of play but rain intervened and prevented a ball being bowled on the last day. Altogether 348 runs were scored in nine and a quarter hours batting, an average of only 37 an hour!

191

The Wars of the Roses

YORKSHIRE v LANCASHIRE
at Headingley June 9,11,12, 1962

Lancashire 308-6dec (Bond 144, Pullar 64) and 112 (Trueman 5-29)
Yorkshire 294 (Sharpe 108*, Greenhough 5-93) and 127-3 (Taylor 60)
Yorkshire won by 7 wickets.

Lancashire batted all day Saturday to score 308 for six with Jack Bond, who went in when the first wicket had fallen for five runs, scoring 144. He was joined in successive century stands by Pullar and Barber. Bond hit 14 fours in a stay of 340 minutes and it was his effort which gave his captain the chance of declaring first thing on the second morning.

Phil Sharpe, who came in at the fall of the third wicket, hit 18 fours and when the last man was bowled with the Yorkshire score on 294, he had carried his bat for 108 out of 176 runs added whilst he was at the crease. Tommy Greenhough's leg-spin had brought him five for 93 but it was to pace that the Yorkshire tail crumbled.

The visitors started the last day at 9 for one but Trueman, who eventually took five for 29, was in an aggressive mood and though Barber and Marner scored a dozen runs each, only Pullar was able to defy him. Lancashire were all out for 112 with 25 of the runs coming from some lusty hitting by Statham for the eighth wicket.

Yorkshire had ample time to get the 127 runs needed to win and chiefly through a polished display by Taylor, who scored 60, obtained them for the loss of three wickets.

JACK BOND (LANCASHIRE)

Jack Bond came from a staunch Methodist family at Little Hulton near Bolton where his father was a cotton spinner and his mother ran the family fish and chip shop. Every Methodist Church had a cricket team where the secretary attended to the equipment and organised practice nets, so it was in this atmosphere of cleaning pads, oiling bats and sometimes making up the numbers in the team that Jack learnt his cricket.

On leaving Bolton School, he joined Walkden in the Bolton League, averaging 44 in his only full season before moving to Radcliffe. His impressive displays with the bat led to him securing a county appointment in 1955. That season saw him play in a couple of games, making his debut against Surrey. He was dismissed by Lock and Laker for 0 and 1 but years later he was fully avenged

when taking a century from both bowlers.

He scored the first of his fourteen centuries in 1959 when he made 101 not out against Nottinghamshire at Trent Bridge. In 1961 he scored 1,701 runs with three centuries to earn his county cap. This was bettered in 1962 when he scored 2,125 runs with a career best 157 against Hampshire at Old Trafford being amongst his five centuries. A successor to Cyril Washbrook, he looked to be establishing himself when West Indian paceman Wes Hall broke Bond's wrist as he attempted to fend off a fearsome delivery in Lancashire's match against the tourists in 1963. It took some time for Bond to recover his old form and over the next few seasons he was in and out of the side, frequently captaining the Second XI. His success in that role led to him acting as deputy captain on a number of occasions when Brian Statham was unfit to play and when the great man retired, Bond was appointed in his place.

In the first season of Bond's leadership, Lancashire rose to sixth place in the County Championship table - the resurgence had begun. In 1969, the year of its inception, Lancashire won the new John Player League Championship and by their shrewd pacing of an innings, tight fielding and accurate bowling, Bond and his men proved themselves masters of limited overs cricket. In 1970, Lancashire won the John Player League Championship for the second year in succession and the Gillette Cup for the first time.

The 1971 season was a little less successful. Third position was maintained in the Championship but the John Player title went to Worcestershire. It was in the Gillette Cup this year however that Lancashire captured the imagination of the public with a series of brilliant victories culminating in victory in the final over Kent. Chasing Lancashire's total of 224 for seven, Kent, with Asif Iqbal on 89, were going well when Bond changed the whole course of the game with a magnificent catch to dismiss the Pakistani international. In 1972 Jack Bond led Lancashire to their third successive Gillette Cup Final victory over Warwickshire. At the end of that season, feeling that his playing days were coming to an end, he announced his retirement. After a short spell on the coaching staff, he left to play for Nottinghamshire for a year. Since the mid 1970s, Bond has coached at King William College on the Isle of Man, been a Test selector, run a public house and been a first-class umpire. He also became manager of Lancashire, helping them to win the Benson and Hedges Cup in 1984, but he left shortly afterwards, leaving people with the memory that it was he who put Lancashire cricket back on top.

LANCASHIRE v YORKSHIRE
at Old Trafford August 4, 6, 7, 1962

Yorkshire 235 (Sharpe 112, Statham 6-68) and 149-1dec (Hampshire 71*, Sharpe 60*)
Lancashire 202 (Bond 109) and 50-1
Match Drawn.

Brian Statham and Colin Hilton shot down Yorkshire's early wickets so quickly that six were out for 79. It was again Phil Sharpe who saved the White Rose side, though he had no support until Trueman arrived at the crease. The pair of them added 80 runs in an hour and when Trueman departed, Sharpe, with some assistance from Don Wilson, went confidently on to his hundred. It was Sharpe's second Roses century of the season and took him 273 minutes.

Lancashire struggled hard to overhaul Yorkshire's total of 235; that they failed by 33 runs was certainly not the fault of Jack Bondf, who came in at the fall of the first wicket at 11 and scored 109 out of 191 in five hours with 2 sixes and 10 fours.

On the last day, John Hampshire with 71 and Phil Sharpe with 60 added an unbeaten 115 in 95 minutes for the second wicket and this enabled Yorkshire to declare at 149 for one. Lancashire were asked to get 183 runs in 143 minutes and were 50 for one with Bond and Barber at the wicket when rain curtailed play.

194

YORKSHIRE v LANCASHIRE
at Bramall Lane June 1,3,4, 1963

Lancashire 151 (Clayton 50) and 123 (Wilson 5-57)
Yorkshire 384-6dec (Boycott 145, Stott 143)
Yorkshire won by an innings and 110 runs.

It seemed as if Yorkshire were lucky to lose the toss as Trueman and Ryan accounted for Lancashire's first five batsmen for 28 runs. Then Grieves and Clayton took the score to 61 before the Australian all-rounder was dismissed. Wicket-keeper Clayton with 50, and to a lesser extent Brian Statham with 33, rescued Lancashire, for without their contributions they would not have reached so mediocre a total as 151.

By the end of play, Yorkshire were 82 for three but on the Monday, Stott and Boycott, who scored his first century for the county, added 249 for the fourth wicket in five and a quarter hours. Boycott scored 145 with his off-side play being especially prominent and Stott 143, a confident innings that contained 19 fours. Their partnership enabled Yorkshire to declare at 384 for six, a lead of 233 runs.

Lancashire were 28 for two overnight but collapsed in a little over ninety minutes on Tuesday to the left-arm spin of Don Wilson, who took five for 57. Only Brian Booth, Marner and Clayton reached double figures as Yorkshire won by an innings and 100 runs, their heaviest victory since 1938.

GEOFF BOYCOTT (YORKSHIRE)

The most prolific, single-minded and controversial of post-war batsman, Geoff Boycott's early interest in the game prompted his family to send the ten-year old to Johnny Lawrence's Cricket School at Rothwell, fourteen miles from his Fitzwilliam home. He joined Ackworth Cricket Club and by the age of thirteen was playing for their first team in the Yorkshire Council. Two years later the bespectacled Boycott joined Barnsley in the Yorkshire League before moving to Leeds, who were then captained by Billy Sutcliffe.

Boycott made his Yorkshire debut in 1962, making just 4 opening against the touring Pakistanis at Bradford. After appearing in a handful of Championship matches he returned to the

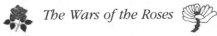

Colts, but in 1963, in the match against Lancashire at Bramall Lane, he scored his maiden century (145), helping Bryan Stott to add 249 for the fourth wicket on a difficult track. Boycott hit another Roses century at Old Trafford and ended the summer with 1,628 runs at an average of 45.22. He began 1964 with three centuries and a 77 in the opening six matches and was selected for the first Test against Australia at Trent Bridge where he scored 48. In the final Test of that series at the Oval, Boycott made his first hundred for England, scoring 113 in the drawn match.

In 1967 Boycott scored the first of seven double-centuries for Yorkshire when he made 220 not out against Northamptonshire. That same summer, Boycott scored 246 not out in the first Test against India at Headingley. It was an innings that brought censure from the selectors and he was dropped for slow scoring.

In 1971 Boycott was appointed Yorkshire captain - but it certainly didn't affect his batting as he scored 2,405 runs at an amazing average of 100.12. Boycott, who carried his bat through an innings on eight occasions, did so for 182 out of 320 against Middlesex at Lord's that summer.

Despite his self-imposed exile of 30 Test matches (1974-77) and three-year banishment for joining a rebel tour of South Africa, Boycott realised his ambition of scoring the then record aggregate of runs in Test cricket - 8,114 at an average of 47.72.

In the match against Australia at Headingley in 1977, Boycott became the first player to score his 100th first-class hundred in a Test match.

Boycott, who lost the captaincy to Hampshire in 1979, later became the centre of a traumatic schism in the Yorkshire Club; sacked as a player in 1983, he was reinstated after his supporters overthrew the committee and elected him on to its successor.

Although Boycott, who went on to play for Yorkshire until 1986, commanded a full range of strokes and was especially adept at cover-driving off the back foot, he was very rarely motivated to take an attack apart. For Yorkshire he scored 32,570 runs at an avaerage of 57.85 and a highest score of 260 not out against Essex in 1970.

On retirement from the game he became a popular, insightful and opinionated television commentator, but, as throughout his playing career, controversy has followed him.

LANCASHIRE v YORKSHIRE
at Old Trafford August 3,5,6, 1963

Yorkshire 345-8dec (Boycott 113, Sharpe 106) and 63-1
Lancashire 237 (Marner 83, Grieves 78, Trueman 5-50)
Match Drawn.

Rain at Old Trafford came down persistently at tea-time on the first day with Yorkshire scoring just under 200 for the loss of one wicket. On the Monday, Sharpe and Boycott went on to defy the Lancashire bowlers by scoring centuries, each in his own characteristic fashion. Boycott's slow-ish but never tedious innings was his second against Lancashire in the seson. Yorkshire, hitting out, lost a few cheap wickets before Close, their new captain, declared at 345 for eight.

Yorkshire's only chance of a win was to dismiss Lancashire cheap-ly twice. The Red Rose county lost three wickets quite cheaply but then Grieves and Marner stayed together until they had evaded the follow-on. Once this partnership had been broken, Trueman tore the rest of the Lancashire batting to pieces to end with five for 50.

However, time had been swallowed up and Yorkshire finished the day and the match with an hour's placid batting for the loss of one wicket.

LANCASHIRE v YORKSHIRE
at Old Trafford May 16,18,19, 1964

Yorkshire 354-3dec (Taylor 153, Boycott 131) and 83-1dec
Lancashire 284-9dec (Pullar 128) and 129-7
Match Drawn.

Geoff Boycott and Ken Taylor were not parted until they had scored 236 for the first wicket. Boycott's 131 was his third Roses century in succes-sive games. Taylor's 153 was equally as powerful. The two batsmen had put Yorkshire into a strong position and their total of 354 for three was judged sufficient to warrant a declaration first thing on Monday morning.

Lancashire's first innings seemed to be a succession of partnerships between Geoff Pullar and whoever happened to be at the other end. Marner and Pullar added 80, whilst Clayton and Pullar put on 64 for the eighth wicket. Pullar was eventually dismissed for 128 on the Tuesday morning, with half of his total coming in boundary strokes.

Lancashire declared 70 runs behind Yorkshire's total before the White Rose county scored a quick-fire 83 for the loss of one wicket before

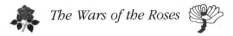

doing likewise. Set to score 154 runs for victory in 105 minutes, Lancashire made a gallant attempt. They lost five wickets for 64 runs, three of them to Fred Trueman who was bowling at his most fiercest. In most circumstances, Lancashire would have put up the shutters but Clayton hit hard and at the close of play, Lancashire were 25 runs short with three wickets in hand. With Geoff Clayton in such a mood, who can say what the result might have been if there had been another thirty minutes play.

YORKSHIRE v LANCASHIRE
at Headingley August 1,3,4, 1964

Lancashire 101 (Illingworth 4-9, Trueman 4-35) and 120 (Nicholson 7-32)
Yorkshire 352 (Binks 75, Hutton 64, Boycott 62, Hampshire 51, Ramadhin 8-121)
Yorkshire won by an innings and 131 runs.

With the exception of Geoff Pullar, who made 29, Lancashire's top-order batsmen succumbed to the fiery pace of Fred Trueman, whilst the other half fell to the leg-breaks of Ray Illingworth. In forty-six deliveries, he took four wickets for 9 runs as Lancashire were bowled out for 101.

When Yorkshire batted, only Padgett and Illingworth failed completely and although West Indian Test bowler Sonny Ramadhin took eight for 121 in 50 dedicated overs, a number of Yorkshire's batsmen enjoyed enough batting practice to give their side a lead of 251 runs. Yorkshire's leading run-getters were wicket-keeper Binks with 75, Hutton 64, Boycott 62 and Hampshire 51.

Faced with this heavy disadvantage, Lancashire again failed disastrously. England opener Geoff Pullar was the only Lancashire batsman to resist. He carried his bat for 33 but received little support from his colleagues. Yorkshire's Rhodesian-born pace bowler Tony Nicholson bowled accurately to take seven for 32. After half an hour's play on the Tuesday morning, Nicholson picked up his last two wickets and Yorkshire had won another crushing victory by an innings and 131 runs.

LANCASHIRE v YORKSHIRE
at Old Trafford June 5,7,8, 1965

Lancashire 218 (Knox 108) and 187 (Trueman 4-59)
Yorkshire 262 (Sharpe 60, Boycott 53) and 111-5
Match Drawn.

Making his debut at Old Trafford was Gerry Knox, a strong and solid batsman who had done sterling work for Northumberland. Against eager

199

bowling, especially by Richard Hutton, who ended up with four for 38, he scored a century. In fact, his score of 108 was almost half of Lancashire's total as they were bowled out for 218.

Boycott continued his run of good Roses scores with an excellent half-century, whilst Phil Sharpe's 60 was typical in its doggedly powerful way. They scored 262, a lead of 44 runs over the Red Rose county.

When Lancashire batted a second time, Trueman was in a hostile mood and the top-order batsmen had to face a barrage of short-pitched deliveries. In fact, the only Lancashire batsman to show any courage against this type of delivery was Ken Higgs who fought hard and unexpectedly. Lancashire were eventually all out for 187, leaving Yorkshire to score 144 in a limited time to win.

They lost more wickets than they were prepared to throw away in haste and when the last over was bowled, they were still 33 short of their target with five wickets in hand.

YORKSHIRE v LANCASHIRE
at Bramall Lane July 31, August 2,3, 1965

Lancashire 175 (Pilling 60, Sullivan 53, Trueman 5-47) and 74 (Wilson 4-35)
Yorkshire 194-3dec (Hampshire 110*, Padgett 72) and 56-3
Yorkshire won by 7 wickets.

Lancashire's first innings total of 175 contained two admirable efforts by two of the county's younger batsmen. Harry Pilling, one of the game's smallest cricketers, made 60, whilst John Sullivan, a promising all-rounder promoted from the second team, scored 53. These two stood up manfully to Fred Trueman, which is more than can be said of their colleagues.

Yorkshire's first innings was short, yet entertaining. Out of the 194 for three, scored before Clsoe declared, Hampshire made 110 not out and Padgett 72.

Lancashire in their second innings had no answer to the spin of Wilson and Illingworth. Baffling them at one end was Don Wilson who took four for 35 and bewildering them at the other was Ray Illingworth, who came on after Fred Trueman had broken through with two early wickets.

All Lancashire could muster was 74, so setting Yorkshire just 56 to win. This was easily achieved for the loss of three wickets. It was Yorkshire's sixtieth victory in 179 Roses matches.

200

The Wars of the Roses

YORKSHIRE v LANCASHIRE
at Headingley May 28,30,31, 1966

Lancashire 57 (Trueman 5-18, Waring 3-23) and 144 (Waring 7-40, Trueman 2-26)
Yorkshire 196-9 (Close 48*) and 6-0
Yorkshire won by 10 wickets.

Headingley's Whitsun game produced a Yorkshire victory, the match ending an hour before time on the second day. But it was won and lost on the first morning when Fred Trueman tore the heart out of Lancashire's batting, taking four wickets for seven runs. Five men were out for 15 and half-an-hour after lunch, Lancashire had given up the ghost and were all out for 57. Trueman, in sparkling form, had taken five wickets for 18 runs.

Boycott failed to get his fourth Roses hundred, but Hampshire, Padgett and Taylor all showed the face of the bat; Brian Close was Yorkshire's top-scorer with an unbeaten 48.

Lancashire began their second innings 139 runs behind and it wasn't long before Trueman drew first blood. The only redeemable feature of Lancashire's innings was a stand between Knox and Lever, who along with Ken Higgs, who was unbeaten on 13, were the only players to reach double figures. Yorkshire's John Waring, from Ripon, took seven for 40 as Lancashire were dismissed for 144, leaving Yorkshire just six to win.

FRED TRUEMAN (YORKSHIRE)

Fred Trueman was Yorkshire's greatest fast bowler, liberally distributing bouncers and bluster from his earliest days in the Yorkshire team, which began with a match against Cambridge University in 1949. He was still working at Maltby Main, often working night shifts in order to play cricket, when in 1950 he was somewhat surprisingly chosen for a Test trial at Bradford. Though he had little opportunity to show what he could do, he did remove Len Hutton's off stump! In 1951, Trueman performed the first of four hat-tricks for Yorkshire, in the match against Nottinghamshire at Trent Bridge. At the end of that summer he was summoned by the RAF for National Service but thankfully for Yorkshire his employers proved to be cricket lovers and

Trueman missed very few matches.

After taking 32 Championship wickets at 14 runs apiece in the opening four games of 1952, there was no question that England had to select him for the first of his 67 Tests. Playing against India at Headingley, he reduced the tourists to 0 for 4 in their second innings by taking three wickets in eight balls. He finished that series with a record 29 wickets. A few problems on his first tour sowed the seeds of his reputation for being a little tricky to handle. It was a tragedy for English cricket that those early difficulties cost him many Tests and several tours.

In 1954 he took eight for 28 before lunch on the first day for Yorkshire in their match against Kent at Dover and followed it up the following season with his second hat-trick against Nottinghamshire at Scarborough. Trueman's third hat-trick came in 1958 against the MCC at Lord's and five years later he performed the feat for a fourth time, and a third against Nottinghamshire, in the match at Bradford. There were match figures of twelve for 62 against Hampshire at Portsmouth in 1960 and twelve for 58 against Leicestershire at Sheffield in 1961

On the 1962-63 tour of New Zealand, Trueman passed Brian Statham's world Test record of 242 wickets, his analysis of seven for 75 remains the record for Christchurch Tests and for Enfgland in New Zealand. In 1963, Trueman set the England v West Indies series record with 34 wickets, including match figures of twelve for 119 at Edgbaston when he ended with a six for 4 spell from twenty-four balls. In 1964 Trueman became the first player to take 300 wickets in Test matches when he dismissed Neil Hawke of Australia, going on to take 307 wickets at 21.57 runs apiece.

For Yorkshire, Trueman took 1,745 wickets at 17.13 runs apiece, whilst his total of 6,852 runs at an average of 15.15 included scores of 104 against Northamptonshire in 1963 and 101 against Middlesex in 1965.

In 1972, having left Yorkshire four years earlier, Trueman played Sunday League cricket for Derbyshire and dismissed three of his former Yorkshire colleagues in a televised match.

Trueman, who was awarded the OBE for his services to cricket in 1989, served the Yorkshire Committee until swept away in the Boycott tide and thereafter refused to stand again although he has remained an honorary life member.

LANCASHIRE v YORKSHIRE
at Old Trafford July 30, August 1,2, 1966

Yorkshire 146-7dec (Close 54*, Lloyd 4-39) Second innings forfeited
Lancashire 1-0dec and 133 (ILlingworth 5-33)
Yorkshire won by 12 runs.

One of the strangest games in Roses history saw Lancashire lose by 12 runs after declaring at 1 for 0 in their first innings with Yorkshire forfeiting their second innings.

The first day saw an hour-and-a-half's cricket and the second day none at all. After lunch on the final day, Yorkshire declared at 146 for seven with Close unbeaten on 54. Lancashire received two balls and astonishingly declared, and perhaps even more astoundingly still, Yorkshire forfeited their second innings, leaving Lancashire to score 147 to win.

Close gave Trueman just three overs and kept Nicholson on long enough for Hampshire to make a brilliant one-handed catch and for Binks to dismiss his sixty-third Roses victim. Close then caught Green and Worsley only inches from the bat and when David Lloyd went at 110, twenty-five minutes still remained. Lancashire's last pair, Greenhough and Goodwin, seemed to be coping well until Close brought Illingworth back. His last ball of the over, bowled from round the wicket, had Greenhough unmistakably leg-before to give Yorkshire their first 'double' since the war.

LANCASHIRE v YORKSHIRE
at Old Trafford May 27,29,30, 1967

Match Abandoned without a ball being bowled.

YORKSHIRE v LANCASHIRE
at Bramall Lane August 5,7,8, 1967

Lancashire 183 (Pullar 104) and 206-6dec (Pilling 82*)
Yorkshire 207 (Close 61, Statham 5-82) and 75-4
Match Drawn.

In a game played at a funereal pace, Lancashire's Geoff Pullar scored 104, his fifth Roses century, out of his side's total of 183 all out. After Tony Nicholson had removed both Barry Wood and Harry Pilling with just three

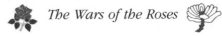

runs on the board, Richard Hutton took the wickets of Atkinson, Snellgrove and Sullivan to leave the visitors on 26 for five. Pullar was then joined by David Lloyd and the two added 94 for the sixth wicket. But the remaining Lancashire batsmen seemed afraid of playing their shots on what was a dubious wicket.

Geoff Boycott fell to Brian Statham before a run had been scored and only Phil Sharpe (45) and Brian Close (61) seemed to bat with any real confidence against the accurate seam bowling of Statham and Higgs. Statham finished with five for 82 as Yorkshire ended their innings with a lead of 24 runs.

In their second innings, Lancashire declared at 206 for six with Harry Pilling scoring an unbeaten 82. Yorkshire's Phil Sharpe took six slip catches in the match, just one short of equalling the county record.

Yorkshire needed 183 for victory but with Boycott top-scoring with 54, settled for a draw, finishing the game on 75 for four.

YORKSHIRE v LANCASHIRE
at Headingley June 1,3,4, 1968

Lancashire 176 (Trueman 5-45) and 116 (Trueman 3-17)
Yorkshire 348 (Padgett 105, Taylor 85, Hampshire 56)
Yorkshire won by an innings and 56 runs.

In a fairly lack-lustre Lancashire batting display, only opener Graham Atkinson with 42 and David Hughes with an unbeaten 30 provided any resistance. Fred Trueman took five for 45, including removing the off stump of the Indian wicket-keeper Farokh Engineer for 13 in what was his Roses' debut.

The placid Headingley wicket held no problems for the home side with Doug Padgett scoring 105, his second Roses century. He was well supported by Ken Taylor (85), Jackie Hampshire (56) and Ray Illingworth (49). Surprisingly, Yorkshire lost their last three wickets without a run being scored, but their total of 348 still gave them a lead of 172 runs.

After losing first innings top-scorer Atkinson in the opening over, Lancashire never recovered and were bowled out for 116 to give Yorkshire victory by an innings and 56 runs. Geoff Pullar hung around to score 35 but all the Yorkshire bowlers took wickets, with Don Wilson being the most successful, taking four for 32 from 26.2 overs.

LANCASHIRE v YORKSHIRE
at Old Trafford August 3,4,5, 1968

Lancashire 162 (Hutton 5-52, Nicholson 4-64) and 151 (Wood 55)
Yorkshire 61 (Statham 6-34) and 189-5 (Close 77*)
Match Drawn.

In what was Brian Statham's last first-class match, Lancashire won the toss and elected to bat. Richard Hutton (five for 52) and Tony Nicholson (four for 64) both bowled well for Yorkshire as the home side were dismissed for 162, opener David Lloyd top-scoring with 26.

Yorkshire faced an awkward last hour or so and, with Statham and Higgs at their best, collapsed to 34 for eight at the end of the first day. When Statham bowled Don Wilson with just four runs added, it looked as if Yorkshire were heading for their lowest score since 1932 when they were bowled out for 46 at Bradford. However, a last wicket stand of 23 by Hutton and Nicholson helped them reach 61 before a disastrous run

The Yorkshire team that was so successful in the 1960's, both in Roses matches and the County Championship:

Back row: Waring, Sharpe, Binks, Wilson, Hutton, Hampshire, Padgett, Boycott,
Front row: Illingworth, Close, Trueman, Taylor

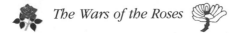

out ended their resistance. Brian Statham had bowled unchanged to take six for 34 in 17.5 overs - it was a majestic piece of bowling.

In Lancashire's second innings, it was Ossett-born opener Barry Wood, with an innings of 55, who helped the Red Rose county to a total of 151.

Needing 253 for victory on what was undoubtedly a bowler's wicket, Yorkshire ended on 189 for five with Brian Close 77 not out. There were some Yorkshire members who argued that Close had enough time to win the match and that the White Rose county made no real effort to do so. Others saw it as a magnificent rearguard action against two of the country's finest opening bowlers.

LANCASHIRE v YORKSHIRE
at Old Trafford May 24,26,27, 1969

Lancashire 243-9dec (Lloyd 66)
No Result.

In a rain affected match, there was only time for Lancashire's first innings. The home side declared at 243 for nine with David Lloyd top-scoring with 66. He was well supported by Indian Test wicket-keeper Farokh Engineer, whose innings of 44 came to an end when he was brilliantly caught and bowled by Chris Old.

The pick of the Yorkshire bowlers was Don Wilson, who after bowling David Lloyd went on to take four for 55 from 20 overs.

YORKSHIRE v LANCASHIRE
at Bramall Lane August 2,4,5, 1969

Lancashire 171 (Lever 57, Old 5-34) and 183 (Engineer 96, C.Lloyd 50)
Yorkshire 290-8dec (Boycott 80, Hampshire 62, Lever 5-61) and 64-6
Match Drawn.

The return match at Sheffield, set aside for Doug Padgett's benefit, resulted in a remarkable finish. Yorkshire, on winning the toss, put Lancashire in to bat and with Chris Old at his best, reduced the Red Rose county to 94 for eight. Todmorden-born Peter Lever, better known for his bowling, then proceeded to score 57 with some hefty blows all around the wicket to take Lancashire to 171 all out.

Lever then took the honours with the ball, taking five for 61 as Yorkshire declared at 290 for eight. Geoff Boycott had made 80 when he was adjudged leg-before to Lever, whilst Jackie Hampshire had scored 62 before being brilliantly caught by David Lloyd off the bowling of Simmons. Lloyd also caught the beneficiary Padgett for 21.

Despite losing David Lloyd and Harry Pilling to the bowling of Chris Old with just 10 runs on the board, Lancashire seemed to be back in the game after the county's two overseas players, Engineer (96) and Clive Lloyd (50), had put on 140 for the third wicket. But they then collapsed against some good bowling by Don Wilson, who took four for 48 from 33.1 overs, and were all out for 183.

Yorkshire were left with just 65 runs to win in 19 overs but with Higgs and Lever bowling with great accuracy, they still required one run to win when Higgs began the last over. In that over, a maiden, Higgs managed to dismiss Leadbeater, Wilson and Hutton - and the game was drawn!

YORKSHIRE v LANCASHIRE
at Headingley May 23,25,26, 1970

Lancashire 381 (Wood 105, Engineer 70, D.Lloyd 64, Nicholson 5-116) and 25-0
Yorkshire 121 (Lever 4-51) and 281 (Boycott 71, Hutton 51)
Lancashire won by 10 wickets.

Lancashire's opening batsmen David Lloyd and Barry Wood put on 151 for the first wickets as Yorkshire's bowlers toiled on a flat Headingley wicket. Lloyd was the first to go, leg-before to Cope for 64, but Wood was the county's top-scorer with 105, his first Roses century. There were also useful contributions from the county's overseas players with Engineer making 70 and Clive Lloyd 45 in a total of 381. Former Rhodesian policeman Tony Nicholson took five for 116.

After Ken Shuttleworth had removed Yorkshire's first three batsmen - Boycott, Padgett and Sharpe - the White Rose county never recovered and with Peter Lever taking four for 51 were bowled out for 121 and forced to follow-on.

Boycott (71) and Hutton (51) were the only Yorkshire batsmen to get to grips with the Lancashire attack, who were without Shuttleworth. The St Helens-born bowler, who modelled his action on Fred Trueman, had suffered an injury whilst bowling in Yorkshire's first innings and was unable to bowl. The home side were dismissed for 281, leaving Lancashire needing just 22 to win. They reached their target without loss to inflict a ten wicket defeat on their rivals

The Wars of the Roses

LANCASHIRE v YORKSHIRE
at Old Trafford August 29,31, September 1, 1970

Lancashire 430-7dec (Wood 144, Hayes 82, Pilling 66, C.Lloyd 64) and 61-1dec
Yorkshire 282-3dec (Boycott 98, Hutton 81*) and 45-1
Match Drawn.

When Yorkshire visited Old Trafford for the second Roses match of the summer, they were only seven points from the top of the County Championship.

However, after Lancashire had won the toss and batted, their first innings total of 430 for seven declared put paid to the White Rose county's chances. Barry Wood scored 144, his second Roses century of the season, and with Harry Pilling (66) put on 183 for the second wicket. There were fine innings from Frank Hayes (82 not out) and Clive Lloyd (64) as Yorkshire's bowlers, with the exception of Richard Hutton (three for 47), were made to suffer.

In reply, Yorkshire did not try to force the pace and after Geoff Boycott had been caught behind by Engineer off the bowling of Lever, two runs short of his hundred, Hampshire and Hutton blunted the Lancashire attack. Both batsmen were undefeated, Hampshire on 49 and Hutton on 81 when the visitors declared at 282 for three.

In a game of declarations, Lancashire had scored 61 for one when they closed their second innings, leaving Yorkshire 210 to win in just over two hours.

However, after losing Geoff Boycott to the first ball of the match, Yorkshire made no effort to go for the runs and at the end of thirty overs, bowled by six Lancashire bowlers, they were 45 for one.

LANCASHIRE v YORKSHIRE
at Old Trafford May 29,31, June 1, 1971

Lancashire 168 (Hutton 6-38) and 75 (Hutton 5-24)
Yorkshire 79 (Lever 5-27) and 103-6
Match Drawn.

After Richard Hutton and Chris Old had demolished the Lancashire top-order, Ken Snellgrove (37) and Farokh Engineer (49) put on 57 for the fifth wicket before Hutton came back to mop up the tail to finish with six for 38 from 19.2 overs as Lancashire were bowled out for 168.

Yorkshire and England opening batsman Geoff Boycott was run out for nine and though Woodford and Padgett took the score to 43, both

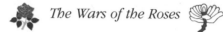

batsmen were dismissed at that total. Hampshire and Leadbeater added 18 for the fourth wicket but then in a devastating spell of bowling by Peter Lever (five for 27 off 24.3 overs) and David Hughes (three for 10 off eight overs), Yorkshire lost their next six wickets for just three runs! A last wicket partnership of 15, in which Geoff Cope scored an unbeaten 13, helped the visitors to reach 79.

Lancashire certainly needed their first innings lead of 89 runs, for in their second innings they were bowled out for just 75 with Richard Hutton taking five for 24 to finish with match figures of eleven for 62.

With just over three hours play remaining, Yorkshire were set 165 to win but with Boycott absent ill, they decided not to go for the target and finished on 103 for six with John Hampshire the top-scorer on 44.

YORKSHIRE v LANCASHIRE
at Bramall Lane, July 31 August 2,3, 1971

Yorkshire 320-5dec (Boycott 169, Hampshire 83) and 54-0
Lancashire 277 (Pilling 56, Engineer 50, Hutton 5-58)
Match Drawn.

In the return game at Bramall Lane, Yorkshire opening batsman Phil Sharpe was dismissed before he had scored a run and though Boycott and Padgett took the score to 80, the latter batsman became Lever's second victim when he edged a fast rising delivery to Engineer. Boycott and Hampshire added 186 for the third wicket before the Thurnscoe-born batsman was run out for 83. Boycott went on to score another monumental century, dominating the Lancashire bowlers to the tune of 169 out of a total of 320 for five declared.

After Lancashire openers Lloyd and Wood had gone cheaply, the rest of the county's top-order made useful contributions - Pilling (56) Snellgrove (48) Engineer (50) and Bond (36) - though Clive Lloyd had to retire hurt after being hit on the forearm by a Tony Nicholson delivery. The Red Rose county were bowled out for 277 with Richard Hutton once again Yorkshire's best bowler with five for 58 from 27.2 overs.

Yorkshire had a first innings lead of 43 runs but then rain interrupted the rest of the proceedings and at the close of play, Yorkshire's opening pair of Sharpe and Leadbeater had taken the score to 54 without loss.

YORKSHIRE v LANCASHIRE
at Headingley May 27,29,30, 1972

Yorkshire 253-8dec (Boycott 105) and 95-9dec (Lever 5-27)
Lancashire 190 (Engineer 69, Nicholson 7-49) and 36-2
Match Drawn.

There was a bleak start to the match which was set aside for Don Wilson's benefit as a cold wind swept the ground, reducing the number of spectators on the first day to around 1,500.

Geoff Boycott scored his fifth century in Roses matches and can seldom have played better. He scored 82 in an opening stand of 119 with Phil Sharpe and went on to score his hundred out of 147. Throughout that time he offered just one chance when on 92 he drove back at shoulder height to Ken Shuttleworth. The St Helens-born paceman eventually bowled Boycott for 105 and finished as Lancashire's most successful bowler with three for 52.

As rain began to fall, Yorkshire declared at 253 for eight.

The wicket began to deteriorate and at times the ball bounced very nastily. Tony Nicholson and Chris Old reduced Lancashire to 21 for three with both Lloyds and Pilling back in the pavilion. Nicholson then removed opening batsman Barry Wood for 39 before a sixth wicket stand of 90 between Engineer (69) and Hughes (32) went some way to repairing the damage. Nicholson took seven for 49 as Lancashire were bowled out for 190.

Rain then caused several interruptions and Yorkshire, who had struggled against the bowling of Peter Lever (five for 27), declared at 95 for nine to leave the visitors needing 159 in just under two hours.

Sadly there was more rain and with Lancashire 36 for two, the game was abandoned.

LANCASHIRE v YORKSHIRE
at Old Trafford July 29,31, August 1, 1972

Lancashire 358-4dec (C.Lloyd 181, Hayes 71*, Pilling 65)
Yorkshire 132 (Hughes 5-59, Simmons 4-34) and 192 (Lumb 56, Hampshire 54, Simmons 6-50)
Lancashire won by an innings and 34 runs.

In a one-sided contest, Lancashire won by an innings and 34 runs, their second Roses victory out of the last nine meetings, the others being drawn.

211

After Chris Old had clean bowled both Lancashire openers, David Lloyd and Barry Wood with just 15 on the board, Pilling and Clive Lloyd added 162 for the third wicket. After Pilling had gone for 65, Lloyd was joined by Frank Hayes and these two took the score to 315 before the popular West Indian was caught and bowled by Richard Hutton for 181. This attacking, aggressive innings and Hayes' unbeaten 71 allowed Lancashire to declare their first innings closed at 358 for four.

Yorkshire, who were without Boycott, had no answer to Lancashire's spin bowlers, Hughes (five for 59) and Simmons (four for 34), and were bowled out for 132.

Following-on 226 runs in arrears, the White Rose county made a slightly better showing with both Richard Lumb (56) and Jackie Hampshire (54) scoring half-centuries. However, Jack Simmons' off-breaks resulted in him taking six for 50 off 30.3 overs to have match figures of ten for 84 as Lancashire dismissed Yorkshire for 192.

LANCASHIRE v YORKSHIRE
at Old Trafford May 26,28,29, 1973

Yorkshire 286-7dec (Lumb 114, Boycott 101) and 69 (Lee 5-20, Lever 4-23)
Lancashire 284-9dec (Pilling 92) and 4-0
Match Drawn.

There have been a number of Roses matches where the weather has saved one side or another from certain defeat and this was one of them.

When Boycott and Lumb put together an opening partnership of 178 before the England opener was leg-before to Shuttleworth for 101, the Red Rose county were in dire straits. Lumb went on to score 114, his first Championship century, but with rain disrupting the latter stages of Yorkshire's innings, they decided to declare at 286 for seven.

With Harry Pilling making a determined 92 before being dismissed by Mike Bore and Hayes (48) and Sullivan (45) also showing good form, Lancashire declared two runs behind Yorkshire's first innings total.

When batting a second time, Yorkshire collapsed to the swing bowling of former Northamptonshire player Peter Lee (five for 20) and England Test star Peter Lever (four for 23) and were dismissed for just 69.

Lancashire were left to make 72 for victory with three-and-a-half hours play ahead of them. But with the Red Rose county four without loss at lunch, rain set in to prevent any further play and so Yorkshire escaped.

YORKSHIRE v LANCASHIRE
at Bramall Lane August 4,6,7, 1973

Yorkshire 99 (Lee 6-43) and 114-2 (Sharpe 62*)
Lancashire 111-8dec
Match Drawn.

The second Roses match of this summer was the last first-class game to take place at Bramall Lane but unfortunately it was it was ruined by rain.

With Peter Lee taking six for 43 from 25 overs, the home side, for whom Phil Sharpe top-scored with 35, were bowled out for only 99. Lee was well supported by John Sullivan, the Lancashire all-rounder taking four for 19 off 11 overs

Lancashire fared little better and, with Tony Nicholson removing the first four batsmen very cheaply, were at one time 38 for six. John Sullivan batted well and was unbeaten on 48 when the Red Rose county decided to declare at 111 for eight.

When Yorkshire batted for a second time, the wicket played much easier and when rain finally brought the curtain down on the game, they were 114 for two with Phil Sharpe 62 not out.

Yorkshire and Lancashire contest the last game
played at Bramall Lane

This was the thirty-eighth Roses game to be played at Bramall Lane with Yorkshire having won 12 and Lancashire eight. Sadly the weather wouldn't allow a full game to be played for the last one.

YORKSHIRE v LANCASHIRE
at Headingley May 25,27,28, 1974

Lancashire 246 (C.Lloyd 65, D.Lloyd 58, Old 4-40) and 213-7dec (C.Lloyd 84*)
Yorkshire 220-9 (Leadbeater 92*, Shuttleworth 7-61) and 124-3 (Boycott 79*)
Match Drawn.

Yorkshire won the toss and put Lancashire in to bat. Despite both Lloyds scoring half-centuries, David (58) and Clive (65), and Harry Pilling (49) before being run out, the visitors batted very slowly in compiling their first innings total of 246. Chris Old, who dismissed both Lloyds, finished with four for 40 from 25 overs.

In reply, Yorkshire, who lost Richard Lumb before he had troubled the scorers, batted even slower, although they weren't helped by Lever and Shuttleworth's over-rate which made this a particularly depressing match for the spectators to watch. Barry Leadbeater was 92 not out when the Yorkshire innings closed at 220 for nine with Ken Shuttleworth having taken seven for 61.

Lancashire scored at over four runs an over in their second innings to set Yorkshire a victory target of 244 in three-and-a-half hours. Clive Lloyd was unbeaten on 84 when the Red Rose county declared at 213 for seven.

Yorkshire made little attempt to go for the runs with captain Geoff Boycott 79 not out at the close. It was an innings which Boycott's detractors were able to use as ammunition against him in the future. Yorkshire ended on 124 for three and though Lever and Shuttleworth bowled slowly, the fact that the White Rose county never made an effort to go for the win rankled with the members and lovers of cricket, whether they were detractors of Boycott or not!

LANCASHIRE v YORKSHIRE
at Old Trafford August 3,5,6, 1974

Yorkshire 263-6 (Hampshire 63*, Boycott 60, Lumb 53) and 170-9dec
Lancashire 216 (Simmons 75, Nicholson 5-74) and 169-5 (C.Lloyd 95)
Match Drawn.

In the return match at Old Trafford, Lancashire captain David Lloyd won

214

the toss and put Yorkshire in to bat. The move looked to have back-fired on him as Boycott (60) and Lumb (53) put on 130 for the first wicket. Jackie Hampshire was undefeated on 63 when the visitors ended the 100 overs on 263 for six.

Lancashire could only reach 216 for nine in their allotted overs, a total that was boosted by some lusty blows by top-scorer Jack Simmons who made 75. Tony Nicholson made life difficult for the Red Rose side's upper order and finished with five for 74 off 32 overs.

In Yorkshire's second innings, all the county's batsmen made useful contributions, enabling the White Rose county to declare at 170 for nine.

Set 224 to win, Lancashire had a setback when David Lloyd and Barry Wood were both dismissed in Chris Old's opening spell. Clive Lloyd, who fell five runs short of a deserved century, played a most entertaining innings until he was bowled by Arthur Robinson. After his dismissal, Lancashire fell behind the clock and when stumps were drawn, were 169 for five.

LANCASHIRE v YORKSHIRE
at Old Trafford May 24,26,27, 1975

Yorkshire 157 and 285-7dec (Boycott 92, Leadbeater 82)
Lancashire 199 (C.Lloyd 58, Old 5-75) and 103-3
Match Drawn

After Richard Lumb had been run out for one at the end of the first over, the remaining Yorkshire batsmen gave a disappointing batting display and with Lancashire's three pace bowlers - Peter Lever (three for 36), Peter Lee (three for 58) and Ken Shuttleworth (three for 25) sharing the remaining wickets, the home side were all out for 157.

Lancashire too could not come to terms with the way the wicket was playing though Clive Lloyd, with an innings of 58, supported by Hayes (41) and Engineer (43), enabled the Red Rose county to finish with a first innings lead of 42. The pick of the Yorkshire attack was Chris Old who took five for 75.

The visitors batted much better in their second innings and with Geoff Boycott (92) and Barry Leadbeater (82) putting on 137 for the second wicket, Yorkshire were able to declare at 285 for seven.

The wicket by now was very slow and Lancashire declined the target of 244 in two-and-three-quarter hours, ending on 103 for three.

215

YORKSHIRE v LANCASHIRE
at Headingley August 23,25,26, 1975

Lancashire 340-5 (Hayes 101, C.Lloyd 100*, Engineer 54) and 191-3dec (C.Lloyd 82, Kennedy 80*)
Yorkshire 210-8dec (Johnson 76, Old 57) and 219-1 (Boycott 105*, Lumb 70)
Match Drawn.

This game seemed destined to end in a draw from the very first ball bowled. Only 17 wickets fell in the three days and in a match which contained a dreadful over-rate throughout its duration, neither side seemed to want to take a risk.

Lancashire won the toss and not surprisingly elected to bat. Engineer, with an entertaining knock of 54, and Kennedy (46) put on 97 for the first wicket whilst both Clive Lloyd (100 not out) and Frank Hayes (101) scored centuries in a Red Rose county total of 340 for five.

A devastating spell of fast bowling by Peter Lever at the start of the Yorkshire innings reduced the home side to 13 for four. Colin Johnson (76) and Chris Old (57) later batted well and Yorkshire declared 139 runs behind Lancashire's first innings total.

Farokh Engineer was clean bowled by Old without a run on the board at the beginning of Lancashire's second innings but a third wicket partnership of 138 by Clive Lloyd (82) and Andrew Kennedy (80 not out) enabled the visitors to declare at 191 for three.

The wicket was still playing well and Yorkshire's target of 331 to win in four-and-a-half hours was not an impossible task. Boycott and Lumb put on 144 for the first wicket before the latter batsman fell leg-before to Lever for 70. Boycott went on to score an unbeaten 105 as Yorkshire finished on 219 for one. The White Rose county scored only 83 runs off the first thirty overs which was not a good advertisement for cricket.

YORKSHIRE v LANCASHIRE
at Headingley May 29,31, June 1, 1976

Lancashire 201-7dec (D.Lloyd 52, Pilling 51) and 27-1
Yorkshire 141 (Ratcliffe 5-30)
Match Drawn.

In a match spoiled by the weather, Lancashire declared their first innings closed at 201 for seven after Harry Pilling (51) and David Lloyd (52) had

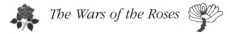

added 96 for the fourth wicket in difficult conditions. Howard Cooper, who dismissed both Lancashire openers Wood and Kennedy and clean bowled Hayes, was Yorkshire's best bowler with three for 45 off 29 overs.

Yorkshire were dismissed for 141 with medium-pacer Bob Ratcliffe taking five for 30 in a spell of very accurate bowling.

The visitors had a lead of 60 runs on the first innings and were 27 for one in their second when torrential rain forced the game to an early finish.

LANCASHIRE v YORKSHIRE
at Old Trafford August 28,30,31, 1976

Yorkshire 260 (Hampshire 83, Carrick 57, Lee 5-78) and 174-6dec (Boycott 103*)
Lancashire 167 (Stevenson 4-25, Robinson 4-61) and 158 (Cope 6-37)
Yorkshire won by 109 runs.

There was some help in the wicket for the bowlers throughout the three days of this match.

Peter Lee and Peter Lever took a wicket apiece as Yorkshire struggled in the game's opening overs, being 18 for two after an hours play. Boycott (34) and Love (38) took the score to 71 but the highlight of the Yorkshire innings was an entertaining knock of 83 by Jackie Hampshire. He was well supported by Phil Carrick, whose dogged knock of 57 helped the visitors to score 260. Peter Lee was the pick of the Lancashire bowlers, taking five for 75 from 34 overs.

Lancashire struggled even more and were dismissed for 167 with many of their batsmen getting themselves out. For Yorkshire Graham Stevenson and Arthur Robinson took four wickets apiece.

When Yorkshire batted a second time, Geoff Boycott scored a timely 103 not out, an innings which helped the White Rose county to declare at 174 for six. Lancashire's chances of scoring the 268 needed for victory seemed remote and with the wicket turning even more, they were bowled out for 158. Peter Lever, Lancashire's last man, was his side's top-scorer with 28 before he became Geoff Cope's final victim. The bespectacled spinner took six for 37 to give Yorkshire victory by 109 runs.

LANCASHIRE v YORKSHIRE
at Old Trafford June 4,6,7, 1977

Lancashire 270-4 (Abrahams 101*, Hayes 90)
Yorkshire 65-6dec
Match Drawn.

Lancashire reached 270 for four in their 100 overs with John Abrahams scoring 101 not out and Frank Hayes 90. The left-handed Abrahams played with a great deal of composure, whilst Hayes played each ball on merit and was unlucky not to join Abrahams in scoring a hundred. The two of them added 168 for the fourth wicket before Stevenson held on to a difficult return catch to dismiss Hayes.

West Indian fast bowler Colin Croft was making his Roses debut for Lancashire and by the close of play he had clean bowled Boycott, Athey and Hampshire in a fiery spell of bowling, the ball rearing dangerously off a length. Yorkshire ended the first day on 55 for five and perhaps fortunately for the White Rose county, rain practically ruined the rest of the game as they only had time to add a further ten runs for the loss of another wicket.

YORKSHIRE v LANCASHIRE
at Bradford August 20,22,23, 1977

Lancashire 302-4dec (Wood 150*, Pilling 67) and 108 (Carrick 6-37)
Yorkshire 234-9dec and 177-5 (Lumb 77, Lee 4-34)
Yorkshire won by 5 wickets.

Playing against Yorkshire at Park Avenue for the first time since the Hedley Verity Memorial Match in 1945, Lancashire scored 302 for four before declaring their first innings closed. Barry Wood, who scored 150 not out, and Harry Pilling (67) put on 145 for the second wicket with the diminutive Ashton-under-Lyne-born batsman playing some lovely cuts and pulls.

Yorkshire's reply started well with Boycott (47) and Leadbeater (43) putting on 85 for the first wicket and though eight of the side reached double figures, the home side declared at 234 for eight, 68 runs behind Lancashire's first innings total.

There was something of a sensational collapse in Lancashire's second innings as they were bowled out for 108. Yorkshire spinner Phil Carrick, who had been out of the side for five weeks through loss of form, took six for 37 from, 21 overs.

218

Set 177 to win, Yorkshire reached their target for the loss of five wickets thanks in the main to Richard Lumb. The tall right-handed batsman, who had also been badly off form, scored 77.

YORKSHIRE v LANCASHIRE
at Headingley May 27,28,29, 1978

Lancashire 123 (C.Lloyd 58, Stevenson 8-65) and 105 (Cooper 6-26, Oldham 4-28)
Yorkshire 260 (Carrick 105, Hampshire 54)
Yorkshire won by an innings and 32 runs.

On a Headingley pitch reported as being unfit for first-class cricket, Yorkshire, without England Test players Geoff Boycott and Chris Old, beat Lancashire by an innings and 32 runs.

Lancashire, who were bowled out for 123, lost their first two wickets with just one run on the scoreboard. Ackworth-born all-rounder Graham Stevenson took eight for 65 with five of his victims being caught behind the wicket by David Bairstow, who went on to take eight catches during the game. Only Clive Lloyd of the Lancashire batsmen showed anything like his true form with a fighting innings of 58.

Yorkshire too made a dreadful start, losing their first four wickets for 20 runs, three of them to Willie Hogg in a devastating opening spell by the Ulverston-born bowler. Then Yorkshire's acting captain, Jackie Hampshire, made 54 and added 88 for the sixth wicket with Phil Carrick, who went on to make his maiden century in Yorkshire's total of 260.

When Lancashire batted for a second time, Yorkshire's medium-pace bowlers, Howard Cooper (six for 26) and Steve Oldham (four for 28), did the damage as the Red Rose county were shot out for 105 to leave the home side the victors by an innings and 32 runs.

LANCASHIRE v YORKSHIRE
at Old Trafford August 26,28,29, 1978

Lancashire 128 (Stevenson 5-61, Old 4-38) and 155 (Hayes 73*, Old 5-47)
Yorkshire 251 (Old 100*, Love 55) and 36-0
Yorkshire won by 10 wickets.

With just ten runs on the scoreboard, Graham Stevenson dismissed Kennedy and Abrahams with successive deliveries - a start Lancashire never recovered from. The county's middle-order collapsed against the

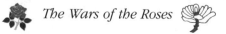

bowling of Old (four for 38) and Stevenson (five for 61) and were all out for 128.

Yorkshire began badly as well, losing their first three wickets with just six runs having been scored. Jim Love with 55 and Chris Old with a superb innings of 100 not out put the visitors into a winning position - finishing 123 runs ahead of Lancashire on first innings scores.

Although Frank Hayes batted well to score 73 not out in Lancashire's second innings, the Red Rose county were bowled out for 155 with Chris Old taking five for 47. As in the first innings he was well supported by Graham Stevenson who took three for 57.

Needing just 33 for victory, Yorkshire reached their target without losing a wicket.

LANCASHIRE v YORKSHIRE
at Old Trafford May 26,28,29, 1979

Lancashire 29-0
No Result.

In a game completely decimated by rain, only 17 overs were bowled on the opening day in which time, Lancashire, who had been put in to bat by the visitors, were 29 without loss.

YORKSHIRE v LANCASHIRE
at Headingley August 25,27,28, 1979

Lancashire 155 (Boycott 4-14) and 270 (C.Lloyd 103)
Yorkshire 322 (Boycott 94, Hampshire 53, Sidebottom 51, Ratcliffe 5-82)
and 104-4 (Hartley 53*)
Yorkshire won by 6 wickets.

After Chris Old and Graham Stevenson had removed both Lloyds and Frank Hayes with just 15 runs on the board, Lancashire never recovered and were bowled out for 155. The top-scorer in the county's disappointing total was Extras with 27, whilst Yorkshire's most successful bowler was Geoff Boycott who took four for 14 off 14.2 overs!

Yorkshire replied with a score of 322 with Geoff Boycott leading the way with 94. Jackie Hampshire (53) and lower down the order Arnie Sidebottom (51) made telling contributions, whilst Lancashire's Bob Ratcliffe stuck to his task to take five for 82 off 41.4 overs.

220

When they batted again, Lancashire, despite losing openers David Lloyd and Barry Wood for 0 and 1 respectively, looked to have saved the game when Frank Hayes and Clive Lloyd put on 135 for the fourth wicket. Lloyd treated the Headingley crowd to a dazzling innings of 103 with Hayes (48) and later Abrahams (53) also batting well. However, with the score at 266 for seven, Lancashire lost their last three wickets for just four runs and were all out for 270.

Yorkshire required 104 to win at over seven runs an over. The target was achieved with Neil Hartley, a right-handed middle-order batsman making the winning hit and finishing on 53 not out.

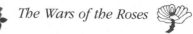

CLIVE LLOYD (LANCASHIRE)

No player has made the same impact on Lancashire cricket as Clive Hubert Lloyd. Arguably Lancashire's greatest-ever batsman, he was born in Georgetown, Guyana where at the age of 12, whilst trying to separate two fighting school friends, he received a blow to the eye. His eyesight was affected and he has been obliged to wear spectacles ever since. Lloyd made his Guyana debut in 1963-64 against Jamaica, following it up with a Test debut for the West Indies against India in 1966-67.

In 1967 he came to England to play as professional for Haslingden in the Lancashire League. When his Haslingden engagement expired, Lloyd accepted a contract with Lancashire. He played in one match in 1968 against the touring Australians before linking up with the county in 1969. Though he failed to score a century in 1969, he helped Lancashire win the new John Player League. Lloyd's first century for Lancashire arrived the following season in the match against Kent at Dartford. The innings of 163 lasted only 145 minutes and included seven sixes. In that season's John Player League he scored 134 not out against Somerset - which was Lancashire's highest score in the competition until equalled by Graham Lloyd against Durham in 1997. Until 1991, Lloyd also held the county's highest score in the Benson and Hedges Cup with 124 not out against Warwickshire. They were a county that Clive Lloyd seemed to take a particular liking to as his highest score for Lancashire of 217 not out came against Warwickshire at Old Trafford in 1971. The Edgbaston side were Lancashire's opponents in the 1972 Gillette Cup Final when Lloyd scored a brilliant match-winning 126.

The captaincy of the West Indies was given to Lloyd in 1974, a position he was to hold for eleven seasons. During his first series as captain he hit a Test century in 102 minutes against India at Bangalore. He went on to 163 with two sixes and 22 fours, an innings that is still the fastest century on record in West Indies' Test matches. In that same series he achieved the highest score of his Test career, 242 not out in a West Indies total of 604 at Bombay.

But it was 1975 that provided something special, a World Cup year, a brilliant summer in England and six centuries for Lancashire, four of them in successive matches. His most spectacular hundred came against Derbyshire at Buxton. He scored 147 not out in 167 minutes, the last 67 runs coming in 37 minutes as he finished with eight sixes and 15 fours. Lloyd also led the West Indies to victory in the World Cup, scoring 102 off 82 balls against Australia in the final. Lloyd was having trouble with his knees around this time and operations were inevitable, the first coming in 1977 after one of his most stunning innings. Both knees were dicey and he shifted the weight from one to the other while hitting sixes in a Gillette Cup match against Surrey at Old Trafford. At the end of 1980, when Gillette ended their sponsorship, Clive Lloyd was awarded the 'Man of the Series' trophy as the player who had made the greatest contribution. In 1981 Lloyd was appointed captain of Lancashire, but unfortunately his three year spell in charge and a further year in 1986 could not produce the winning formula.

In first-class matches for Lancashire, Lloyd scored 12,764 runs at an average of 44.94, the second highest average behind Ernest Tyldesley of Lancashire players. At international level, he appeared in 110 Tests and scored 7,515 runs at an average of 46.67 to be without doubt one of the world's finest batsmen.

YORKSHIRE v LANCASHIRE
at Headingley May 24,26,27, 1980

Lancashire 234 (Cockbain 57, Stevenson 4-70) and 182-8 (Abrahams 54, Stevenson 5-71)
Yorkshire 257 (Carrick 63, Bairstow 61)
Match Drawn.

Yorkshire won the toss and put Lancashire in to bat and though a number of batsmen made useful scores - Cockbain (57) Hughes (40) and David Lloyd (36) - nobody went on to build a big score and the visitors were all out for 234. Graham Stevenson again bowled well for Yorkshire, taking four for 70 off 30 overs, whilst David Bairstow was in fine form behind the stumps, taking six catches.

The Bradford-born wicket-keeper was in good form with the bat too, scoring 61 runs in entertaining fashion as Yorkshire scored 257. In fact, the White Rose county were in trouble at 97 for six at one stage, but when Phil Carrick, who top-scored with 63, joined Bairstow, they added 104 for the seventh wicket.

Lancashire soon knocked off the 23 runs they were in arrears and, thanks to a brave knock of 54 by John Abrahams, they saved the game, finishing on 182 for eight. Graham Stevenson again bowled well, taking five of the wickets to fall at a cost of 71 runs.

223

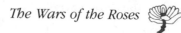

LANCASHIRE v YORKSHIRE
at Old Trafford August 23,25,26, 1980

Yorkshire 346-7dec (Boycott 135, Athey 71, Lumb 65) and 265-5dec (Love 105*, Hampshire 89)
Lancashire 310-5 (Hayes 94*, Reidy 75, Kennedy 55) and 305-7 (C.Lloyd 101, D.Lloyd 61, Reidy 60)
Lancashire won by 3 wickets.

On an easy paced Old Trafford wicket, both sides produced some entertaining cricket.

Yorkshire won the toss and had no hesitation in batting. Openers Geoff Boycott, who scored 135, and Richard Lumb (67) put on 178 for the first wicket and with Bill Athey hitting a quick-fire 71, the White Rose county scored 346 for seven before declaring. Lancashire replied with 310 for five and though left-handers Andrew Kennedy (55) and Bernard Reidy (75) made half-centuries, top-scorer Frank Hayes was left stranded on 94 not out at the end of the allotted overs.

After Willie Hogg had removed Geoff Boycott for three and Bill Athley for 30, following the earlier dismissal of Richard Lumb, Jim Love (105 not out) and Jack Hampshire (89) put on 177 for the fourth wicket. Nine runs later Yorkshire declared, setting Lancashire 302 to win in four hours.

Hampshire's declaration was thought by many to be too generous, especially the way the wicket was playing. Yorkshire's captain came in for much criticism, mostly unjustified, though in the end this fine game of cricket did go Lancashire's way.

The home side won by three wickets with Clive Lloyd scoring a magnificent 101, helped by David Lloyd (61) and Bernard Reid (60) - although if the West Indies captain hadn't been dropped at 68 and again at 70, it could have been a completely different story.

LANCASHIRE v YORKSHIRE
at Old Trafford May 23,25,26, 1981

Yorkshire 348-9dec (Love 154, Allott 6-105)
Lancashire 310-8 (Hayes 126)
Match Drawn.

There was never really any chance of a finish in the game at Old Trafford which was continually interrupted by rain.

224

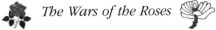

Batting first, Yorkshire declared at 348 for nine with Jim Love scoring a superb 154 before being bowled by Paul Allott. He shared in two partnerships of over a hundred - 109 for the fourth wicket with Neil Hartley (32) and 131 for the fifth wicket with David Bairstow (49). Paul Allott bowled well in long spells for Lancashire to finish with six for 105 from 33.2 overs.

Lancashire replied with 310 for eight with Frank Hayes top-scoring with a fine innings of 126. He shared in a third wicket stand of 103 with David Lloyd (47) whilst Reidy (38) and Hughes (37) also made useful contributions.

YORKSHIRE v LANCASHIRE
at Headingley August 29,31, September 1, 1981

Yorkshire 149 (Hartley 53, Holding 4-39, Allott 4-63) and 181 (Holding 6-76, Allott 4-78)
Lancashire 346 (C.Lloyd 145, Hughes 54)
Lancashire won by an innings and 16 runs.

Put in to bat, Yorkshire lost early wickets to Lancashire's opening bowlers, Allott and Holding, and at one stage were 36 for six as Peter Lee joined in on the act. They recovered to reach 149, thanks in the main to captain Neil Hartley who scored 53. For Lancashire, Michael Holding took four for 39 and Paul Allott four for 63.

Lancashire too found runs difficult to come by in the early part of their innings and half the side were out with just 79 on the board. Then David Hughes (54) was joined by Clive Lloyd and the two of them proceeded to put on 145 for the sixth wicket. Lloyd went on to score 145 himself as Lancashire took their first innings total to 346.

The two Lancashire pacemen proved too much for Yorkshire again when the home side batted for a second time, taking all ten wickets between them. Despite good efforts from Arnie Sidebottom (47) and Jackie Hampshire (40), Yorkshire were dismissed for 181 to give Lancashire victory by an innings and 16 runs.

West Indies Test star Michael Holding had ten wickets in the match at a cost of 11.5 runs apiece.

225

 *The Wars of the Roses*

YORKSHIRE v LANCASHIRE
at Headingley May 29,30,31, 1982

Lancashire 351-8dec (Hughes 126*) and 255-6dec (D.Lloyd 81)
Yorkshire 317-6dec (Athey 90, Bairstow 70*) and 197-5 (Lumb 72, Boycott 68)
Match Drawn.

Batting first on what seemed a fairly placid Headingley wicket, Lancashire's opening pair of Kennedy and Fowler gave the Red Rose county a solid start before both players lost their wicket when seeming set to amass big scores. Chris Old dismissed both Lloyds, David and Clive, before David Hughes and John Abrahams (57) put on 134 for the fifth wicket. Hughes went on to score an unbeaten 126 enabling the visitors to declare at 351 for eight.

West Indian paceman Colin Croft accounted for Geoff Boycott, who was well caught by Andrew Kennedy for 13, and after Lumb had been run out, Love went without troubling the scorers. Bill Athey (90) and Kevin Sharp (43) added 114 for the fourth wicket before both batsmen were out with the score on 188. Bairstow with an unbeaten 70 and Phil Carrck with 44 allowed Yorkshire to declare their innings at 317 for six.

In a game of declarations, a fine innings of 81 from David Lloyd, supported by Hughes (44) and Abrahams (38 not out) saw Lancashire close their second innings at 255 for six, leaving Yorkshire 290 to win in just over three hours.

The White Rose county made a good start with Boycott (68) and Lumb (72) putting on 144 for the first wicket. However, Colin Croft wrecked Yorkshire's middle-order with a devastating spell of pace bowling and they were then content to bat out time, finishing on 197 for five.

LANCASHIRE v YORKSHIRE
at Old Trafford August 7,9,10, 1982

Lancashire 310-6dec (C.Lloyd 100, Simmons 61*) and 30-0dec
Yorkshire Forfeited first innings and 142-3 (Boycott 62)
Match Drawn.

In a game in which over seven hours were lost to rain on the first two days, Lancashire's captain Clive Lloyd scored his sixth Roses century - a record for the Red Rose county.

Alan Ramage removed both Fowler and Cockbain in a good opening spell, but with Abrahams (41), O'Shaughnessy (41 not out) and Simmons (61 not out) all making useful contributions, Lancashire declared at 310 for six.

226

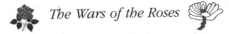

Yorkshire forfeited their first innings on the final day and Lancashire declared in the ninth over of their second innings to leave the White Rose county needing 341 to win.

Lumb and Athey went cheaply and though Boycott and Love added 66 for the third wicket before the England opener was adjudged leg-before to Peter Lee, the target was far too demanding.

LANCASHIRE v YORKSHIRE
at Old Trafford May 28,30,31, 1983

Lancashire 301-4dec (Fowler 156*, Hayes 116) and 24-0
Yorkshire 228 (Carrick 83)
Match Drawn

After the entire first day had been washed out, Lancashire, put in to bat, took maximum batting points thanks to a second wicket stand of 222 in 192 minutes by Graeme Fowler and Frank Hayes. Fowler scored 156 not out - a career-best innings that took his average for the season to 136! Hayes had made 116 before Stevenson removed his off stump as Lancashire declared at 301 for four.

The temptation to forfeit innings was resisted and Yorkshire spent most of the final day fighting off the threat of the follow-on. Ian Folley removed both Yorkshire openers, Boycott and Lumb, and with Allott dismissing Athey, Yorkshire were 33 for three. O'Shaughnessy bowled well to take four for 73 but a stand of 73 by Bairstow (40) and Carrick (83) helped the visitors avoid the follow-on with three wickets standing.

With Yorkshire eventually all out for 228, there was just time for Lancashire to face a handful of overs and with wicket-keeper David Bairstow opening the bowling, they were 24 without loss when play ended.

YORKSHIRE v LANCASHIRE
at Headingley August 6,8,9, 1983

Lancashire 344 (D.Lloyd 73, Simmons 52) and 256-3dec (O'Shaughnessy 100*,
Fowler 75, Abrahams 50)
Yorkshire 305-4dec (Moxon 153, Love 67*, Athey 63) and 90-7
Match Drawn.

Yorkshire's Simon Dennis was awarded his county cap just before the start of this Roses match and celebrated with two early wickets - Fowler and

Abrahams both caught behind by Bairstow. However, Lancashire's remaining batsmen all made useful contributions and with David Lloyd (73) and Jack Simmons (52) leading the way, the visitors made 344.

Martyn Moxon led Yorkshire's reply with a career-best 153, which included a six and 17 fours - his driving through the off-side being a feature of his innings. He was well supported by Athey (63) and Love (67 not out), enabling the White Rose county to declare at 305 for four after only 87 overs in order to make a game of it.

Lancashire though were in no hurry at the outset of their second innings in which Steve O'Shaughnessy, opening the batting, scored 100 not out. Fowler scored a quick-fire 75, his first 50 runs coming from only 60 balls and John Abrahams 50 as Lancashire finally declared at 256 for three.

Setting Yorkshire a target of 296 in two-and-a-half hours on what seemed to be a good batting track, the home side's supporters were disgusted when no attempt was made to go for the runs. Moxon was again his side's top-scorer with 39 but with O'Shaughnessy (three for 14) and Simmons (two for 8) bowling well, Yorkshire struggled to avoid defeat, finishing on 90 for seven.

YORKSHIRE v LANCASHIRE
at Headingley May 26,27,28, 1984

Yorkshire 188 (Bairstow 62, Allott 6-31) and 16-2
Lancashire 288-7dec (Fowler 107, Ormrod 60)
Match Drawn.

Batting first, Yorkshire collapsed on an easy-paced Headingley wicket which offered a little early movement. Paul Allott, keeping a full length, made the most of the conditions, dismissing both Moxon and Sharp as the White Rose county slumped to 12 for four. Though Hartley (44) and Carrick (38) made useful contributions, Yorkshire's top-scorer in their first innings total of 188 was David Bairstow, who made 62 from 58 deliveries including 3 sixes and 8 fours. Paul Allott finished with six for 31, his best figures in a Roses match.

Graeme Fowler with 107 completed his second Roses century, a year to the day after the first, and with Alan Ormrod (60) put on 159 for the first wicket - the best against Yorkshire for 39 years.

Even when rain washed out the whole of the second day, Lancashire held a clear advantage and this made their approach on the final day all the harder to understand. O'Shaughnessy and Hughes were it seemed content just to occupy the crease and it was only when Fairbrother (42 not out) and Maynard (32 not out) were together that the scoring rate accelerated. Abrahams declared at 288 for seven but when stumps were drawn, Yorkshire, who might well have struggled had Lancashire left themselves more time to try and get them out, were 16 for two.

LANCASHIRE v YORKSHIRE
at Old Trafford August 4,6,7, 1984

Lancashire 151 (Jarvis 6-61)
Yorkshire 124-5
Match Drawn.

In yet another Roses game that was decimated by the weather - the first and last days were lost to rain and only 78.3 overs were possible on the second - Lancashire were bowled out for 151 on a lively wicket.

Yorkshire's young seam bowler, 19-year-old Paul Jarvis from Redcar, took a career-best six for 61. Bowling well within himself, his figures could have been even better had Yorkshire's slip fielders held all their chances.

When Yorkshire batted, they only had time to take their score to 124 for five. Neil Hartley was 37 not out, the same score made by Martyn Moxon who was one of Paul Allott's three victims.

LANCASHIRE v YORKSHIRE
at Old Trafford May 25,26,27, 1985

Yorkshire 205 (Hartley 52, Patterson 6-77) and 58-4
Lancashire 269 (Fairbrother 128, Folley 69)
Match Drawn.

West Indian pace bowler Patrick Patterson, playing in only his third County Championship match, took three wickets in his first six overs and with O'Shaughnessy chipping in with the wicket of Kevin Sharp, Yorkshire were struggling at 26 for four. They recovered to reach 205 with Neil Hartley scoring 52. No other Yorkshire batsman could come to terms with the extra pace and bounce that Patterson found as he finished with six for 77 off 25 overs.

Lancashire too lost quick wickets at the start of their innings and ended the first day on 16 for two. Nightwatchman Ian Folley took his score to 69 whilst Neil Fairbrother hit his first Roses century and his highest score as the two of them added 142 for the fourth wicket. In the end, Lancashire were bowled out for 269, a lead of 64 runs.

In their second innings, Yorkshire were in trouble at 58 for four as

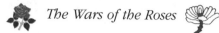

Paul Allott took three wickets for four runs in his first five overs. Sadly, rain then intervened and ruined a game in which an exciting finish looked a distinct prospect.

YORKSHIRE v LANCASHIRE
at Headingley August 10,12,13, 1985

Lancashire 327-8dec (Fairbrother 147, Hartley 5-91)
Yorkshire 328-9dec (Moxon 127)
Match Drawn.

On a Headingley wicket of unreliable bounce, Neil Fairbrother completed his second Roses century of the summer in a little under four hours with one six and 19 fours. He was well supported lower down the order by wicket-keeper Chris Maynard (43) and pace bowler David Makinson (40 not out). Lancashire had scored 327 for eight when Abrahams declared their innings closed.

Patterson and Allott made early inroads into the Yorkshire batting, reducing the home side to 95 for four, but Martyn Moxon, who occupied the crease for over six hours in his innings of 127, made sure that the White Rose county were not dismissed cheaply.

Though rain cut into the Yorkshire innings, their batsmen made little or no effort to score quickly, whilst Lancashire for their part bowled their overs very slowly and set ultra-defensive fields.

YORKSHIRE v LANCASHIRE
at Headingley May 24,26,27, 1986

Lancashire 296 (Maynard 132*, Allott 65, Jarvis 5-86) and 268-7dec (Mendis 62)
Yorkshire 314 (Carrick 50) and 90-1
Match Drawn.

Lancashire were soon in trouble, losing early wickets to Jarvis and Sidebottom, who reduced the Red Rose county to 47 for five. However, the Yorkshire pacemen were kept on for far too long and this enabled Lancashire wicket-keeper Chris Maynard to score his first century in first-class cricket. His innings of 132 contained one six and 14 fours. He was well supported lower down the order by Paul Allott, who scored a very useful 65. Paul Jarvis took five for 86, his early figures being somewhat damaged later in the innings by one or two lusty blows by the tail-enders.

Yorkshire made a solid reply to Lancashire's total of 296 with Phil

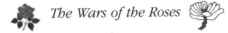

Carrick making a half-century and four other batsmen reaching the forties. The home side were dismissed for 314, a lead of 18 runs.

In their second innings, Lancashire lost wickets steadily but thanks to a fine innings of 62 by Sri Lankan-born opener Gehan Mendis, who held the innings together, they were able to declare at 268 for seven. A number of dropped catches didn't help Yorkshire's cause.

Set 251 to win in 75 minutes plus 20 overs, the White Rose county showed no interest in the target and were 90 for one when stumps were drawn.

LANCASHIRE v YORKSHIRE
at Old Trafford August 2,4,5, 1986
Lancashire 170 (Mendis 54) and 251-6 (Fairbrother 116*, Abrahams 80)
Yorkshire 399-7dec (Metcalfe 151, Moxon 147, Love 53*)
Match Drawn.

Despite making a good start with openers Mendis (54) and Fowler (35) putting on 79 for the first wicket, the only other Lancashire batsman to reach double figures was Paul Allott, who made a quick-fire 36 lower down the order.

With the wicket improving, Yorkshire passed Lancashire's first innings total of 170 without losing a wicket. Openers Martyn Moxon and Ashley Metcalfe went on to put on 282, the highest Yorkshire opening stand in a Roses match and the third best by a county first-wicket pair at Old Trafford. Moxon made 147 and Metcalfe 151 before Jim Love hit a rapid 53 not out to enable David Bairstow, the Yorkshire captain to declare at 399 for seven, a lead of 229.

By the close of play on the second day, Lancashire had lost two wickets for 14 runs but on the final day, John Abrahams batted over four hours for 80 and with Neil Fairbrother scoring his third Roses century off 213 balls, Lancashire managed to save the game, finishing on 251 for six.

MARTYN MOXON (YORKSHIRE)

Barnsley-born Martyn Moxon came from a cricketing family, his father being an excellent league cricketer and coach to the Wombwell Cricket Lovers. Moxon captained Yorkshire Schools at Under-15 and Senior Schools levels and in 1979 captained the North of England Under-19 tour to Canada.

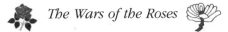

Moxon scored 116 against Essex at Headingley in 1981 on his first-class debut and then 111 against Derbyshire at Sheffield in his next match to become the first Yorkshire player to score hundreds in each of his first two Championship matches.

Despite this early success, Moxon had to wait until 1984 for a regular place in the Yorkshire side after scoring 153 against Lancashire in his first Roses match the previous year. He would have made his England debut that year against West Indies at Lord's but for a rib injury sustained earlier in the summer.

On the following tour of India, he missed a glorious chance of establishing his place as England's regular opening batsman when he had to return home to attend the funeral of his father.

In 1986, Moxon scored 123 and 112 not out against the Indians at Scarborough and won selection for his first Test against New Zealand at Lord's. He made a sound 74 in his first Test innings before losing the selectors' confidence by falling to Richard Hadlee's bowling four times in succession. As Graham Gooch's deputy he played two innings of great tenacity to head England's averages for the 1987-88 series against New Zealand and was unlucky to be denied his maiden Test century twice in successive innings. At Auckland he was out after being kept on 99 for 18 agonising minutes and when a well-timed sweep for three runs off Bracewell early in his innings had been signalled as leg-byes, the bowler subsequently admitting that the ball had come off Moxon's bat! Having become the ninth England player (and fourth Yorkshireman) to perish on 99, he was then left 81 not out when rain washed out the last two days of the Wellington Test. Moxon played in 10 Tests, scoring 455 runs at an average of 28.43.

Moxon had a sound technique and limitless patience - attributes strengthened by watching Geoff Boycott at close quarters in his early days and, like his mentor, he too changed his spectacles for contact lenses.

A quiet, studious man with university qualifications, Moxon captained Yorkshire from 1990 to 1995 and, though he was an excellent slip fielder and occsionally useful medium-pace swing bowler, it was as a batsman that he made his name. Moxon scored 21,116 first-class runs at an average of 42.83 and a highest score of 274 not out against Worcestershire in 1994 before being appointed Yorkshire's Director of Coaching in 1998.

233

LANCASHIRE v YORKSHIRE
at Old Trafford June 13,14,15, 1987

Lancashire 402-3dec (Mendis 156, Fowler 77, Varey 59) and 96-0dec
Yorkshire 179-1dec (Moxon 88*, Metcalfe 78) and 223-9 (Blakey 124*)
Match Drawn

Lancashire made full use of a superb batting wicket at Old Trafford, with
Mendis and Fowler putting on 153 for the first wicket before the England
left-hander fell to Phil Carrick for 77. Mendis went on to score 156, an
innings that contained 16 fours, before skipper David Hughes, who was
43 not out, declared at 402 for three. Rain interrupted the second day's
play and Phil Carrick was forced to declare his side's innings at the
overnight score of 179 for one.

Lancashire batted for twenty over before declaring to set Yorkshire
320 for victory in 79 overs. It seemed a generous declaration by the home
side, especially in view of the easy-paced wicket, but fine bowling by
Patrick Patterson, who took three wickets in 14 balls, supported by Paul
Allott and Jack Simmons, had Yorkshire struggling. Only Richard Blakey,
who batted for all but the opening over to score 124 not out, prevented
Lancashire from winning the game. He was well supported by Stuart
Fletcher, who was given not out by umpire David Evans after a bat-pad
chance off Jack Simmons. The Lancashire spinner later accused Fletcher
of cheating! Simmons was suspended by the Lancashire committee for a
week following his public outburst.

YORKSHIRE v LANCASHIRE
at Headingley August 1,3,4, 1987

Lancashire 356 (Fowler 83, Watkinson 81, Shaw 6-64) and 180-0dec
(Mendis 100*, Atherton 76*)
Yorkshire 250-2dec (Sharp 81*, Blakey 79*, Moxon 54) and 102-0 (Moxon 51*)
Match Drawn.

After winning the toss, Yorkshire surprisingly put Lancashire in to bat on
a wicket that offered very little help to the bowlers after being subjected
to fifteen tons of pressure in a rolling exercise to eradicate the ground's
uneven bounce.

Fowler was in fine form, scoring 83 in partnerships with Mendis
(22), Atherton (44) and Fairbrother (21) before Lancashire's innings lost its

momentum. Mike Watkinson hit a quick-fire 81 from 116 balls, including 4 sixes and 6 fours,help the Red Rose county to a first innings total of 356. In reply, Yorkshire had progressed to 168 for two when rain washed out the rest of the second day. Yorkshire captain Phil Carrick declared at 250 for two, giving Lancashire a 106-run lead in an attempt to keep the game alive.

Yorkshire used seven bowlers in Lancashire's second innings, including Chris Shaw who had taken six for 64 in their first knock, but they failed to break up Mendis (100 not out) and Fowler (76 not out), who helped Lancashire reach 180 for 0 declared. Yorkshire were set a target of 287 in just over an hour plus 20 overs but Moxon and Metcalfe, who took the score to 102 without loss, showed no interest in the challenge.

On a remarkable last day, 368 runs had been scored without the fall of one wicket!

YORKSHIRE v LANCASHIRE
at Headingley July 30, August 1, 1988

Lancashire 154 (Mendis 58, Sidebottom 4-32) and 156
Yorkshire 293 (Love 77, Sidebottom 55, Allott 5-85) and 18-0
Yorkshire won by 10 wickets.

After winning the toss and electing to bat, only Gehan Mendis with 58 made use of an easy-paced pitch as Lancashire were bowled out for 154. The leading wicket-taker was Arnie Sidebottom, who took four for 32 including a spell of four for 4 in 21 balls. Lancashire were hampered by the loss of Wasim Akram with a groin strain but Paul Allott, who was suffering with a damaged foot, bowled well to take five for 85 from 32 overs as Yorkshire scored 293. Top-scorer was Jim Love with 77 but it was a partnership of 78 between Arnie Sidebottom (55) and Phil Carrick (37) that enabled Yorkshire to lead by 139 on the first innings.

Lancashire again batted irresponsibly in their second innings with only Fairbrother (43) and Hegg (31) coming to terms with the medium-pace bowling of Sidebottom, Hartley and Fletcher, who between them dismissed the Red Rose county for 156.

Needing just 18 to win, Yorkshire claimed the extra half-hour and won by 10 wickets to end the sequence of 12 draws by the counties.

LANCASHIRE v YORKSHIRE
at Old Trafford August 30,31, September 1,2, 1988

Yorkshire 224 (Hartley 127*, Allott 5-70) and 171-8 (Fitton 6-59)
Lancashire 218 (Hayhurst 57, Carrick 5-62, Booth 5-98)
Match Drawn.

In a bid to accommodate television schedules, play on each day began at
10.30 a.m, the earliest ever start for a County Championship match.
Having won the toss and elected to bat, Yorkshire made a disastrous start,
losing their first six wickets for just 37 runs with Paul Allott claiming four
of them. Enter Peter Hartley to hit a magnificent maiden century, 127 not
out, an innings containing 11 fours and a six. He and Stuart Fletcher
added 91 for the last wicket to give the White Rose county's total an air
of respectability.

Lancashire, who had reached 38 for two at the end of the first day's
play, struggled against the spin of Carrick and Booth, who both claimed
five wickets apiece in the home side's total of 218. It was then the turn of
the Lancashire spinners and in particular Dexter Fitton, who took six for
59 in what was only his second Championship match. After just short of
an hour-and-a-half's cricket on the third day, play was washed out along
with the entire fourth day, thus spoiling what promised to be a most interesting finish to the game.

LANCASHIRE v YORKSHIRE
at Old Trafford August 19,21,22, 1989

Lancashire 293 (Atherton 115*) and 228-3dec (Mendis 103*, Watkinson 51*)
Yorkshire 192 (Blakey 56, Wasim Akram 5-44) and 148 (Blakey 62, Wasim
Akram 5-51)
Lancashire won by 181 runs.

Michael Atherton, who was awarded his county cap before play got
underway, held the Lancashire first innings together with his first century
of the summer. After Mendis and Fowler had put on 52 for the first wicket, Atherton arrived at the crease to totally dominate the proceedings with
an unbeaten 115 in the home side's total of 293. The only other Lancashire
player to make a contribution was Mike Watkinson with 48. By the close
of play on the first day, Moxon and Metcalfe had taken the Yorkshire
score to 46 for 0.

236

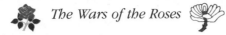

Moxon fell to Fitton early on the second day but Metcalfe (44) and Blakey, who hit 56, put the White Rose county in the driving seat before a devastating spell of bowling by Wasim Akram destroyed Yorkshire after lunch.

Lancashire then took complete control and at the end of the second day were 137 for two, a lead of 238. On the final day, Mendis completed his second century of the season and Mike Watkinson an unbeaten 51, enabling Lancashire to declare at 228 for three.

Yorkshire, set 330 to win in 81 overs, never recovered from a fine spell of opening bowling by Paul Allott and though Richard Blakey hit his second fifty of the match, Wasim Akram again took five wickets as Yorkshire were bowled out for 148.

YORKSHIRE v LANCASHIRE
at Scarborough September 8,9,10,11, 1989

Lancashire 347 (Fairbrother 161, Fowler 58) and 369-8dec (Fowler 123,
Fairbrother 67, Mendis 66, Batty 5-118)
Yorkshire 237 (Pickles 62, Fitton 5-53) and 295 (Robinson 117)
Lancashire won by 184 runs.

Lancashire completed their first Roses 'double' for 29 years, winning the game with comparative ease. On winning the toss, Lancashire decided to bat and though the ball was moving off the seam right from the start, Graeme Fowler put bat to ball and scored a quick-fire 58 before falling to Phil Carrick. The Lancashire innings was dominated by another left-hander, Neil Fairbrother, whose score of 161 contained 3 sixes and 23 fours.

In reply to Lancashire's first innings total of 347, Yorkshire made a bright start but off-spinner Dexter Fitton ripped through the middle-order to finish with five for 53. Chris Pickles (62) and Arnie Sidebottom (40) helped Yorkshire reach 237.

Despite some promising bowling by Jeremy Batty, who took five for 118, Lancashire's batsmen scored freely in their second innings with Graeme Fowler leading the way with 125.

Set 480 to win, Yorkshire's batsmen collapsed for a second time and only Phil Robinson, with a superb innings of 117 from 142 balls in 160 minutes, showed any real resistance.

For Lancashire, Mike Watkinson, pressed into service following Fitton's inability to find a length, took three for 36 to wrap up victory for the Red Rose county.

237

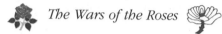

NEIL FAIRBROTHER (LANCASHIRE)

It is highly appropriate that Neil Harvey Fairbrother developed into a nimble-footed left-handed middle-order batsman and outstandingly agile cover fielder like the Australian Test cricketer whose names he was given.

It was with Manchester Association side Grappenhall that the young Fairbrother first came to the notice of Lancashire, making his debut at Old Trafford against Kent in 1982. He did not bat in that match, his debut innings coming the following season in the match against Warwickshire at Edgbaston.John Abrahams was captaining Lancashire in Clive Lloyd's absence and agreed with Warwickshire captain Bob Willis early in the day to close Lancashire's innings at 250, which was 146 in arrears, to set up a victory chase. Fairbrother was 94 when 250 was reached and Abrahams, having given his word, would not go back on it. Willis could have given Fairbrother the necessary deliveries to have reached a historic hundred but immediately turned on his heels at 250 and left the field, much to the disgust of a number of players and indignation of cricket supporters.

Since then, Fairbrother has made up for that with more than 18,000 runs and 40 centuries. They include one triple and three doubles for Lancashire. His highest score was 366 at the Oval against Surrey in 1990. His innings broke a number of records - the highest score by an Englishman this century, the highest score at the Oval, beating Len Hutton's 364 not out, the highest score against Surrey and the highest by a player batting at number four - he also became the first player to score 100 runs or more in all three sessions of a day's play and with Mike Atherton put on 364, a record for Lancashire's third wicket.

In May 1990 he scored exactly 1,000 runs in all competitions - 674 in the County Championship, 125 in the Refuge Assurance League and 201 in the Benson and Hedges Cup. In 1991 he hit three hundreds in succession - 107 not out against Glamorgan at Aigburth and 109 and 102 not out against Somerset at Taunton.

Neil Fairbrother's Test record of 219 runs at 15.64 is a travesty of his true ability. He has played in 66 one-day internationals for England, scoring 1,918 runs at an average of 40.80, including a magnificent 113 against the West Indies at Lord's in 1991.

Fairbrother led the county in the Benson and Hedges Cup Final of 1991 and in the Refuge Assurance Cup Final of 1991 when they lost both matches to Worcestershire before being appointed officially David Hughes' successor in September 1991. However, his form was so diminished by the trials of leadership that after two seasons in charge he stepped down. In 1995 his benefit realised £206,000 - it was a year in which he signed a new five-year contract to keep this most popular of cricketers with Lancashire until at least the year 2000.

YORKSHIRE v LANCASHIRE
at Headingley August 4,6,7, 1990

Lancashire 369-9dec (De Freitas 66, Atherton 64, Mendis 54) and 133-7 (G.Lloyd 70)
Yorkshire 188 (Atherton 5-26) and 328 (Metcalfe 146)
Match Drawn.

Lancashire took early control of this Roses match with Mendis (54) Fowler (43) and Atherton (64) making sure the Red Rose county got off to a good start. Phil DeFreitas gave the innings a boost with 66 from 85 balls, including three giant sixes and 6 fours. Lancashire declared at 369 for nine and just before the end of play captured the wicket of Yorkshire captain Martyn Moxon, caught by Fowler off the bowling of Atherton. The Lancashire leg-spinner went on to produce his best figures of five for 26 as Yorkshire fell away to be bowled out for 188.

239

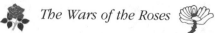

Lancashire enforced the follow-on but Ashley Metcalfe was in magnificent form, scoring 146 off 325 balls. It was just as well for the Yorkshire middle-order, with the exception of Chris Pickles who scored 39, collapsed again.

Lancashire needed 148 to win in just 13 overs and despite losing wickets at regular intervals, almost made them. Graham Lloyd scored a superb 70 from just 38 balls, including 4 sixes, as he and Mike Atherton added 74 in six overs! As Yorkshire pushed eight of the fielders onto the boundary, Lancashire had to settle for a draw, finishing the game on 133 for seven.

LANCASHIRE v YORKSHIRE
at Old Trafford August 18,19,20,21, 1990

Lancashire 433 (Watkinson 138, Atherton 108, Fairbrother 99, Carrick 5-98)
and 73-1dec (Fowler 50*)
Yorkshire 190-3dec (Moxon 90*, Robinson 70) and 266-9 (Carrick 57, Moxon 50,
Watkinson 5-105)
Match Drawn.

Despite losing openers Mendis and Fowler cheaply, Lancashire ended the first day on 417 for eight. Mike Atherton scored 108, his seventh century of the season, and Neil Fairbrother was dismissed by Hartley just one run short of his century off only 86 balls. The county's top-scorer was Mike Watkinson, who was caught off the bowling of Carrick for 138. Sadly, rain washed out the entire second day and it needed two declarations on the third day, following Lancashire being bowled out for 433, to bring Yorkshire into the game.

The White Rose county declared their first innings closed at 190 for three with captain Martyn Moxon undefeated on 90. Lancashire declared at 73 for one, with Fowler scoring an unbeaten 50, to leave Yorkshire needing 317 for victory.

Moxon and Metcalfe gave Yorkshire another good start but then Watkinson and Atherton began to get amongst the wickets. Lancashire almost clinched victory but Kevin Sharp, whose right thumb was broken by a Wasim Akram delivery in the first innings, held out with last man Batty for the final few overs of the 95 Lancashire bowled to help save the match.

LANCASHIRE v YORKSHIRE
at Old Trafford August 2,3,5, 1991

Yorkshire 318 (Kellett 81, Robinson 58, Pickles 50, Wasim Akram 5-91)
and 238-4dec (Metcalfe 113*)
Lancashire 276-8dec (Atherton 114*) and 105-1 (Mendis 59*)
Match Drawn.

There was a sensational start to this Roses match when Lancashire's Wasim Akram dismissed both Moxon and Byas in the opening over of the game. However, Yorkshire recovered and, with Simon Kellett scoring a Championship-best 81, and Robinson and Pickles hitting half-centuries, they were able to total 318. In the remaining overs, Mark Robinson removed both Lancashire openers to leave the Red Rose county at 21 for two.

Michael Atherton dominated proceedings on the second day, his innings of 114 not out enabling Lancashire to declare 42 runs behind Yorkshire at 276 for eight.

During the course of that innings, Phil Carrick bowled Phil de Freitas to claim his 1000th first-class wicket.

Ashley Metcalfe continued his fine run of form with an innings of 113 not out, allowing Moxon to declare at 238 for four and set Lancashire a victory target of 281 runs at about four an over. Mendis and Atherton took Lancashire to 105 for one off 25 overs when sadly rain intervened to ruin what promised to be a most interesting finish.

YORKSHIRE v LANCASHIRE
at Scarborough September 3,4,5,6, 1991

Yorkshire 501-6dec (Robinson 189, Byas 120, Gough 60*, Blakey 59)
and 224-6dec (Moxon 115)
Lancashire 403-7dec (Mendis 114, Speak 73, Crawley 52, Lloyd 51, Hartley 5-100)
and 294 (Austin 101*, Gough 5-41)
Yorkshire won by 48 runs.

After Phil DeFreitas and Peter Martin had reduced Yorkshire to 18 for three, David Byas and Phil Robinson proceeded to add 251 in 70 overs for the fourth wicket. Byas scored 120, hitting one six and 20 fours after being dropped on one, whilst Robinson hit a career-best 189 with one six and 27 fours. Blakey, Carrick and Gough also got amongst the runs as Yorkshire declared at 501 for six.

In reply, Lancashire too were able to declare their innings on 403

241

for seven. Top-scorer was Gehan Mendis with 114 whilst Speak, Lloyd and Crawley, in his first Championship innings, all hit half-centuries.

Martyn Moxon scored 115 in Yorkshire's second innings, adding 145 for the fourth wicket with Phil Robinson, who ended on 79 not out as the White Rose county set Lancashire a victory target of 343 in a minimum of 80 overs.

Darren Gough made early inroads into the Lancashire batting to leave the visitors reeling at 99 for seven, eventually finishing with figures of five for 41 from 18 overs. Phil DeFreitas, with 50 off 28 balls, and Ian Austin, who hit the season's fastest century in 68 minutes off 61 balls, helped Lancashire mount a serious challenge. Austin's innings contained 6 sixes and 13 fours but just when it seemed the impossible might happen, Hartley returned to dismiss Martin after he and Austin had put on 82 runs for the last wicket.

YORKSHIRE v LANCASHIRE
at Headingley July 31, August 1,2, 1992

Lancashire 399-8dec (Fairbrother 166*, Speak 59, Lloyd 56) and 182-3dec
(Atherton 53*)
Yorkshire 300-3dec (Kellett 91, Moxon 90, Tendulkar 56*) and 283-6
(Kellett 89, Blakey 63)
Yorkshire won by 4 wickets.

Lancashire won the toss and on a wicket offering little assistance to the bowlers, Neil Fairbrother helped himself to an unbeaten 166 as Lancashire declared at their overnight total of 399 for eight. The Lancashire captain, who hit 5 sixes and 18 fours in his stay at the crease, was missed when he had scored 80. He mistimed a drive against Robinson straight to Batty at mid-off but the Yorkshire bowler couldn't hold on to it. Speak and Lloyd both hit half-centuries and Phil Carrick, bowling defensively, picked up four wickets as a reward for his accuracy.

When Yorkshire replied, Peter Martin bowled a good spell with the new ball and was unlucky not to pick up a few wickets. However, Moxon (90) and Kellett (91) got to grips with the bowling and were unlucky not to reach deserved centuries after putting on 169 for Yorkshire's first wicket. Sachin Tendulkar, playing in his first Roses game, scored an unbeaten 56 as Yorkshire declared their innings closed at 300 for three.

It was apparent that both sides were working their way towards a run chase on the last afternoon, a fact borne out when Lancashire captain Neil Fairbrother set the home side a target of 282 in a minimum of 55 overs after nightwatchman Peter Martin had scored 46 and Mike Atherton an unbeaten 53 in a total of 182 for three declared.

242

Kellett was again in sparkling form and his innings of 89 formed the backbone of Yorkshire's second innings. He was well supported by Blakey with 63 and though Phil DeFreitas dismissed both batsmen, he obviously lacked match fitness for they cost him 48 runs off his 11 overs. Lancashire employed Barnett and Watkinson bowling spin in an attempt to buy wickets but their options were limited and with Tendulkar hitting 48, Yorkshire won by four wickets.

LANCASHIRE v YORKSHIRE
at Old Trafford August 26,27,28,29, 1992

Lancashire 384-6dec (Atherton 119, Lloyd 77*, Fairbrother 67)
and Second innings forfeited.
Yorkshire First innings forfeited and 121 for 3
Match Drawn.

After torrential rain had washed out the first two days play of this Roses match, only 65 overs were possible on the third day. However, that was still enough for Mike Atherton to score his fourth Roses century in consecutive years, all at Old Trafford.

Crawley departed with the score on six and then Nick Speak went for 42 with Lancashire on 71. Atherton and Fairbrother put on 103 for the third wicket and then Atherton and Lloyd added exactly 100 before Atherton was bowled by Batty for 119. Lancashire batted on until lunchtime on the final day when DeFreitas hit Batty for 5 sixes and 2 fours before a declaration and a double forfeiting of innings left Yorkshire to make 385 for victory in at least 71 overs.

A heavy shower cut out 16 overs and more rain ended the game at a quarter-past five with Yorkshire on 121 for three.

YORKSHIRE v LANCASHIRE
at Headingley April 29,30, May 1,3, 1993

Yorkshire 319 (Blakey 95, Kellett 62, Barnett 5-83) and 258 (Moxon 91, Martin 5-35)
Lancashire 200 (Lloyd 116) and 261 (Lloyd 88, Stemp 6-92)
Yorkshire won by 116 runs.

With the two counties only due to meet once in the new style County Championship, they decided to institute a challenge match which was granted first-class status by the TCCB. Competing for a vase newly commissioned by Aynsley China, and sponsored on this occasion by Trans-Pennine Express, Yorkshire took first knock on a slow pitch which allowed a little turn.

There were useful contributions from Moxon (48), Kellett (62) and Byas (44) but the pick of the Yorkshire batsmen was wicket-keeper Richard Blakey who fell five runs short of what would have been a richly deserved century in a White Rose county total of 319.

In reply, Graham Lloyd batted superbly to score 116 from 159 balls as Lancashire could only muster 200 against some tight Yorkshire bowling, for whom Paul Jarvis took three for 20 off 13.3 overs.

Martyn Moxon had scored 64 when he was hit on the foot and had to retire. During his absence, Peter Martin and Phil DeFreitas picked up some cheap wickets before the Yorkshire captain returned to take his score to 91. He too became one of Martin's victims, the Lancashire paceman finishing with five for 35.

Set 378 to win, Lancashire made a solid start but again, the only batsman to come to terms with the spin of Richard Stemp, who took six for 92, was Graham Lloyd who scored 88 as the visitors fell 116 runs short.

LANCASHIRE v YORKSHIRE
at Old Trafford August 19,20,21,23, 1993

Yorkshire 242 (Grayson 64, Vaughan 64, Wasim Akram 8-68) and 258 (Byas 73, Richardson 50, Wasim Akram 4-57)
Lancashire 167 (Mendis 55) and 314 (Crawley 80, Robinson 6-62)
Yorkshire won by 19 runs.

Michael Vaughan became the first Lancashire-born player for 73 years to play for Yorkshire and in what was his first-class debut, top-scored with Paul Grayson, both batsmen scoring 64 in Yorkshire's first innings total of 242. For Lancashire, Pakistan Test all-rounder Wasim Akram was in devastating form, taking eight for 68 off 23 overs.

With the exception of Gehan Mendis, who scored 55, Lancashire's batsmen had no answer to the pace and movement of Hartley and Gough, who claimed four wickets apiece as the home side fell 75 runs short of Yorkshire's total.

Akram continued to trouble Yorkshire's batsmen and only Byas (73) and West Indian Test player Richie Richardson (50) put up any real resistance in their second innings total of 258.

Needing 334 for victory, Lancashire made a solid start and began the final day on 137 for two. Early in the first session, both Crawley (80) and Speak (40) fell victim to Mark Robinson, who took six of the first seven wickets to fall at a cost of 62 runs. All of Lancashire's batsmen made useful contributions but they fell 20 runs short of what would have been a record score to win against their old rivals.

244

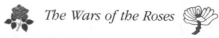

WASIM AKRAM (LANCASHIRE)

One of the world's best all-rounders, Wasim Akram was born in Lahore, Pakistan, where as in a schoolboy's dream, he progressed into first-class cricket.

His first Test match for Pakistan came when he was just 17 and he took ten wickets against New Zealand in his second Test. He was the youngest cricketer ever to do so. It was a taste of things to come.

His introduction into English cricket came in 1986 when he played for Burnopfield in the north-east for three months. After a series of impressive performances with the 1987 Pakistani touring party, Lancashire were quick to offer him a six-year contract.

He made his impact felt early on with an unbeaten hundred at the end of May 1988 against Somerset. The match against Surrey at Southport in late July was full of incident. Wasim achieved a hat-trick and then hit 98 off 78 balls with four sixes and nine fours - two more runs would have provided him with the fastest century of the season at the time. In 1989 he topped the Lancashire bowling averages with 50 wickets at 19.86 runs apiece, but the following season only played in six Championship matches due to injury. In 1991 he returned to something like his old self and, after hitting 122 against Hampshire at Basingstoke for his highest-ever Lancashire score, he looked to be heading for 100 wickets when a foot injury ruled him out halfway through the season. He again topped the county bowling averages with 56 wickets at 22.33 runs each. In 1992 he toured England with Pakistan and did not play for Lancashire. He topped the Pakistan bowling averages in the five-match series with 21 wickets at 22.00 runs each and a best of six for 67 at the Oval in the final Test to help his team to a 2-1 series win. At the end of the season he was chosen as one of Wisden's 'Five Cricketers of the Year'.

He returned to top the county's bowling averages in 1993 with 59 wickets at 19.27 runs apiece including match figures of twelve for 126 against Yorkshire including a career best of eight for 68 in the first innings. He did only manage to play in six games the following season but improved these figures against Somerset at Southport, taking eight for 30 and thirteen for 147 in the match.

In 1995 he had his best season for Lancashire, taking 81 wickets at 19.72 runs apiece.

The Pakistan captain hit a career best unbeaten 257 in the first Test against Zimbabwe in October 1996 and broke two world records - a Test record eighth wicket stand of 313 with Saqlain Mushtaq and the most sixes in a Test. Arguably the world's best new-ball operative when he has the golden star of Pakistan on his chest, he frequently frustrated when wearing the red rose, a sequence of injuries preventing him from playing a full summer for Lancashire. Having taken 912 first-class wickets at 21.34 runs apiece, Wasim Akram finished playing for Lancashire at the end of the 1998 season.

LANCASHIRE v YORKSHIRE
at Old Trafford April 28,29,30, May 2, 1994

Lancashire 354 (Speak 105, Gallian 57, Gough 5-75) and 225-4dec (Crawley 77, Gallian 71)
Yorkshire 275 and 305-3 (Moxon 161*)
Yorkshire won by 7 wickets.

Despite losing its sponsor, the 'friendly' Roses match continued and once again was won by Yorkshire. The counties' overseas players, Wasim Akram of Lancashire and Richie Richardson of Yorkshire, along with Mike Atherton, did not take part.

Lancashire opted to bat in pleasant conditions and Gallian (57), Fairbrother (44), Watkinson (47) and Martin (43 not out) all made valuable contributions. However, it was Nick Speak who top-scored with an innings of 105 in the Red Rose county's total of 354. In reply, Yorkshire fell 79 runs short of the home side's total and when Crawley and Gallian put on 154 for the first wicket of Lancashire's second innings, it seemed as if the game was slipping away from Yorkshire. Mike Watkinson eventually declared at 225 for four, setting Yorkshire a target of 305 in 74 overs for victory.

The White Rose county reached their goal with three overs remaining, thanks in the main to skipper Martyn Moxon, who hit an unbeaten 161, and Richard Blakey, whose unbeaten 40 included a massive six off Barnett to win the game.

247

YORKSHIRE v LANCASHIRE
at Headingley August 11,12,13,14, 1994

Yorkshire 214 (Moxon 69, Grayson 51*) and 314
(Byas 104, Grayson 95, Parker 50, Martin 5-68)
Lancashire 404 (Speak 143, Austin 50) and 125-3 (Gallian 50)
Lancashire won by 7 wickets.

Rather surprisingly, Yorkshire decided to bat first on a Headingley wicket of uneven bounce. Their total of 214 was due in the main to three men, captain Martyn Moxon (69), David Byas (40) and Paul Grayson (51 not out), whilst for Lancashire Peter Martin and Glen Chapple took four wickets apiece.

Lancashire too struggled and were 56 for three when Nick Speak came to the wicket. The Manchester-born batsman hit 3 sixes and 18 fours in an innings of 143, ably supported by Ian Austin, who scored 50 as Lancashire ended their innings with a lead of 190.

David Byas scored 104, his first century at Headingley, and was well supported by Paul Grayson, with 95, as the pair added 142 in 42 overs. Peter Martin was again in fine form with the ball for Lancashire, taking five for 68 off 24.4 overs.

Warren Hegg, the Lancashire wicket-keeper, held five catches in each innings.

Requiring 125 for victory, Lancashire reached their target for the loss of three wickets with Jason Gallian scoring 50.

YORKSHIRE v LANCASHIRE
at Headingley April 27,28,29, May 1, 1995

Yorkshire 417-7dec (Byas 193, Blakey 77*, White 72) and 288-6dec (Bevan 108, Moxon 84, White 50)
Lancashire 271 (Atherton 129) and 215 (Hegg 64, Gough 7-28)
Yorkshire won by 219 runs.

In the third non-Championship meeting of recent years, a full strength Yorkshire side proved too strong for a depleted Lancashire side whose problems were added too when Peter Martin fell ill and Ian Austin damaged a shoulder.

Yorkshire, and in particular David Byas, made good use of batting first on a wicket of good pace and even bounce. Byas hit a career-best 193 from 250 balls, with a six and 34 fours, as Yorkshire declared at 417 for seven.

Mike Atherton scored his first Roses century away from Old

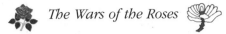

Trafford but only Ian Austin with a quick-fire 49 gave him any support as Lancashire just avoided the follow-on.

Australian Michael Bevan made sure the home side kept in control of the game with a powerful innings of 108, enabling Martyn Moxon to declare the innings closed a second time and set Lancashire 435 to win.

Despite a defiant 93-run stand between wicket-keeper Hegg and Gary Yates, Lancashire never looked like getting anywhere near the required total. Darren Gough produced a career-best performance to take seven for 28 and give his side victory by 219 runs.

DARREN GOUGH (YORKSHIRE)

The Barnsley-born seamer made his Yorkshire debut as an 18-year-old at Lord's in April 1989 - the first product of Yorkshire's cricket school to appear in the County Championship - where he made a startling entry. The wicket of former England captain Mike Gatting was one of five the teenager claimed in the match. However, after this remarkable start, a back injury ruined the rest of the season and Gough didn't return until the end of August. The next three seasons rarely hinted that he would develop into a consistently accurate quick bowler but in 1993 his off-cutter developed and he also began to bowl the yorker with devastating effect. That season he took 55 wickets at 25.74 and produced his career-best figures of seven for 42 against Somerset at Taunton. It was an eventful year for he was selected to go to Holland with an England XI, chosen as Whittingdale Young Cricketer of the Month in July and awarded his county cap in September because of his success with the ball.

In 1994 he played in the first of 56 one-day internationals against New Zealand. His debut was encouraging, two wickets including Martin Crowe's in his first over and an invigorating display of quick bowling had him hailed as England's new fast bowling hero. Unfortunately his hopes of immediate Test match recognition were dashed by a nipped side muscle which incapacitated him for four weeks. When he did make his Test debut at Old Trafford, he revived England's innings with a lusty 65.

In 1995, Gough took four wickets in five balls, including the hat-trick in the match against Kent at Headingley, and followed this with his best figures of seven for 28 (ten for 80 in the match) against Lancashire in a non-Championship match also at Headingley.

The following summer he had his best season with the ball, taking 66 wickets at 22.69 runs apiece but also scored his maiden first-class century with a knock of 121 against Warwickshire at Headingley.

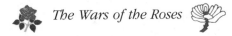

At Test level, Gough's best figures with the ball came in front of his home crowd at Headingley when he took six for 42 against the touring South Africans, helping England to a surprise 2-1 series win. On the 1998-99 tour of Australia, Gough performed the hat-trick for the first time for England in the Sydney Test and, at the time of writing, has taken more than 150 wickets for his country at an average of below 30. In first-class matches, Gough, who has always possessed the ability to bowl fast, has taken well over 500 wickets, a total he is surely going to add to for both Yorkshire and England over the coming years.

LANCASHIRE v YORKSHIRE
at Old Trafford August 17,18,19,21, 1995

Yorkshire 505 (Bevan 95, Metcalfe 79, Byas 76, Silverwood 50) and 96-1 (Moxon 50*)
Lancashire 238 (Crawley 83, Atherton 61) and 362 (Atherton 100, Crawley 58)
Yorkshire won by 9 wickets.

For the first time in a good number of years, the Roses match was televised on satellite TV. England captain Mike Atherton had intended resting from this game but had to play when Neil Fairbrother cried off with a strained hamstring. It was a good job that he did otherwise Yorkshire's victory margin might have been even greater.

Yorkshire won the toss and elected to bat, making good use of a rather placid Old Trafford batting strip to score 505. Australian Test player Michael Bevan came within five runs of his century and Ashley Metcalfe, in his first first-class match of the season, played his biggest Championship innings for four years in scoring 79. Chris Silverwood struck a maiden 50 off 46 balls and was the last man out attempting to hit a third successive six!

Batting in the middle-order, Atherton made 61 to support John Crawley's fighting innings of 83, but Lancashire had to follow-on when they were dismissed for 238.

The Red Rose county showed more spirit in their second innings and Atherton scored his sixth century to equal Clive Lloyd's record for Lancashire in Roses games. John Crawley scored his second half-century of the game but Lancashire were all out for 362 in the fifth over of the final morning.

Yorkshire reached their target of 96 before lunch for the loss of one wicket.

251

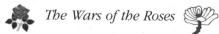
MIKE ATHERTON (LANCASHIRE)

Educated at Manchester Grammar School and Cambridge University, where he excelled as a player and captain, Mike Atherton made his Test debut at 21 and impressed with his technique, temperament and composure at the crease.

At Manchester Grammar School, he smashed batting records and at the age of sixteen captained the England Under-19s, which reinforced the suspicion at that time that he would one day lead England through the Long Room at Lord's.

His career choice was confirmed after an unbeaten 73 as a freshman for Cambridge University against a rampant Essex attack. Captain of Cambridge University, where he hit three centuries and a highest of 151 not out against Middlesex at Fenners, he also led the Combined Universities on their enterprising giant-killing run in the 1989 Benson and Hedges Cup.

He made his Lancashire debut against Warwickshire in 1987, a summer in which he scored 1,193 first-class runs to become the first batsman since Paul Parker in 1976 to make over 1,000 runs in a debut season. He scored his maiden century for Lancashire against Sussex at Hove in 1988 when he made 152 not out. In 1989 he was awarded his county cap and selected to play for England in two Tests against the Australians, scoring 47 at Trent Bridge.

Atherton continued to score runs by the ton for Lancashire and he trod in some famous footprints at Trent Bridge in June 1990 to become, at twenty-two, the youngest Englishman to make a Test hundred since the 21-year-old David Gower achieved the feat in India in 1978. This summer was also his first full season with Lancashire and no-one at Old Trafford did more to lead Lancashire's assault on the Britannic Championship, Benson and Hedges Cup and Refuge Assurance League. Atherton ended that summer of 1990 with 1,170 runs at an average of 78.00.

In his early days with the county, Atherton was a wily leg-spinner and in 1990 produced his best figures with six for 78 against Nottinghamshire at Trent Bridge. His highest score for Lancashire is the undefeated 268 he made against Glamorgan at Blackpool in 1999.

In 1993, Atherton followed Percy Chapman, Gubby Allen, Peter May, Ted Dexter, Mike Brearley and others from the fields of Fenners to the tenacy of the captain's locker in the England dressing-room. Atherton has played over 100 Tests - 52 as captain, an England record - and scored nearly 7,000 runs at an average of almost 40 with his mammoth innings of 185 not out against South Africa in the second Test at Johannesburg in November 1995 his highest score.

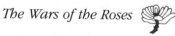

LANCASHIRE v YORKSHIRE
at Old Trafford April 18,19,20, 1996

Lancashire 212 (Elworthy 88, Wharf 4-29) and 24-1
Yorkshire 237-9dec (Kettleborough 88, Morris 60, Green 6-41)
Match Drawn.

In a rain-affected match, the fourth non-Championship meeting petered out into a draw. The game was reduced to three days as both sides had four players in the England 'A' v The Rest match, but when only 21.1 overs were possible on the opening day, a win for either side looked out of the question.

South African all-rounder Steve Elworthy, who had replaced Wasim Akram for the summer, top-scored with 88 in a Lancashire total of 212.

In reply, Yorkshire took their total to 237 for nine before declaring with Richard Kettleborough (85) and Alex Morris (60) the pick of the batsmen. For Lancashire, 20-year-old pace bowler Richard Green took six for 41.

Lancashire had just started their second innings when a further outbreak of rain brought the game to an early conclusion.

YORKSHIRE v LANCASHIRE
at Headingley August 22,23,24,26, 1996

Yorkshire 529-8dec (White 181, Blakey 109*, Moxon 66, Vaughan 57)
Lancashire 323 (Fairbrother 86, Watkinson 64) and 231-7 (Speak 77, Fairbrother 55)
Match Drawn.

Despite dominating proceedings throughout the four days, Yorkshire had to settle for a draw after amassing a large first innings total. Their score of 529 for eight declared was due in the main to a sixth wicket stand of 252 between Craig White and Richard Blakey. White scored a career-best 181 and Blakey completed his first century for four years with an unbeaten 109.

After losing a couple of early wickets, the Lancashire batsman began to put bat to ball with Fairbrother (86) and Watkinson (64) the most successful. Just when it seemed as if the Red Rose county would avoid the follow-on, Darren Gough took three for one in 17 balls to leave Lancashire 206 runs adrift.

In their second innings, only Nick Speak with 77 and Neil Fairbrother with 55 were able to combat the in-swinging yorker of Darren Gough, who took four for 48. Only 13 overs play was possible on the final day as rain fell to save Lancashire from what seemed a certain defeat.

254

YORKSHIRE v LANCASHIRE
at Headingley April 16,17,18,19, 1997

Yorkshire 289 (Parker 85*, Wood 81, Yates 4-46) and 298 (Chapman 80, Martin 4-53)
Lancashire 482 (Lloyd 225, Austin 83) and 106-4
Lancashire won by 6 wickets.

Lancashire won the toss and asked Yorkshire to bat on a slow, low pitch which made timing the ball difficult. However, Yorkshire's opening batsman, debutant Matthew Wood scored a promising 81 and Bradley Parker an unbeaten 85 in a total of 289.

In reply, Lancashire had struggled to 173 for six when Graham Lloyd and Ian Austin produced a record seventh wicket partnership of 248 in only 31 overs. Lloyd plundered 225 runs from only 151 balls, reaching his century in 76 balls and hitting 10 sixes and 25 fours. Austin's 83 helped Lancashire reach 482, a lead of 193 runs.

In Yorkshire's second innings, only Colin Chapman with 80 and Gavin Hamilton, who was run out for 49, showed their true form in a disappointing performance against some average Lancashire bowling.

Needing 106 for victory, Lancashire achieved their goal just after lunch on the final day.

LANCASHIRE v YORKSHIRE
at Old Trafford August 27,28,29,30, 1997

Yorkshire 419-9dec (Vaughan 105, Byas 61, Silverwood 58,
White 52) and 176-5 (McGrath 76)
Lancashire 277-8dec (Hegg 50*)
Match Drawn.

Yorkshire controlled this match from the outset with Michael Vaughan (105) leading a solid effort from their top-order. Other major contributors were Byas (61), Silverwood (58) and White (52) as the White Rose county declared at 419 for nine.

Only an unbeaten 50 from wicket-keeper Warren Hegg prevented Lancashire from following-on and they were able to declare their innings closed at 277 for eight. Opening batsman Jason Gallian was fined £250 and reprimanded about his future conduct by the club after he had knocked out two of his stumps with his bat after being bowled by Paul Hutchison.

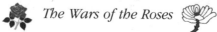

Yorkshire had taken their second innings total to 176 for five by the end of the third day but heavy overnight rain meant that the final day had to be abandoned without a ball being bowled. The visitors, who were 318 runs ahead, had planned to bat a few more overs and then leave Lancashire a challenging target for victory.

YORKSHIRE v LANCASHIRE
at Headingley August 14,15,16,17, 1998

Lancashire 484 (Crawley 180, Lloyd 56) and 215 (Hegg 85, Crawley 56,
Hutchison 5-39)
Yorkshire 457-8dec (Byas 101, Lehmann 71, Blakey 67*, Hamilton 56)
and 183 (Keedy 5-35, Yates 4-69)
Lancashire won by 59 runs.

For the first time in any County Championship match, twelve different players batted for Lancashire. Ian Austin left Headingley at lunch-time on the second day when he was called into England's one-day squad for the injured Mark Ealham of Kent. This then meant that pace bowler Richard Green, who was already on the field as a substitute fielder for the injured Wasim Akram could play a full part as Austin's replacement under ECB rules. Austin, in fact, would have left the ground much earlier but was selected for a random drugs test and had problems in providing a sample!

Lancashire, who won the toss and elected to bat, had John Crawley to thank for them reaching a total of 484, their highest total in Yorkshire. Crawley, who scored 180, the highest for Lancashire in a Championship match in Yorkshire, was well supported by Lloyd (56) and Austin (49).

Yorkshire batted well in reply with Vaughan (45), Lehmann (71), Blakey (67 not out) and Hamilton (56) all amongst the runs. The White Rose county's top-scorer though was captain David Byas (101), who was caught by Lancashire coach Dav Whatmore, on the field as a substitute. Byas was able to declare Yorkshire's innings closed at 457 for eight, 27 runs behind the visitors.

An outstanding spell of pace bowling by Paul Hutchison reduced Lancashire to 22 for four and though he finished with figures of five for 39, Crawley (56) and Hegg, who top-scored with 85, helped Lancashire to set their rivals 243 to win off 60 overs.

The Yorkshire batsmen succumbed to the spin of Gary Yates (four for 69) and Wakefield-born Gary Keedy (five for 35) as they fell 59 runs short of their target.

256

LANCASHIRE v YORKSHIRE
at Old Trafford August 19,20,21,22, 1999

Yorkshire 67 (Green 4-21) and 277 (Byas 66, Martin 5-67)
Lancashire 314 (Flintoff 160) and 34-0
Lancashire won by 10 wickets.

No play was possible until 2.10 p.m. on the opening day of the 1999 Roses match because of heavy overnight and morning rain, but Lancashire's seamers made up for lost time in spectacular style after David Byas had elected to bat. Richard Green claimed Championship-best figures of four for 21, Glen Chapple three for 22 and Peter Martin three for nine in 11.2 overs as Yorkshire were bowled out for 67, their lowest Roses total since 1968.

By the end of the first day, Lancashire had taken their score to 91 for three. After resuming on his overnight score of 45, Preston-born all-rounder Andy Flintoff became the first Lancastrian to score 100 runs before lunch in a Roses match. He plundered 111 from only 98 deliveries and powered on past his previous best of 158 set at Bristol against Gloucestershire earlier that season. Eventually out chipping Michael Vaughan to Anthony McGrath at mid-wicket, his innings of 160 contained 2 sixes and 25 fours. Lancashire were eventually bowled out for 314, a first innings lead of 247.

Yorkshire fared much better in their second innings, with Michael Vaughan and Matthew Wood sharing an opening stand of 50 and captain David Byas reaching a 102-ball half-century. However, Peter Martin bowled superbly to take five for 67 and Flintoff followed his career-best score with two wickets as Yorkshire were all out for 277.

Needing just 31 to win, Mark Chilton and skipper John Crawley knocked off the runs to complete a 10-wicket victory.

LANCASHIRE V. YORKSHIRE
at Old Trafford June 29,30, July 1, 2000

Yorkshire 164 (Blakey 56, Chapple 4-27) and 151 (Keedy 4-47)
Lancashire 269 (Hegg 58, Silverwood 4-67) and 47-1
Lancashire won by 9 wickets

Lancashire completed their first hat-trick of Rosess Championship victories for more than a century, beating Yorkshire by nine wickets. The last time this had happened was as far back as 1892-93.

257

Yorkshire reached lunch on the first day on 126 for 2 but then lost their last eight wickets for 38 runs in 21 overs.

Lancashire made a disastrous start in reply, with captain John Crawley out for a golden duck off the second ball of the innings. Mark Chilton (35) and Sourav Ganguly (44) helped Lancashire to recover, but by the close of play they were 149 for 5. A fighting knock of 58 by wicket-keeper Warren Hegg, ably supported by Chris Schofield (23) and Glen Chapple (24), helped the home side to a first innings lead of 105.

With Gary Keedy bowling well in tandem with Gary Yates, Yorkshire ended the day on 130 for seven, with only David Byas (30) and Richard Blakey (32) putting up a fight.

The weather looked likely to frustrate Lancashire, but when play got underway they wasted little time in polishing off the Yorkshire second innings, Mike Smethurst almost finishing off with a hat-trick. Despite losing Crawley shouldering arms, Chilton and Fairbrother steered Lancashire home within 13 overs, the latter ending the match in emphatic fashion with a straight six off Ian Fisher.

YORKSHIRE V. LANCASHIRE
at Headingley July 28,29,30,31, 2000

Lancashire 267 (Hegg 75, Hoggard 4-70) and 127 for 2 (Crawley 46*)
Yorkshire 376 (Lehmann 83, Byas 81, Fellows 46)
Match drawn

Yorkshire officials, already angered by a Lord's decision to withdraw Darren Gough from this top-of-the-table clash, were stunned to learn that he had been permitted to play in a one-day game for the Academy XI against Barnsley!

Nevertheless, the White Rose county made light of Gough's absence through most of a grim opening day, reducing Lancashire to 128 for 6 on an untrustworthy pitch. Warren Hegg then transformed an old-fashioned day of attrition with a sparkling 75, racing to his 50 in only 62 balls. Lancashire were eventually all out for 267.

Though Australian Test star Darren Lehmann top-scored for the home side with 86, it was skipper David Byas who was the home side's hero, painstakingly compiling 81. Gary Fellows chipped in with a county best score of 46 as Yorkshire took a 109-run lead.

On the third day it was Lancashire skipper John Crawley who defied the Yorkshire attack as the Red Rose county ended the day on 127 for 2, wiping out the first innings deficit, but sadly this clash ended in disappointment as rain prevented any play on the final day.

258

Appendix

BATTING

Leading Run-getters:

Player	County	Runs	Ave.
1. H.Sutcliffe	Yorkshire	3006	52.73
2. G.Boycott	Yorkshire	2509	52.27
3. C.Washbrook	Lancashire	2209	40.90
4. D.Denton	Yorkshire	2093	29.48
5. W.Rhodes	Yorkshire	2055	27.77
6. M.D.Moxon	Yorkshire	1995	53.91
7. E.Tyldesley	Lancashire	1869	32.22
8. L.Hutton	Yorkshire	1831	43.59
9. G.H.Hirst	Yorkshire	1816	25.16
10. N.H.Fairbrother	Lancashire	1804	53.05
11. J.T.Tyldesley	Lancashire	1685	24.42
12. A.N.Hornby	Lancashire	1665	23.45
13. P.Holmes	Yorkshire	1613	39.34
14. J.W.H.Makepeace	Lancashire	1600	27.54
15. M.Leyland	Yorkshire	1538	39.43
16. K.J.Grieves	Lancashire	1509	29.59
17. C.H.Lloyd	Lancashire	1492	51.44
18. J.Sharp	Lancashire	1481	25.53
19. G.Ulyett	Yorkshire	1399	21.52
20. J.H.Hampshire	Yorkshire	1355	30.79

Highest Scores:

Player	County	Score	Venue
1. G.D.Lloyd	Lancashire	225	Headingley 1997
2. M.Leyland	Yorkshire	211*	Headingley 1930
3. L.Hutton	Yorkshire	201	Old Trafford 1949
4. R.H.Spooner	Lancashire	200*	Old Trafford 1910
5. H.Sutcliffe	Yorkshire	195	Sheffield 1931
6. D.Byas	Yorkshire	193	Headingley 1995
7. P.Robinson	Yorkshire	189	Scarborough 1991
8. C.H.Lloyd	Lancashire	181	Old Trafford 1972
9. C.White	Yorkshire	181	Headingley 1996
10. A.Ward	Lancashire	180	Old Trafford 1892
11. J.P.Crawley	Lancashire	180	Headingley 1998
12. E.Tyldesley	Lancashire	178	Sheffield 1922
13. W.Watson	Yorkshire	174	Sheffield 1955
14. C.Washbrook	Lancashire	170	Headingley 1948
15. G.Boycott	Yorkshire	169	Sheffield 1971
16. N.H.Fairbrother	Lancashire	166*	Headingley 1992
17. F.Lee	Yorkshire	165	Bradford 1887
18. E.Tyldesley	Lancashire	165	Headingley 1927
19. H.Sutcliffe	Yorkshire	165	Old Trafford 1939
20. M.D.Moxon	Yorkshire	161*	Old Trafford 1994
21. N.H.Fairbrother	Lancashire	161	Scarborough 1989
22. L.Hall	Yorkshire	160	Bradford 1887
23. A.Flintoff	Lancashire	160	Old Trafford 1999
24. G.Fowler	Lancashire	156*	Old Trafford 1983
25. G.H.Hirst	Yorkshire	156	Old Trafford 1911
26. C.Washbrook	Lancashire	156	Old Trafford 1948
27. G.D.Mendis	Lancashire	156	Old Trafford 1987
28. J.D.Love	Yorkshire	154	Old Trafford 1981
29. K.Taylor	Yorkshire	153	Old Trafford 1964
30. M.D.Moxon	Yorkshire	153	Headingley 1983
31. A.C.MacLaren	Lancashire	152	Bradford 1897
32. C.Hallows	Lancashire	152	Old Trafford 1929
33. E.Paynter	Lancashire	152	Bradford 1932
34. L.Hutton	Yorkshire	152	Headingley 1952
35. A.A.Metcalfe	Yorkshire	151	Old Trafford 1986
36. B.Wood	Lancashire	150*	Bradford 1977

**Graham Lloyd - his 225 at Headingley in 1997
is the highest score in a Roses match**

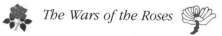

Most Centuries:

A total of 185 centuries have been scored in the series. Of these
Lancashire have scored 93 and Yorkshire 92. The leading centurions are:

Player	County	No.
1. G.Boycott	Yorkshire	10
2. H.Sutcliffe	Yorkshire	9
3. M.A.Atherton	Lancashire	6
P.Holmes	Yorkshire	6
C.H.Lloyd	Lancashire	6
6. N.H.Fairbrother	Lancashire	5
M.D.Moxon	Yorkshire	5
G.Pullar	Lancashire	5
9. D.Byas	Yorkshire	4
L.Hutton	Yorkshire	4
A.C.MacLaren	Lancashire	4
G.D.Mendis	Lancashire	4
R.H.Spooner	Lancashire	4
E.Tyldesley	Lancashire	4

Century in each innings of a match:

P.Holmes (Yorkshire)   126 and 11   Old Trafford 1920
E..Lester (Yorkshire)   125* and 132   Old Trafford 1948

Three Centuries in a match:

Bradford 1887   L.Hall(Y) 160, F.Lee(Y) 165, W.Robinson(L) 111*
Headingley 1901   F.Mitchell(Y) 106, A.C.MacLaren(L) 117, A.Wood(Y) 100
Sheffield 1919   P.Holmes(Y) 123, H.Sutcliffe(Y), 132 C.Hallows(L) 102*
Old Trafford 1926   H.Makepeace(L) 126, E.Tyldesley(L), 139 P.Holmes(Y) 143
Headingley 1948   L.Hutton(Y) 100, C.Washbrook(L) 170, E.H.Edrich(L) 121
Old Trafford 1964   G.Boycott(Y) 131, K.Taylor(Y) 153, G.Pullar(L) 128
Headingley 1975   F.C.Hayes(L) 101, C.H.Lloyd(L) 100*, G.Boycott(Y)105*
Old Trafford 1980   G.Boycott(Y) 135, J.D.Love(Y) 105*, C.H.Lloyd(L)101
Old Trafford 1986   N.H.Fairbrother(L), 116* A.A.Metcalfe(Y) 151, M.D.Moxon(Y) 147
Headingley 1995   D.Byas(Y) 193, M.G.Bevan(Y) 108, M.A.Atherton(L) 129

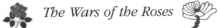

Five Centuries in a match:

Old Trafford 1948   L.Hutton(Y) 104, E.Lester(Y) 125* and 132,
                            C.Washbrook(L) 156, J.T.Ikin(L) 106

Scarborough 1991   P.E.Robinson(Y) 189, D.Byas(Y) 120, M.D.Moxon(Y)
                            115, G.D.Mendis(L) 114, I.D.Austin(L) 101*

Highest Partnerships:

LANCASHIRE

1st	181	R.H.Spooner/J.W.H.Makepeace	Old Trafford 1912
2nd	223	R.H.Spooner/J.T.Tyldesley	Old Trafford 1905
3rd	244	C.Washbrook/J.Ikin	Old Trafford 1948
4th	202	J.L.Hopwood/C.Hawkwood	Headingley 1933
5th	131	C.Washbrook/R.B.Rae	Bradford 1945
6th	145	C.H.Lloyd/D.P.Hughes	Headingley 1981
7th	248	G.D.Lloyd/I.D.Austin	Headingley 1997
8th	134	C.Maynard/P.J.W.Allott	Headingley 1986
9th	141	J.T.Tyldesley/W.Huddleston	Sheffield 1914
10th	64	A.Appleby/W.Hickton	Sheffield 1871

YORKSHIRE

1st	323	P.Holmes/H.Sutcliffe	Sheffield 1931
2nd	288	H.Sutcliffe/A.Mitchell	Old Trafford 1939
3rd	186	G.Boycott/J.H.Hampshire	Sheffield 1971
4th	249	G.Boycott/W.B.Stott	Sheffield 1963
5th	170	J.V.Wilson/N.W.D.Yardley	Old Trafford 1954
6th	252	C.White/R.J.Blakey	Headingley 1996
7th	120	R.Moorhouse/Lord Hawke	Old Trafford 1895
8th	130	E.Smith/Lord Hawke	Headingley 1904
9th	162	W.Rhodes/S.Haigh	Old Trafford 1904
10th	108	Lord Hawke/L.Whitehead	Old Trafford 1903

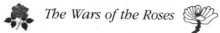

Highest Score on each ground:

	Lancashire	Yorkshire
Bradford	354 in 1897	590 in 1887
Dewsbury	53 in 1886	112 in 1886
Holbeck	34 in 1868	250 in 1868
Huddersfield	232 in 1885	301 in 1885
Hull	259 in 1914	329 in 1914
Leeds-Headingley	484 in 1998	489 in 1921
Liverpool	317 in 1958	177 in 1913
Manchester-Old Trafford	509-9dec in 1926	528 in 1938
Middlesbrough	180 in 1959	348 in 1959
Scarborough	403-7dec in 1991	501-6dec in 1991
Sheffield-Bramall Lane	385 in 1928	484-7dec in 1931
Whalley	75 in 1867	188 in 1867

BOWLING

Leading wicket-takers:

	Ovs	Mdns	Runs	Wkts	Ave.
1. W.Rhodes (Yorks)	2018.3	672	4053	237	17.10
2. G.H.Hirst (Yorks)	1407.1	433	3031	175	17.22
3. J.Briggs (Lancs)	1562.4	640	2683	170	15.78
4. A.Watson (Lancs)	2035	1120	2284	168	13.59
5. T.Emmett (Yorks)	1216.1	567	1773	162	10.94
6. R.Peel (Yorks)	1292.4	591	1753	138	12.70
7. A.Mold (Lancs)	1022.5	420	1906	128	14.89
8. F.S.Trueman (Yorks)	982.5	225	2307	128	18.02
9. J.B.Statham (Lancs)	1146.3	292	2671	123	21.71
10.W.Brearley (Lancs)	608.2	102	2018	115	17.57
11.S.Haigh (Yorks)	691	227	1814	108	17.46
12.J.H.Wardle (Yorks)	974.4	371	2014	99	20.34
13.H.Dean (Lancs)	809.4	253	1721	95	18.11
14.W.McIntyre (Lancs)	810.1	268	1033	91	11.37
15.R.Tattersall (Lancs)	697.2	247	1561	91	17.15
16.H.L.Verity (Yorks)	715	274	1308	87	15.03
17.R.G.Barlow (Lancs)	912.1	464	1194	86	14.00
18.W.E.Bowes (Yorks)	770.2	256	1420	84	16.90
19.G.G.Macaulay (Yorks)	948.5	283	1884	83	22.69
20.A.Appleby (Lancs)	857.2	353	1081	78	13.83

Best Bowling:

1. G.H.Hirst (Yorks)	9-23	Headingley 1910
2. J.H.Wardle (Yorks)	9-25	Old Trafford 1954
3. E.Robinson (Yorks)	9-36	Bradford 1920
4. A.Mold (Lancs)	9-41	Huddersfield 1890
5. J.Iddon (Lancs)	9-42	Sheffield 1937
6. H.Dean (Lancs)	9-62	Liverpool 1913
7. A.G.Steel (Lancs)	9-63	Old Trafford 1878
8. W.Brearley (Lancs)	9-80	Old Trafford 1909
9. G.Freeman (Yorks)	8-11	Holbeck 1868
10.J.Briggs (Lancs)	8-19	Headingley 1893
11.R.G.Barlow (Lancs)	8-22	Huddersfield 1878
12.E.Peate (Yorks)	8-24	Old Trafford 1880
13.W.Huddleston (Lancs)	8-24	Old Trafford 1909
14.H.Dean (Lancs)	8-29	Liverpool 1913
15.W.McIntyre (Lancs)	8-35	Bradford 1874
16.C.H.Parkin (Lancs)	8-35	Old Trafford 1919
17.E.P.Robinson (Yorks)	8-35	Headingley 1939
18.W.Rhodes (Yorks)	8-43	Bradford 1900
19.R.Tattersall (Lancs)	8-43	Headingley 1956
20.W.Bates (Yorks)	8-45	Huddersfield 1878

Best Match Analysis:

1.H.Dean (Lancs)	17 for 91(9-62 & 8-29)	Liverpool 1913
2.E.Peate (Yorks)	14 for 80(6-56 & 8-24)	Old Trafford 1880
3.R.Tattersall (Lancs)	14 for 90(6-47 & 8-43)	Headingley 1956
4.A.G.Steel (Lancs)	14 for 112(5-49 & 9-63)	Old Trafford 1878
5.J.Briggs (Lancs)	14 for 122(6-76 & 8-46)	Old Trafford 1891

Hat-Tricks:

1.G.Freeman (Yorks)	Holbeck 1868
2.G.Ulyett (Yorks)	Sheffield 1883
3.S.Haigh (Yorks)	Old Trafford 1909
4.G.G.Macaulay (Yorks)	Old Trafford 1933
5.G.G.Macaulay (Yorks)	Old Trafford 1934
6.K.Higgs (Lancs)	Old Trafford 1968

266

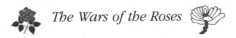

WICKET-KEEPING

Leading wicket-keepers:

	Ct	St	Total
1. D.L.Bairstow (Yorks)	98	3	101
2. D.Hunter (Yorks)	65	27	92
3. J.G.Binks (Yorks)	68	4	72
4. W.Hegg (Lancs)	58	6	64
5. R.Pilling (Lancs)	37	25	62
6. R.J.Blakey (Yorks)	50	12	62
7. A.Dolphin (Yorks)	33	14	47
8. G.Duckworth (Lancs)	28	15	43
9. A.Wood (Yorks)	31	11	42
10.C.S.Smith (Lancs)	33	9	42

Victims in a match:

	Total	Ct	St	
1. W.K.Hegg (Lancs)	10	10	0	Headingley 1994
2. D.L.Bairstow (Yorks)	9	9	0	Old Trafford 1971
3. W.K.Hegg (Lancs)	9	8	1	Old Trafford 1993
4. G.Pinder (Yorks)	8	6	2	Sheffield 1872
5. D.L.Bairstow (Yorks)	8	8	0	Headingley 1978

FIELDING

Leading catchers:

1. J.Tunnicliffe (Yorks)	65
2. A.C.MacLaren (Lancs)	48
3. G.H.Hirst (Yorks)	46
4. A.N.Hornby (Lancs)	37
5. D.B.Close (Yorks)	35
6. R.G.Barlow (Lancs)	34
7. K.J.Grieves (Lancs)	33
8. W.Rhodes (Yorks)	31
9. P.J.Sharpe (Yorks)	31
10.J.V.Wilson (Yorks)	31
11.A.Watson (Lancs)	29
12.E.Wainwright (Yorks)	29
13.D.P.Hughes (Lancs)	26
14.G.Ulyett (Yorks)	26
15.M.D.Moxon (Yorks)	25
16.J.Simmons (Lancs)	25
17.F.H.Sugg (Lancs)	23
18.P.Holmes (Yorks)	23
19.A.Mitchell (Yorks)	23
20.J.Briggs (Lancs)	22
D.Lloyd (Lancs)	22
H.Sutcliffe (Yorks)	22

Most Catches in a match:

1. L.O.S.Poidevin (Lancs)	7	Old Trafford 1906
2. J.Tunnicliffe (Yorks)	6	Old Trafford 1893
3. P.J.Sharpe (Yorks)	6	Sheffield 1967

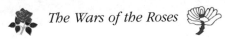

Summary of Venues and Results:

Venue	Total	Wins Lancs	Yorks	Draws
Bradford	19	3	11	5
Dewsbury	1		1	
Holbeck	1		1	
Huddersfield	5	3	1	1
Hull	1	1		
Leeds-Headingley	50	9	15	26
Liverpool	2	2		
Manchester-Old Trafford	120	25	32	63
Middlesbrough	2	2		
Scarborough	2	1	1	
Sheffield-Bramall Lane	43	8	13	22
Whalley	1		1	
TOTALS	**247**	**51**	**77**	**119**